THE CLASSICS
OF WESTERN
SPIRITUALITY

SHOWINGS

TRANSLATED FROM THE CRITICAL TEXT
WITH AN INTRODUCTION BY
EDMUND COLLEDGE,O.S.A.
AND
JAMES WALSH,S.J.

PREFACE BY
JEAN LECLERCQ, O.S.B.

PAULIST PRESS
NEW YORK • RAMSEY • TORONTO

Cover Art:
The artist, POMONA HALLENBECK is a native of the southwest. Pomona now lives in New York City and teaches at schools and workshops in New York, Texas, New Mexico and Canada. She also does textile designs and multimedia education materials. Of her cover for *Julian of Norwich*, she explains: "During a critical illness in her 30th year, Julian encountered the devil . . . Death. During this confrontation, the awareness came that there was no death . . . that Love flowed through even that seeming experience . . . there was no separation. The vision of the Passion as she experienced it at this time revealed that an all-embracing Love controlled, healed, strengthened, and enlightened. Love was the Source, the Energy, the Joy. The vision clarified for her the Divine Christ in us all, no matter how *we* perceive ourselves . . . that is part of our very existence . . . undeniable.

"Therefore, through the illumination of the cross, the Passion of the Christ Jesus, the cruciform halo, Julian sees/perceives the past, the present and the future through the Christ-ness of her own Be-ing . . . beyond the human frailty of what *seems*, through the revelation of the Passion via her own soul. The all-pervading care and protection of the loved encompasses her own consciousness as a Constant. Ultimately, Julian presents us with the immediacy of the Christ *Within*. The crucified Christ becomes the channel for communication with that Source of Perfection which is our Heritage."

Design: Barbini Pesce & Noble, Inc.

Library of Congress
Catalog Card Number: 77-90953

ISBN: 0-8091-2091-7 (Paper)
ISBN: 0-8091-0234-X (Cloth)

Published by Paulist Press
Editorial Office: 1865 Broadway, New York, N.Y. 10023
Business Office: 545 Island Road, Ramsey, N.J. 07446

Printed and bound in the
United States of America

CONTENTS

The Editors of this Volume:

EDMUND COLLEDGE, O.S.A., has specialized in the study of the devotional literature, Latin and vernacular, of England, the Low Countries and the Rhineland in the later Middle Ages. He is the author of studies and modern English translations of Ruysbroek, Tauler and Suso; he published in 1957, in collaboration with Joyce Bazire, a critical edition of *The Chastising of God's Children*, and, in 1961, an anthology, *The Medieval Mystics of England*. He taught English Language and Philology at Liverpool University from 1937 until 1963 when he resigned his Readership there, and entered the English novitiate of the Augustinian Friars Hermit. He taught at the Pontifical Institute of Medieval Studies in Toronto until his recent retirement. He continues to direct students and to do international research on spiritual texts.

FR. JAMES WALSH, S.J., born in Lancashire in 1920, was educated at the Catholic College, Preston, Lancashire. He joined the Society of Jesus in 1938, took an honours degree in the Classical Languages and English Language and Literature at Oxford University, and was ordained a priest in 1952. After taking a doctorate in Ascetical and Mystical Theology at the Gregorian University, Rome, in 1957, he was appointed assistant editor of *The Month*. In 1961, he founded *The Way*, a quarterly periodical of spirituality, with Fr. William Yeomans, S.J., and remains its editor. He is also Vice-Postulator for the Cause of the English and Welsh Martyrs, and for the Cause of Mother Cornelia Connelly, Foundress of the Society of the Holy Child Jesus. His special study is fourteenth-century English Spirituality. He has published *The Revelations of Divine Love of Julian of Norwich* (Burns & Oates Orchard Series 1961, and Harper, New York), and *The Knowledge of Ourselves and of God* (Mowbrays Fleur de Lys Series 1961). He has published articles on Medieval Spirituality in the *Revue d'Ascetique et de Mystique* and *Archives d'Histoire Doctrinale et Litteraire du Moyen Age*, as well as contributing regular articles on spirituality to *The Month* and *The Way*. He edited and introduced the book, *Pre-Reformation English Spirituality*. He is now preparing an edition of the works of the author of *The Cloud of Unknowing*.

JEAN LECLERCQ, O.S.B., a medieval historian, is a Benedictine monk. He has written some 70 books and 700 articles in a 40 year career. He is presently a Professor in the Institute of Religious Psychology, Gregorian University, Rome. His permanent residence is the Abbey of Clervaux in Luxembourg.

Acknowledgements

In their critical edition the present editors have acknowledged help received and obligations incurred during the years in which it was in preparation. To that acknowledgment they would now add this expression of their gratitude to the Paulist Press for accepting a modernized version of Julian's *Showings* as the first volume of the new series they are publishing, and to their friends Denise Critchley, J. C. Marler, Bernard Muir and Michael Sargent for a generous and sympathetic cooperation on which the editors have learned that they can rely.

Marylake, King City, Ontario.
Southwell House, London.

Preface

It is not inappropriate to open a series on Western spirituality with the works of Julian of Norwich. She wrote about the central problems of the spiritual life, particularly those related to the encounter between the soul and God. Her writings are now considered to have universal and permanent value. As a woman, she represents the feminine teacher and feminine insight that are less rare in the Western Christian tradition than many of our contemporaries might think. Her teaching is timeless, meeting some of the urgent needs of those seeking God in our age and answering many of the crucial problems of spiritual development and contemplative consciousness.

In their introduction the editors have, in admirable fashion, provided the reader with information on Julian's life, the history of her writings and the content of her teaching. What we propose to do in this preface is to situate her in a tradition and to suggest her relevance to our time.

Women as Church Teachers

The women who dedicated themselves to God during the Middle Ages seem to have been less numerous than the men, but they were not less influential. Like the monks, they were of two kinds: nuns living in communities and hermitages, and anchoresses living alone. The communities of 14th and 15th-century England numbered one hundred and thirty-six, and more than half of them had less than ten members.[1] Consequently, we must beware of projecting onto these mediaeval convents the image—not to say the myth—of those large communities which became the dream of monastic founders in the 19th century as a result of the romantic restoration of a Middle Ages which had never existed. There was probably little difference between these small convents and the communities of anchoresses with their maids or companions. In that age women and men who successfully sought to be alone with God had an enormous impact on the people of their area precisely because they were able to achieve divine solitude. Sometimes their influence extended beyond their immediate environs to a larger region or group of nations.[2] They fulfilled a social function of praying, counseling, reconciling, settling political conflicts; and some of them, like Richard Rolle of Hampole, also fulfilled the function of teaching. This is not to imply that they had to preach to the people or to elaborate for students the doctrinal deposit of the Church. They were asked, however, on occasion to share their spiritual insight and experience either orally or in writing.

Throughout history women exercised various church ministries: as the deaconesses of the Apostolic and post-Apostolic generations, the women who converted their husbands in the first centuries or in the new barbarian kingdoms of the 6th to 8th centuries, the nuns who have deserved the title of

---

1. David Knowles, C.N.L. Brooke, Vera C.M. London, eds., *The Heads of Religious Houses, England and Wales, 940-1216* (Cambridge: Cambridge University Press, 1972).

2. H. Mayr-Harting, "Functions of a Twelfth-Century Recluse," *History*, 60 (1975), 337-352.

missionaries among the Anglo-Saxon and Germanic people of the same period. Some women, moreover, chiefly from the 12th century on, had a real teaching role in the Church, for example, Hildegard of Bingen, who was called a "prophetess", Mechtild of Magdeburg, Mechtild of Hackeborn, Gertrude, Catherine of Genoa and others. St. Catherine of Siena was recently granted, along with St. Teresa of Avila, the official title of Doctor of the Church.[3] This public recognition has, like many canonizations, a sociological reason—i.e., each society needs models; the Church authority endeavors, usually with a certain "prudent" delay, to meet these needs. Our times require feminine models. These saintly women did not expect to receive the title before proceeding to exercise their doctoral function. In the disputations of the masters of 13th and 14th-century scholastic theology, the question was often asked whether or not women had a right to be depicted with the halo of the Doctors; the answer was always negative in spite of the fact that women had been actually teaching. To be sure, they did not teach in the same manner as the majority of the Schoolmen. Although most of the latter are forgotten and their sophisticated "questions" remain buried in a few manuscripts, the existential message of the women who encountered God never ceases to be transcribed, translated and published. One of these prophetesses, St. Catherine of Siena, had such an impact on the church politics of her time that the Pope's return from Avignon to Rome has been attributed to her influence. She did not fear to write to the Roman Pontiff in such strong terms as "I want" and "I demand".

The character and the content of these feminine teachings were varied. St. Catherine of Siena and St. Bridget of Sweden were involved in politics; St. Hildegard possessed an encyclopedic learning. Later, St. Teresa was to demonstrate a remarkable skill in constitutional law, making contributions

---

3. Jean Leclercq, "Deux nouveaux Docteurs de l'Eglise," *La Vie spirituelle*, 123 (1970), 135-146, with bibliographical references.

which were masterpieces. St. Juliana of Liège was the inspiration behind the feast of Corpus Christi and of all the liturgical developments it occasioned. Other devotions and celebrations had their impetus from private revelations received by holy women; these devotions were later approved by the local and Roman authorities. What all these women had in common was a spiritual experience out of which emerged both practical and doctrinal implications. Although they did not all use the term, nevertheless they all had "revelations" of some kind, which added nothing to the content of Christian revelation as such, but which complemented the official teaching of the active Churchmen since these messages sprang forth from their contemplation. These messages and revelations were not so much concerned with practical considerations as with the quality of prayer life and the theological formulations proceeding from the prayer experience. A new dimension was made possible because these teachers were women; they opened new horizons to the teaching authority of the Church which, if it had remained exclusively a masculine stronghold, would have been limited and partial. It would have missed the characteristic genius of the feminine with its intuitive approach to reality. In relation to God this is the only effective approach. It is in this context that Julian of Norwich acquires her more comprehensive significance.

Contemplation and Theology:
The Experience

Present-day anthropological and religious research is concerned with the creation of symbols, images, texts and the ideas that they convey. This concern extends to the texts of Scripture, to the writings received from tradition, to rituals and also to private revelations. This current research considers how the passage is made from the deep level of experience to the surface level of expression. Julian presents us with a typical example of a theology based on mystical experience, which certainly does not exclude the activity of reason but which can in no way be reduced to the rational. To do so would do great harm to the experience and would alter its essential meaning. In Julian's texts, we can see the passage from desire—hence the frequency and importance of the language of "longing", of "desiring"—to union in prayer and love, culminating in a loving prayer, through the mediation of an active experience. She translates her mystical experience into conceptual terms, as most mystics do, and she deduces the meaning from the experience; she makes explicit in rational terms what is in its very nature extra-rational. She is not merely passive; she does not only receive. She gets "suggestions" and "sharings"; she then has "doubts". She even asks "questions"; finally, she accepts. She consents and she "chooses". "Bodily visions" and "corporeal sights" stimulate her search for understanding. The "revelation" is never sufficient; it is a grace and God takes all the initiative, but there must be human effort. The extraordinary does not dispense with the ordinary; there is need of asceticism, of reflection and study and of humble, daily prayer.

During this process a phenomenon occurs that we must be willing to acknowledge and attempt to understand; it is what Julian calls "a bodily sickness". She evokes it in realistic terms; she says that "her body was dead". She "felt as if the upper part of her body was beginning to die"; she actually believed that she was at the point of death. "The greatest pain that I felt was my shortness of breath and the ebbing of my life" (pp. 127-129). Is this an example of what contemporary psychologists call "creative illness" or "creative malady"? After all, have not many great mystics from St. Paul to St. Thérèse of Lisieux experienced such states of physical depression and humiliation? This weakness, illness or lack of energy is a consequence of the mystical state, which overpowers the human frame. The intensity of mystical encounter is often too great to bear without some side effects; thus, the reality of bodily sickness. Is it not important to remember what the Apostle proclaimed? "Strength is

made perfect in weakness".[4] The combination of organic
symptoms and mystical graces in the case of St. Francis of Assisi
has recently been submitted to a precise study in the light of the
historical evidence at our disposal. In the case of Julian, we have
no other evidence than what she herself gives us; we must depend
on what she mentions and reveals of her symptoms. We can see,
however, that for her, as for other Christian mystics, her infir-
mity is a God-given opportunity to reaffirm that all her energy
and wisdom are the fruits of grace. "I trusted in God . . . and
suddenly in that moment all my pain left me. It was by God's
secret doing and not natural . . . " (pp. 127-128). Her actions
and her writings prove that she was not a neurotic. Yet she had
to integrate, in a unity far beyond mere human possibilities, the
total experience of a bodily weakness, of an enlightened mind,
of a loving grace and of a mystical vision. The sign that this
process was genuine was its final result, that is, peace.

The Understanding

Contemplative experience leads to and overflows into doctrinal teaching. The mystic understands the meaning which the
experience has for faith and for the contents of faith; it is, again, a
translation of the mystical experience from its proper domain in
the actuality of its remembrance into that of the human sphere,
mediated by finite and most inadequate categories. Julian
touches on all the main issues of theology, e.g., creation, man,
nature, life, the Incarnation, the death and glorification of
Christ, grace, sin, the Church, Mary and the world to come.
Her primary focus, however, is on three great mysteries, or
rather three aspects of the same mystery: God, man and their
reconciliation. Furthermore, she sees everything in the light of
Christ-the-Servant. It is through Christ that she reaches God;
for her, "the Trinity is God, and God is the Trinity. The

4. 2 Cor. 12:9.

Trinity is our maker, our protector, our everlasting lover, our endless joy and our bliss, from our Lord Jesus Christ and in our Lord Jesus Christ" (p. 181). Here Julian seems to deduce the necessity of the Trinity as the being of God from her experience of God's inner dynamism. What about the place of the Holy Spirit? The Spirit is mentioned in both the long and the short text; what is said of him is sufficient to show that she situates him exactly in his relationship to the Father and to the Son, in the role of the three persons, and in his proper function. The Father, Son and Spirit are at work in Creation (p. 208). "God is the Holy Spirit" (p. 335). "Our light will be full, which light is God our creator, the Father and the Holy Spirit in Jesus Christ our savior" (p. 340). "I understand that the Father was pleased, by 'bliss' that the Son was honored, and by 'endless delight' the Holy Spirit. The Father is pleased, the Son is honoured, the Holy Spirit takes delight" (p. 146).

If the Spirit is equal in nature with the Father and the Son, it is through Him that they give us themselves: "In our good Lord the Holy Spirit we have our reward and our gift for our living and our labors" (p. 293-294), "which working belongs to the third person, the Holy Spirit" (p. 294). Christ Jesus is the one in whom dwells the Father and the Holy Spirit (p. 295). He is the one who inspires, teaches (p. 244), moves (p. 246), leads (p. 288), renews (p. 292), touches (p. 324), gives "gentle strength" (p. 324), encourages contrition (p. 324), allows operation (p. 325), dispenses mercy and grace (p. 329). Thus, on this point also, we find in Julian a rigorous precision, especially concerning the relationship of the Spirit to the Church; the Spirit is always given in the Church (pp. 150, 155, and 229). She has a sense of the Church: she speaks of "the faith which the Holy Church teaches me to believe" (p. 234), of "our mother Holy Church, who is Christ Jesus" (p. 302). "God is the teaching of Holy Church and God is the Holy Spirit" (p. 335). We are "drawn and counseled and taught, inwardly by the Holy Spirit, and outwardly through the same grace by Holy Church" (p. 228). On the occasion of a concrete example—a penitent going to confession—we can see how all this works. "The Holy Spirit leads him to confession . . . then he accepts the penance for every sin imposed by his confessor, for this is established in Holy Church by the teaching of the Holy Spirit" (p. 155). There is, therefore, no dichotomy, no conflict between the inspiration and the institution.

Julian sees man as a sinner. Sin is a historical reality, a personal and a collective as well as a universal phenomenon, embracing everyone; it is a mystery, which Julian realistically expresses in two words, evil and the devil. Yet this sinner is forgiven and saved because God shared in his human condition, in his pain and in his joy. Now we can and we must share in this pain and joy of God made man in Jesus Christ; "every man needs to experience this, to be comforted at one time, and at another to fail and to be left to himself" (p. 140). Joy and sorrow, which are given by God, transform our human joy and sorrow into that of Christ. In order to rest in God, which is the true meaning of Sabbath, man has to experience and to realize that nothing comes from himself (p. 132). Such is the attitude of true spiritual poverty, a complete dependence upon God for everything.

This is humility; it is not an empty nothingness, but a capacity for universal communion. "I am in the unity of love with all my fellow Christians" (p. 134); it is a personal love, even cosmic in scope, which leads to eternal joy (p. 134). A fundamental optimism pervades all of this experience and this teaching. Joy and sorrow alternate (pp. 161/202), but it is joy or the fulness of joy which dominates. She expresses this joy with a humor which at times breaks into laughter (p. 201-202).

God As Mother

Of all the doctrinal issues that she considers, the one which makes Julian's contribution the most timely, the most in tune with certain trends in contemporary theology, is her insistence on referring to God as Mother. This was not new, but part of a long tradition. The Church has always been aware of the maternal aspect of God and has given it expression in her theological formulations, particularly in the notion of providence. The editors indicate some previous examples and possible sources—St. Augustine, St. Anselm, St. Mechtild, the author of the *Ancrene Riwle;* and some parallels among writers of Julian's time, such as St. Bridget of Sweden and St. Catherine of Siena. More instances have been mentioned by other historians. There is the case of the motherly image attributed to God by Isaiah when he wrote: "Like a son comforted by his mother, will I comfort you",[5] and that attributed to Jesus by himself when he said: "O Jerusalem! Jerusalem! How often have I longed to gather your children as a hen gathers her brood under her wings".[6] There is also the allusion to "the Father's loving breasts" and to "the milk of the Father" in Clement of Alexandria,[7] and to the Spirit as feminine in the time of St. Irenaeus.[8] In the 12th century several Cistercian authors made use of maternal imagery to speak not only of male authority figures, but of God and of "Mother Jesus" as a symbol of tenderness and of supportive love.

Julian, therefore, did not invent the theme. What makes her contribution original, however, is the theological precision with which she applies this symbolism to the Trinitarian interrelationships, as the editors have adequately shown. What we wish to emphasize here is the beauty and the relevance of the theme. Here we find a conspicuous example of harmony between theology and poetry. In the Trinity, "fatherhood means power and goodness" (p. 296); motherhood means wisdom and lovingness.[9]

---

5. Is. 66:13.

6. Mt. 23:37. Other texts are quoted by J. Edgar Bruns, *God as Woman, Woman as God* (New York: Paulist Press, 1973), pp. 33-59.

7. Elaine H. Pagels, "What Became of God the Mother? Conflicting Images of God in Early Christianity," *Signs: Journal of Women in Culture and Society,* 2(1976), 302.

8. Antonio Orbe, S.J., "Los valentinianos y el matrimonio espiritual," *Gregorianum,* 58 (1977), p. 51.

9. On the traditional association of wisdom and womanhood, cf. Bruns, *op. cit.,* pp. 36-41, where he quotes texts and gives a bibliography.

This last idea is associated with, and illuminated by, themes borrowed from the Song of Songs and from courtly literature. God as Mother is, at the same time, "true spouse", "beloved wife" and "fair maiden" (p. 293). In Christ motherhood means mercy and "all the sweet loving offices", in the Holy Spirit "help and grace". The purpose of all this imagery is to evoke a totality, which Julian expresses well as "all one love" (p. 297).

What a richness of prayerful variations Julian develops around this main theme. "My kind Mother, my gracious Mother, my beloved Mother, have mercy on me" (p. 301). How many other titles the whole text of Julian allows us to add to this litany: heavenly Mother, courteous, wise, true, fair, sweet, loving, precious Mother. What matters more than all of these attributes is the deep reality included in what she names with a totally human, not merely feminine, tenderness, in "this fair lovely word Mother" (p. 298). Here we have poetry, but not a mere sentimental poesy as if it were only a maudlin panegyric to the "feelings of a mother". There is here a full theology of the Trinitarian life. There is also a description of God's *praxis*, of the offices and services of a mother towards her children, as he fulfilled them in his Son, Jesus Christ. He gave us life, his life, in his Incarnation and in his death. He nourishes us through the preaching of the Church; he makes us grow through his grace, adapting himself to each of us in his infinite love.

Such a theological approach is relevant in a time when recent studies point to the presence of God as Mother in many religious traditions,[10] especially in Hinduism, from high antiquity to Ramakrishna in the 19th century and to his present-day disciples and admirers. As John Moffitt said in a paper submitted to a Pan-Asian monastic conference in India a few years ago: "It may be that Christians have little or no need for concepts such as these in their own approach to God. But it is not beyond the range of possibility that they may find them of the greatest help in developing a sympathetic and respectful

10. *Ibid.*, pp. 6-31.

approach to God as understood in non-Christian religions. I think it highly important that we try to understand the concept of God as Mother and all that it entails, not merely historically and as reflected in textbooks, but as it may be found today in living Hindu experience".[11]

This interfaith consideration does not exclude the psychological interpretations that modern thinkers may tend to give to this motherly imagery in terms of the unconscious or of the archetypes. There is still much to do along this line. Let it suffice here to say that the underlying concern of Julian is that of the totality. What she develops is not the idea of femininity as opposed to or distinct from that of masculinity, but that of the motherhood of God as complement to that of his fatherhood. She does not introduce in her approach to God the vocabulary and the symbolism of sex, which according to its very etymology means a section, a part, a division, the opposite of a totality. She conceives the quality of a mother as present in the Trinity, as well as that of a Father, a Son and their Spirit. It is the plenitude of life, of love, which is proper to each of them and common to the three of them as a unity of the same substance. To be sure, she describes the motherhood of God better and more often than his fatherhood. We can easily understand this; after all, Julian remains thoroughly feminine. In no way does she wish to substitute the idea of the motherhood of God for that of his fatherhood; she wants to unite them. She works for an integration of all that is best of what we can conceive and experience of God. This theological synthesis is the result of her own psychological, spiritual and mystical integration. Through her experience and her understanding, she grasps the total mystery of God, as far as this is possible in this life, and she wants to communicate to us a glimpse of it. Her attempt is noble indeed.

---

11. John Moffitt, "God as Mother in Hinduism and Christianity," a paper submitted to the Second Encounter of Christian Monks, Bangalore, 1973, to be published.

The Courtesy of God

Courtly poets, including women troubadours, sometimes ended their songs with a dedication called an "envoy", which they presented to the person or the persons for whom they wrote. This was an expression of their *cortesie*, their "courtesy". Julian made extensive use of this term. At the origins of courtly literature in the 12th century, courtesy was almost exclusively applied to secular persons and their love activity. Progressively it was used by great spiritual men like St. Francis of Assisi, and from the time of Dante was applied to the Virgin Mary and even to God himself. Once more we can see that Julian's doctrine unfolds in a tradition. She presents us with an example of Christian humanism, the art of expressing a divine love in human terms. In her, the courtly language is not only frequent, but also quite explicit: God is "most familiar and courteous" (p. 189). "Let us beware that we do not accept this familiarity so carelessly as to foresake courtesy. For our Lord himself is supreme familiarity, and he is as courteous as he is familiar, for he is true courtesy" (p. 331). "All this familiar revelation of our courteous Lord is a lesson of love and a sweet, gracious teaching from himself, in comforting of our soul" (p. 334). "Our courteous Lord, touching us, moves us and protects" (p. 334). Elsewhere, with a remarkable precision, Julian associates this concept of courtesy with those of "service" and of "reward" (p. 268), the latter being equivalent to what the Provençal court poets called the *merce*, the recompense of their endeavors which is the union. Here these concepts and images are transposed and elevated to the sublime level of God, "our reward and our gift for our living and our labour, endlessly surpassing all that we desire in His marvelous courtesy" (p. 294).

To whom has this spiritual courtly literature been dedicated? For whom is the "envoy" supposed to be given? Certainly not for an elite of sophisticated thinkers, though even they, if they had kept a simplicity of heart, might have been enlightened and moved to conversion by her sublime teaching. Her style is so simple and so clear that it can reach every sincere reader, as it expresses the mystical insights of a soul united with God. She is not theatrical, nor does she strive for surprising effects. Her language, however, like that of St. Gregory the Great is smooth, pacifying, enriched only by a plain musicality that the new translation succeeds in rendering. Furthermore, this harmony of prose is but a manifestation, an irradiation, of the delicate equilibrium which is proper to the teaching. It has its source in her experience, which is equally marked by an intensity and a balance.

Both in her method and in her teaching, she presents an integration of elements which have not always been so easily unified. With great facility she reconciles the human and the mystical, the body and the spirit, the ordinary and the extraordinary, affectivity and intelligence, feeling and reflection, culture and piety, knowledge and spirituality, learning and love, philosophy and theology, theology and psychology, deep teaching and literature, poetry and rigor of thought, beauty and truth, experience and doctrinal insights, imagination and reason, emotions and transcendent values, fidelity to tradition and freedom in its interpretation, objective—even literal—reading of the Scriptures and the capacity to find the fuller meaning, speculation and practice, unity of prayer and its varieties, passivities and activities in the encounter with God, monastic and scholastic ways of contemplating the mysteries of faith and, finally, the human and the divine.

In theology the emphasis placed on one aspect of Christian dogma has sometimes led to the neglect of other aspects or to their minimization. In Julian, however, we find an equal emphasis placed on the Trinity and the Incarnation, the suffering of Christ and his glory, his uniqueness and the role of Mary, the present Church and eschatology, the pain and joy of the Christian, his sinfulness and his hope, his work and the necessity of grace, the personal and the universal, human life and its relation to the cosmos, as well as to eternity.

Such an integration is never presented whole or taken for granted, nor is it received from God suddenly, once and forever. It is the result of an endless progression. In describing it in herself, Julian invites us to share in her own experience, to take the same way she does from evil to glory and to come to the conscious realization of God's presence. The kind of journal which she writes becomes a handbook of patience, avoiding both an attitude of depression and a constant enthusiasm. She wants to show that the path to joy is one of quiet humility in sufferings and in consolations, of calm and peace in everything which occurs between souls and their motherly God, their courteous Lord.

J. Leclercq

Fordham University
July 30, 1977

Foreword

U ntil the present editors completed their "critical edition"—that is, a text made from all available sources, manuscript and others, presented in their original language (in this case the English of the 15th century) and providing students with the evidence that can enable them to judge for themselves whether editors' decisions are sound—of Julian of Norwich's *Showings*, her book in the short and long forms in which she herself composed it had been available only in modernized versions, none based on a complete examination of every document and none presenting, as does the critical edition and this new modernization, both versions of the text in one volume. With no wish to disparage the many excellent previous renderings of Julian's writings, it may be said that they all (including that by James Walsh) are now superseded. Any comparison of Walsh's earlier modern English text with that offered here will show in how many places the editors have now come to different and, they believe, truer understanding of what Julian is saying. In particular, they have achieved this through recognition and analysis, as the key to her thought, of her mastery of

rhetorical figures, a mastery wholly concealed by such manuscripts as the two in the Sloan collection, the scribes of which
neither understood nor followed the text as Julian had composed
it.

Introduction

Julian of Norwich's *Revelations* (*Showings*, as she herself more often called them) have been known to the reading public since the English Benedictine Serenus Cressy published his modernized version of the long text in 1670. Even Pierre Poiret's French translation of Cressy's book seems to have been more widely known than the English, until the beginning of this century, when the British Museum (now officially designated the 'British Library') bought the unique manuscript of the short text which, since the dissolution of the monasteries, had passed from one private owner to another. Since then, there have been very many modern English versions of one witness or another.[1] Although numerous beginnings have been made on critical texts—that is, editions of the original language, displaying and evaluating all the evidence—the task was only successfully completed this year, when the present writers issued their edition of both short and long texts made from all the copies known to survive. In this modernized edition they seek to record what they consider Julian to have written (indicating the places where

---

1. For some of these, see the Bibliography.

this still cannot be certain); and in what follows here they present a modified statement of their own knowledge and beliefs about Julian and her book. This is intended not for professional mediaevalists, but those seeking precise indications of the evidence on which this statement is based will find it clearly set out in *Showings*[2].

It is beyond doubt that Julian is a historical character, although we know singularly little about her, apart from what she chooses to tell us and what can be deduced from the evidence furnished in her book. There are four bequests in wills of the late 14th and early 15th centuries that probably were made to her and would show her as then living the solitary, enclosed life of an anchoress (but with a maidservant to tend her) in a cell adjoining the parish Church of St. Julian in Conisford at Norwich, opposite the house of the Augustinian Friars. The friary long since has disappeared, but the church still stands; yet the cell, destroyed by enemy action in World War II and rebuilt, was itself a reconstruction. In the 18th century the Norfolk antiquarian Francis Blomefield, who had seen the British Museum manuscript of the short text then owned by a fellow antiquary, reported the anchor-hold as razed to the ground.

But the most important independent witness to Julian's historicity is the egregious Margery Kempe, the discovery and recognition of whose *Book* was the crowning event in the career of the distinguished American mediaevalist Hope Emily Allen. Margery tells us how she had recourse to Julian in her cell as one well known to be an expert in spiritual guidance, and in their introduction to the critical text of *Showings* the editors have indicated how closely the teaching and the techniques recorded by Margery in her account agree with what we find in Julian's writings. In addition, it is very evident that she never told Margery that she had received visions or had written a book about them. Had it been otherwise, Margery, naively proud of

---

2. Edmund Colledge, O.S.A., and James Walsh, S.J., eds., *A Book of Showings to the Anchoress Julian of Norwich* (Toronto: Pontifical Institute of Mediaeval Studies, 1978).

the knowledge of spiritual literature that she, an illiterate laywoman, had been able to acquire, would hardly have failed to mention the matter.

A few basic facts can be gleaned from Julian's book. In chapter 2 of the long text (p. 177) she writes of having received her revelations on May 13, 1373. In chapter 3 (p. 179), and in chapter ii of the short text (p. 127), she tells us that she was then thirty and a half years old. The introductory paragraph of the short text (p. 125), evidently not written by Julian, states that in 1413 she was still alive, a recluse in Norwich, and the last of the bequests that probably were made to her would show that this was still so in 1416. In the short text she describes her mother as present with others at her bedside when she was thought to be dying, a circumstance which has given rise to much controversy. But this is all. We do not know where she was born, who or what her family were, what her religious history was or when she died. Had it not been that she was convinced that she was divinely commanded to write down her record of her visions, she might have been no more today than one among the thousands of names of those who in mediaeval England lived as solitaries for the love of God, but of whom nothing else is known.

As regards Julian's external life and her character, the editors have come to the following conclusions, guided by their deductions from what she wrote. Though in several places she protests that she is ignorant ('lewd') and that at the time of the visions she knew (not, be it noted, 'knows') 'no letter', this is nothing but a well-known, often-employed rhetorical device, appealing for benevolence from the reader by dispraising the writer's abilities. The frequently made statement that Julian was illiterate is a fiction; she is saying no more than that when she received her revelations she lacked literary skills, skills which she later mastered better than most of her contemporaries. In *Showings* the evidence has been set out in detail; Julian became such a master of rhetorical art as to merit comparison with Geoffrey Chaucer, whose own greatest achievement in this field, his translation of Boethius's *Consolation of Philosophy* (being written, the experts tell us, about 1380, when Julian also was at work on her book) she may well have known. In adapting the rhetoricians' figures and modes of thought to the needs of English prose, Julian was herself a pioneer. In other matters, however, she shows herself the inheritor of centuries-old traditions.

Accordingly, all that she wrote points to her profound knowledge and flexible use of the Latin Vulgate text, and she seems to have been familiar with a wide range of the classical spiritual writings that were the foundations of the monastic contemplative tradition of the Western Church. Let one example here suffice: Her doctrines, in her age equally singular, of the godly will of the soul, never separated from God by sin, and of 'God our Mother' point to her deep familiarity with the writings of William of St. Thierry, who, it may be observed, has never received for such teaching the adverse criticism often accorded to Julian. And to the best of our knowledge, William's writings had not, at Julian's time, been translated into English, although the leading modern authority has recently demonstrated that for his most popular treatise, the *Golden Letter*, there exists one distinctive textual tradition established, it would seem, as Latin manuscripts were copied and circulated among the monasteries of England.

We have no means of knowing where and how Julian gained her learning, partly because so little is known about the facilities for girls' education in her times. But the evidence of her book points to certain conclusions. From the way in which she associates herself with those who in their youth have dedicated themselves to the contemplative life, it seems clear that she had entered a religious order when still young; if this is so, it must have been there that she acquired her academic training. And from what she writes at the end of the long text (that is, as she tells us elsewhere, in 1393): 'This book is begun by God's gift and his grace, but it is not yet performed' (p. 342), the editors consider that, now that the labours of composition are ending, she is obliquely stating her intention to dedicate herself to a more intense form of contemplative living, to retire, as others before and after her did, from monastic life to the yet more severe rule of solitary enclosure. The first of the four wills mentioning her shows that by the following year she had achieved this.

The manuscript tradition of her own work indicates that until the mid-17th century it enjoyed only limited circulation. In contrast with the plethora of surviving copies of the writings of Richard Rolle, Walter Hilton and the author of *The Cloud of Unknowing* (there are so many that until now only the *Cloud* corpus has received adequate editorial treatment, from Phyllis Hodgson), for Julian there are singularly few. Of the short text there exists no more than one copy, that in the 'Amherst MS' (called so after its last private owner), MS British Museum Additional 37790. This is a considerable anthology of shorter spiritual classics, some of them little known in England. The manuscript contains also the only surviving text of *The Treatise of Perfection of the Sons of God*, an English translation via Latin of one of John Ruysbroek's works. This translation shows clear marks of Carthusian provenance; and though the manuscript's handwriting dates it c. 1450, all that we can say certainly of its early ownership is that it was in the hands of James Grenehalgh of Sheen Charterhouse, who has inscribed in it his celebrated monogram, c. 1500.

For a detailed description of the contents of the 'Amherst MS' and for accounts of the long-text witnesses, *Showings* must be consulted. There is only one such witness which predates the Dissolution—Westminster, an anthology with a series of extracts from the long text written by a professional scribe c. 1500. Although until now everyone had accepted the Bibliothèque Nationale catalogue's dating of MS Fonds anglais 40 as 'early 16th-century', that is not so. It is an attempt made c. 1650 to imitate an early 16th-century hand. Nonetheless, this remains the most important long-text manuscript. Cressy's printed text was undoubtedly made from it, probably during the brief period when he served as chaplain in Paris to the English

Benedictine nuns, whose house had recently been founded from Cambrai. At that time its prioress was a daughter of Elizabeth, Lady Falkland, to whom Cressy dedicated the printed edition. Of the two Sloan manuscripts, the second was copied from the first in the same house; at one point, where in the first a chapter number was omitted, it is supplied in the elegant Roman numerals of the second scribe. Finally, there is the 'Upholland Anthology', with a series of long-text extracts written by several Cambrai nuns in the mid-17th century, and one brief quotation in a manuscript, also produced at Cambrai, now owned by Colwich Abbey. All these circumstances point to one conclusion: that the Westminster extracts apart, we owe the preservation of the long text to the piety and learning of Augustine Baker and his spiritual school among the exiled English Benedictine monks and nuns in the Low Countries and France.

If we seek the reasons for the comparative lack of popularity of this work, until the Baker school rescued it from oblivion, they are not hard to find. Julian's book is by far the most profound and difficult of all mediaeval English spiritual writings, with little of the popular appeal (so often deplored by Hilton and the *Cloud*-author) of Rolle and of his imitators; at the same time it was written with a sobriety that distinguishes it from Hilton's fluent, at times facile, piety and from the *Cloud*-author's eccentric vivacity. Julian is hard going. In her own times there seem to have been few willing to attempt it. Though the external circumstances which occasioned her writing are startling enough (in the whole of literary history there can be few other first-hand accounts of the experience of being at the point of death), the visions, when they came, were of a stark simplicity, conveying deep meaning at a variety of levels, which thereafter for twenty years continued to perplex Julian and which today can still perplex us. To trace the different modes, 'bodily', 'bodily and yet more spiritual' and 'spiritual', in which Julian perceived the visions were given, we have one most excellent guide in Paul Molinari's study, to which the editors are greatly indebted and often refer. But Julian's own perplexity occasioned one notable circumstance, that she drafted her book first as the short text (how soon after the receiving of the visions we cannot tell) and then as the long text, the conclusion of which was being written in 1393, and that this long text as we have it is the product of much editorial rewriting by Julian.

A first reading of the two texts side by side shows an outstanding difference. In the short text there is no mention— barely any hint—of the long text's chapter 51, the extended allegory of the lord and the servant, nor do we find in the short text anything comparable with the teaching on the 'godly will' or on 'God our Mother', which, as the editors have demonstrated in *Showings*, are logically derived from the allegory and represent Julian's profound speculations on it. Two judgments are possible: Either the allegory is Julian's own later invention to justify the doctrines (in which case, in representing the allegory as she does as a part of the revelation, Julian would be guilty of falsification), or she suppressed the allegory when she wrote the short text for reasons no longer obtaining when the long text was composed. There is plain evidence that the second judgment is the right one.

Unlike the brief prologue to the short text, chapter 1 of the long text, summarizing the revelations in sequence, seems to be Julian's own work; otherwise she could not number in her frequent cross-references the succeeding chapters as she does, and, furthermore, the chapter bears many of the distinctive marks of her very individual style. But when we come to the account of Revelation XIV (of which chapter 51 and the subsequent development of 'God our Mother' are by far the most notable ingredients), all that we read is: '. . . that our Lord God is the foundation of our beseeching. In this, two fair qualities were seen. One is proper prayer; the other is true trust, and he wishes them both to be equally generous. And so our prayer is pleasing to him, and he in his goodness fulfils it'. This takes account of chapters 41, 42 and 43, dealing with prayer, but not of the remainder of the revelation. Many previous commentators have assumed that originally this fourteenth showing on prayer ended with chapter 43, but this is not the case. The entire revelation develops Julian's mature thinking on what had become for her an obsessive problem, how what she knew to be true of sin, damnation and the anger of God can be reconciled with what she had been shown of the loving workings of mercy and grace upon the soul in contemplative union with God. Thus the revelation culminates in the parable of the lord and the servant, chapter 51, explaining precisely how the relationship between God and man persists despite human inadequacy and frailty; and in the concluding chapters of this revelation, chapter 52 shows this contemplative relationship to be Trinitarian, chapter 53 declares how creation and redemption come together in Christ, the head of human nature, chapter 54 tells how all incorporated into Christ are so affected. Chapter 55 defines the precise nature of this incorporation in terms of Christ's relationship with the Father and the Spirit, and the two following chapters demonstrate how this knowledge in faith of God in Christ enables creatures to grow in understanding of their own nature, and to receive the gifts which flow from mutual indwelling:

> For the same virtues which we have received from our substance, given to us in nature by the goodness of God, the same virtues by the operation of mercy are given to us in grace, renewed through the Holy Spirit; and these virtues and gifts are treasured for us in Jesus Christ. For in the same time that God joined himself to our body in the maiden's womb, he took our soul, which is sensual, and in taking it, having enclosed us all in himself, he united it to our substance. In this union he was perfect man, for Christ, having joined in himself every man who will be saved, is perfect man (p. 292).

The conclusion of the revelation, chapters 58-63, develops Julian's teachings on the creating and redeeming activity within the Trinity of the second person; and in this development she employs the image and doctrine of 'God our Mother', to which presently we shall revert. The revelation concludes with Julian's emphasis on what is for her the most sublime expression of man's relationship with God in contemplative prayer: the acceptance of the soul's feebleness and failing of insight and understanding, which understanding comes from a loving trust in God which finds its truest human analogy in the relationship of the child with its parents.

It seems, therefore, that when Julian composed the summaries of the revelations for chapter 1 of the long text, she had not yet received the most important of the insights which it now expounds, insights all logically developed from the lord-and-servant allegory, and that at that time it was still her intention to suppress the allegory, as she had in composing the short text, because she did not understand it. But, as she now tells us, she had come to distinguish two kinds of mystery, those which it is God's will to preserve as hidden until he may wish to make them plain, and those, such as had been revealed to her in the showings, which

> . . . *are mysteries to us, but not only because he wants them to be mysteries to us, but also because of our blindness and our ignorance. And therefore he has great pity, and therefore he wants to make them plain to us himself, so that we may know him and love him and cling to him. For everything which is profitable for us to understand and know our good Lord will most courteously show to us by all the preaching and teaching of Holy Church (p. 235).*

And at the very end of the long text she tells us:

> *For truly I saw and understood in our Lord's meaning that he revealed it because he wants to have it better known than it is. In which knowledge he wants to give us grace to love him and to cleave to him, for he beholds his heavenly treasure with so great love on earth that he will give us more light and solace in heavenly joy, by drawing our hearts from the sorrow and the darkness which we are in. And from the time that it was revealed, I desired many times to*

know in what was our Lord's meaning. And fifteen years after and more, I was answered in spiritual understanding, and it was said: What, do you wish to know your Lord's meaning in this thing? (p. 342).

The conclusion is inescapable: In 1388, if not later, she at last understood for the first time the totality of the revelations, and what is now found in the long text but is unrepresented in the short text and in the long text's introductory, summarizing chapter shows us which mysteries in the revelations were unlocked for her and described by her only after final enlightenment was hers.

The minor, running discrepancies between the two versions are commented on in the footnotes to the text. Some show modifications of her own attitudes; she is notably more at pains in the later version to insist on the relevance and applicability of the whole revelation to every Christian soul, notably less willing to seem to be adopting a censorious attitude towards anyone. Others plainly indicate the widening and deepening of her theological interests and perceptions; nowhere is this more apparent than in her extraordinary understanding of contemplative prayer as the working of mercy and grace, desire and fulfillment according to the teaching of Gregory the Great and Bernard of Clairvaux, as well as in her ability to use William of St. Thierry's speculative thinking in her development of her doctrines of the 'godly will' and of 'God our Mother'. The whole tone of the long text, in contrast to the earlier version, is of an assured tranquillity; and the second version displays to a quite remarkable degree her progress in mastering the rhetoricians' skills. To this last feature of her writing no modern English version can do justice; the present editors can only refer interested readers to the footnotes of *Showings*, and to the Appendix to that edition, for illustration and discussion of this matter.

In the introductory summary of the long text, Julian wrote of the first revelation, 'in which all the revelations which follow are founded and connected'; and in the Introduction to *Showings* it is suggested that 'Revelation I stands to the other fifteen in their final version as the Prologue stands to the rest of St. John's Gospel'. The first revelation records Julian's vivid awareness that the Word has been spoken to her and that she has seen his glory. She recounts that when she was young, she had asked for the grace, in her thirtieth year, of a sickness which might seem, to her and to all others, as if it would be mortal, and for the gift of three wounds, of true contrition, loving compassion and longing with her will for God.

The editors have remarked in the Introduction to the critical text on the 'Franciscan' influences in Julian's early piety, and especially on that of popular devotions to the Passion. These gifts, she makes plain, were to lead to the fulfillment of her longing for union with God; and she is clear that the sickness which was granted to her in her thirtieth year, and the miraculous cure which followed, were God's immediate preparation for her to receive the revelations which ensued. She tells us that at the outset she received three graces: the first was the cure, the second what she clearly considers to be a divine impulse to pray for the second wound she had so long ago desired:

> Then suddenly it came into my mind that I ought to wish for the second wound as a gift and a grace from our Lord, that my body might be filled full of recollection and feeling of his blessed Passion, as I had prayed before, for I wished that his pains might be my pains, with compassion which would lead to longing for God (p. 180),

and, although she continues that 'I never wanted any bodily vision or any kind of revelation from God', the third grace, a sight of Christ's head bleeding under the crown of thorns, followed at once.

Her first description of this opening bodily sight, in chapter 4 of the long text and in the corresponding chapter iii of the short, is very austere, in particular by contrast with Revelations II and VIII; and in the long text the reason for this becomes clear, when she writes that 'suddenly the Trinity filled my heart full of the greatest joy, and I understood that it will be so in heaven without end to all who will come there' (p. 181). There is no reference throughout this revelation to the dolours of the Passion. The stress is on the consolation which the vision brought; and she tells us of her first reaction to the sight of Christ, glorified and exalted, yet on his Cross:

> *I accepted it that at that time our Lord Jesus wanted, out of his courteous love, to show me comfort before my temptations began; for it seemed to me that I might well be tempted by devils, by God's permission and with his protection, before I would die (p. 182).*

After the bodily sight of the bleeding head, in the short text she next records 'a spiritual sight of his familiar love' (chapter iv, p. 130), whereas in the long text there follows first the vision of Mary, seen 'spiritually in her bodily likeness' (chapter 4, p. 182), which in the short text is placed after the showing of 'everything which is made'. Julian does not seem in either text to intend to record all the various elements of Revelation I in chronological order. In the long text she tells us that the bodily sight persisted until many things had been seen and understood, and she makes this observation after she has referred a second time to the revelation to her of Mary (chapter 7, p. 187), which second reference is not found in the short text, though she will conclude Revelation I by telling us that

> *all this was shown in three parts, that is to say, by bodily vision and by words formed in my understanding and by spiritual vision (chapter 9, p. 192, and cf. chapter vii, p. 135).*

And although she also offers us six headings under which she arranges its total contents, none of this refers to chronological succession.

When she writes of 'words formed in my understanding', she means the locutions which she reports so often through what the rhetoricians called *ratiocinatio*, 'reasoning by question and answer'. In Revelation I we read:

> At the same time as I saw this sight of the head bleeding, our good
> Lord showed a spiritual sight of his familiar love. I saw that he is to
> us everything which is good and comforting for our help. He is our
> clothing, who wraps and enfolds us for love, embraces us and
> shelters us, surrounds us for his love, which is so tender that he may
> never desert us. And so in this sight I saw that he is everything
> which is good, as I understand. And in this he showed me something
> small, no bigger than a hazelnut, lying in the palm of my hand, as
> it seemed to me, and it was as round as a ball. I looked at it with the
> eye of my understanding and thought: What can this be? I was
> amazed that it could last, for I thought that because of its littleness
> it would suddenly have fallen into nothing. And I was answered in
> my understanding: It lasts and always will, because God loves it;
> and thus everything has being through the love of God (chapter 5, p.
> 183, and cf. chapter iv, p. 130).

She never considers this reasoning as any kind of negative exercise of her own intellect. It has often been noticed that the locutions are of different kinds; but even here, when it is Julian's own reflection on what she has been shown that produces the questions, she is convinced that she cannot of herself find the answers.

In the Introduction to *Showings*, the editors have pointed out how closely Julian's convictions about her locutions resemble what Teresa of Avila has to say in her *Autobiography* and in *The Interior Castle* about her own experiences of such silent 'words' from God. They are very distinctly formed, much more clearly understood than if heard by ear, of themselves convincing that they come from God, carrying authority, producing sudden change in the soul, persisting in the memory. All these are indeed Julian's beliefs about the 'words formed in her understanding'.

Although her editing of Revelation I in the long text shows her as then no longer seeking to restrict what she had to say to those vowed to the contemplative life, and not wishing to seem to condemn the active life as such, nonetheless the whole of the first revelation in the long text can be said to serve as an introduction to contemplative prayer and the way of thinking conducive to it. She tells us first in chapter 4 of the God who communicates himself to us, by associating the great names of the Trinity with his 'familiarity' and 'courtesy'. Next she shows Mary as the model of that reverent contemplation in wisdom and truth. Chapter 5 begins with an image of 'familiar love' compounded from Scripture: the Psalmist's words about the universe clad in the majesty of the transcendent God, united to the detail from Luke of the swaddling clothes of the manger at Bethlehem; and the revelation of the little thing like a hazelnut has its purpose, to explain that the God who seeks us, and he alone, has and is what can fulfil us. The chapter ends with her own petitionary prayer for this unitive life, the expression of this natural yearning of the soul that is itself a response to the inspiration of the Spirit of God:

> God, of your goodness give me yourself, for you are enough for me, and I can ask for nothing which is less which can pay you full worship. And if I ask anything which is less, always I am in want; but only in you do I have everything (p. 184).

Chapter 6, after Julian has described her own devotional life (in terms which indicate how closely she must have followed the pattern established, a century and a half before her, by the *Ancrene Riwle*), concludes with one of her finest passages, which will later be given theological definition when she expounds the doctrine of the Trinity as 'creating nature'. Here she presents us with the images of mother, father and nurse as symbolizing divine goodness; it is the fulness of what God has to give and longs to give which 'the soul seeks and always will, until we truly know our God, who has enclosed us all in himself (p. 186). All true prayer, she concludes here, is consummately unitive; it is the expression of a mutual giving which God has made possible for us and has demonstrated to us in the incarnate Jesus.

> *For our natural will is to have God, and God's good will is to have us, and we can never stop willing or loving until we possess him in the fulness of joy (p. 186).*

In chapter 7 Julian returns again to the revelation of Mary, because in her she has seen that this unitive prayer of petition is the asking and receiving, in the one movement, of divine wisdom, truth and love. It is Mary of the Visitation as well as of the Annunciation whose love and reverent fear will express themselves in an abundant charity towards Christ's brethren. This contemplation of Mary, as Julian will show with greater precision in Revelation XI, is not an end in itself, but a sight 'through which I am taught to know myself and reverently to fear my God' (chapter 25, p. 222). So Julian naturally adverts again to the sight of the head bleeding, which now in the long text she sees as expressing for her the paradox of Crucifixion and Resurrection, life and death, joy and suffering. But, as throughout this revelation, it is consolation which dominates, and she moves to a final manifestation of the 'familiar love'. This particular showing, which she calls an 'example', adding that it was shown bodily, she did not record in the short text. Plainly it anticipates the revealed allegory of the lord and the servant, and must in the short text have been suppressed because of its close relations to this still incomprehensible vision. It, too, is an allegory, of the condescension displayed by a king or a noble to a poor servant, giving the servant greater joy than rich gifts offered in a distant manner, followed by her own gloss, 'So it is with our Lord Jesus and us . . .' (p. 188), which, significantly, concludes with her observation about the application to the contemplative life of the rule of faith, hope and love. A revelation is an operation of divine love; the insights it gives into mysteries is a grace freely given. But when the time of the revelation is past, and what was seen has disappeared, its fruits are preserved by the grace of the Holy Spirit to the end of life. We need not doubt that she is here writing, in 1395 or later, of how there have been preserved for her the showings and their fruits which she had been given twenty years or more ago. The 'example' is deceptively simple, and it is a commonplace in contemporary literature; but for Julian it was revealed 'so exalted that this man's heart could be ravished and he could almost forget his own existence in the joy of this great familiarity' (p. 188). It is clear that she is now seeing it in the light of the great parable of the lord and the servant.

The importance which Julian attaches, in the long text, to this first revelation has already been remarked. The point is made again when we notice how carefully she has reorganized and rewritten, in chapters 9 and 10 of the long text, what she had set down in chapters v, vi and vii of her first version. To begin with, she adds immediately to her own brief analysis of the contents of the showing that a movement of the heart in love towards all her brethren accompanied the entire revelation, and is integral to her evaluation of it. It is therefore logical that she should go on to provide an example of this movement, and her remark to those at her bedside, 'Today is my Doomsday' (p. 190), is precisely that: 'I said this because I wished them to love God better, and to make them mindful that this life is short, of which they could see me as an example'. She therefore inserts these two passages, with which she originally closed the revelation in the short text, here into chapter 8. She also recalls an experience which she seems to have forgotten when she was composing the short text: the wonder and perplexity which she felt at this point. She was convinced that she was going to die, and yet the purpose of the whole revelation was not, as she had previously thought, to comfort her in the moment of death, if, as now appeared, 'this vision was revealed for those who would go on living' (p. 191). The pericope neatly introduces the next section (which had been the beginning of chapter v in the short text), gives added weight to the apologia, 'disregard the wretch to whom it was shown . . .' (as though she were saying, 'What more useless vehicle of God's love and goodness could there be than one who was at the point of death?) and illustrates the claim that it is as though Jesus had shown it directly to all whom he loves. The same theme dominates chapter 9. What is remarkable here is that although she still uses much of what she wrote in her short text, the whole tone and temper have changed. Previously she conveyed a certain apprehension in her humility, as though her readers might not believe her when she proclaimed her unworthiness:

> *I pray you all for God's sake, and I counsel you for your own profit, that you disregard the wretched worm, the sinful creature to whom it was shown (chapter vi, p. 133).*

and also a certain fear that if she protests too much, her revelations might not be received at all. Now, however, she is serene, balanced and at peace with herself; and even the most captious must believe her as she allies herself with 'you who are simple, to give you comfort and strength; for we are all one in love' (chapter 9, p. 191). She no longer needs to protest, as she seems to do in the first version, that 'I am not good because of the revelation, but only if I love God better'; she can state it quite straightforwardly, and round it off with a deceptive rhetorical simplicity and with quiet conviction: 'And inasmuch as you love God better, it is more to you than to me'. With deft touches, such as the insertion of 'I hope', she is able to avoid possible theological inaccuracies and misinterpretations, such as that she is claiming absolutely to be in a state of grace and to be confirmed in that state. Finally, she perceives that any apologia about the publication of private revelations demands, not only for the sake of prudence, but for theological assessment, a clear and lucid profession of faith. This she supplies in the long text, where, in a sense, she goes beyond it. She tells us that the faith 'was always in my sight' throughout the revelation, which informs us that in spite of the sickness, she was in full possession of her faculties. But it also tells us that she came to her revelations with a constant mental background to all that she saw or heard furnished by her previous deep meditation and contemplation on the truths of her faith.

Julian's account of Revelation II is contained in chapter 10 of the long text. It begins with her description of what she saw in the face of the crucified Christ, which substantially agrees with the short text, but after the reasoning 'If God wishes to show you more, he will be your light' (p. 193) the rest of chapter 10 is original. Her mind seems to be engaged by a succession of images and ideas, derived from her reading and meditation, presented afresh to her as lights from God. She enjoys the consoling knowledge that she would be as safe on the seabed, in God's presence, as anywhere else in the universe; but, more, this appeals to her faith, the dogmatic fact that it is in God that we live and move. Her concern that she could see so little of what she longed for is now resolved by faith: 'It is God's will that we believe that we see him continually, though it seems to us that the sight be only partial'.

The recollection of the 'bodily sight' of the Crucifixion presents itself repeatedly to her mind. When she writes: 'And then several times our Lord gave me more insight' (p. 194), plainly she is describing not the first reception of the vision but the insights she has received since it happened, and, perhaps, since she wrote the short text. The vision was given to make her see how Christ who is God suffered death, which came into the world by man (I Corinthians 15.21). Characteristically, she makes her point by a 'contrary', a visual contrast: '. . . our foul, black death, which our fair, bright, blessed Lord bore for our sins'; and she continues without interruption: 'It made me think of the holy Vernicle at Rome'. She knows of the Vernicle's wonder-working reputation, but that is of no interest to her; she wants to penetrate the representation of Christ's suffering humanity, to perceive its spiritual significance.

To do this she has recourse to fundamentals of the Christian faith: that the Trinity made man in their image and likeness (Genesis 1.27), and that only man's Creator could restore fallen man. She dwells on the contrast between our foul, black mortality and Christ's radiant beauty; but this is no sentimental *Brautmystik*, but witnesses to the theological insights she has been given, and which she wants for others, into the mystery of the Redemption. She refers readers to what she will write on this topic in chapter 18, a clear indication of how carefully the long text was drafted.

Then follows a third and final exposition of the theme of 'seeking and seeing'. The soul 'cannot do more than seek, suffer and trust' (p. 195); and the more that she does this, the more is she pleasing to God. Ordinary grace is needed for this to be begun; for it to be perfected in 'illumination by finding' is of the special grace of the Holy Spirit. When the work is completed, God will have contributed his grace and guidance, the soul her disposition from the humility given to her. But whether the soul seeks or sees, the greatest honour she can pay to God is to surrender herself to him. Seeking is 'common to all', and every soul is given the grace for this. Grace must form in us three dispositions: zeal and joy, perseverance and resignation, and perfect trust.

The authority with which her thinking develops, the clarity and precision of her language, and the ease and subtlety with which this complex of inspirations and the associations which they suggest to Julian is resolved make this chapter a truly remarkable and wholly professional performance.

At the end of this revelation Julian writes: '. . . it is his will that we know that he will appear, suddenly and blessedly, to all his lovers' (p. 196). At the beginning of Revelation III she writes: 'And after this I saw God in an instant of time' (p. 197). It is important for her transition here from II to III that she stress the sudden nature of her sight of God. Firstly, this is a 'ghostly sight', following one which was bodily and repulsive, the image of Christ's face after he had been crowned with thorns and mocked. It was only after she had received enlightenment several times that this 'bodily sight' instructed her on seeking and finding God, so that eventually she learns that the finding will be as sudden as it is blissful. So this 'ghostly sight' with which Revelation III begins is precisely the finding of God; and she sees him in an instant of time, 'in a point', *in puncto*, *in ictu oculi*, as the Latin Vulgate text of I Corinthians 15.52 writes of the resurrection of the body. Secondly, in the short text this vision is made the immediate answer to her prayer for more light, and in the long text she is told: 'He will be your light; you need none but him' (p. 193).

In this intellectual vision Julian unobtrusively shows her acquaintance with scholastic metaphysics. Thomas Aquinas, quoting the *Glossa ordinaria*, had written: 'God is in all things by his presence, his power and his substance', and he had briefly explained this: '. . . by his power, because all things are within his power, and by his presence, because all things are open to his sight, and by his substance he is present in all things as the cause of their being'.[3] But Julian's purpose is to express her contemplative awareness of the reality of his presence. Nothing could be more detrimental to contemplative life and prayer than doubt that the rational creature is at the centre of the divine concern of a God who is ever at work in his creation:

> *This vision was revealed to my understanding, for our Lord wants to have the soul truly converted to contemplation of him and of all his works in general (p. 198).*

In the previous chapter Julian had touched upon a cause of unease in contemplatives, the feeling of insecurity which the awareness of evil, and especially of personal sin, can bring. The Christian must learn to live with this, but it can be done only with the help of prayer proceeding from faith informed by a sound theology; and to this end Julian employs her considerable skills and erudition, her knowledge of the sapiential books, her sympathetic understanding of Chaucer's insights into *De consolatione philosophiae*, and her grasp of the teaching of John and

---

3. *Summa theologiae* I.8.3 *in corp.*

Paul on the mysteries of faith, the Trinity and the Incarnation. All this finds striking expression in the final summary of this revelation:

> *So was the soul examined, powerfully, wisely and lovingly, in this vision. Then I saw truly that I must agree, with great reverence and joy in God (p. 199).*

The fourth, fifth and sixth revelations seem to form a group in themselves. Revelation IV, chapter 12, recounts a bodily sight; Revelation V, chapter 13, is a locution, 'With this the fiend is overcome'; Revelation VI, chapter 14, is another locution, 'I thank you for your service. . .'. The bodily sight of chapter 12 is the only one in which Julian is shown any other mystery of the Passion besides the crucified Christ in his last moments. Here there is possibly an unusual discrepancy between the two texts. The long text reads:

> *And after this as I watched, I saw the body bleeding copiously in representation of the scourging . . . (199);*

but the short text has:

> *And after this as I watched I saw the body bleeding copiously, the blood hot, flowing freely, a living stream. . . . And I saw this in the furrows made by the scourging (p. 137).*

The short text clearly refers to the furrows made by the scourges; she is not seeing in the vision the scourging itself. However, as is indicated in the notes to *Showings*, the long text's *in semyng of the scoregyng* would appear to mean that she was granted an imaginative and not a corporeal vision of the actual flagellation at the pillar. One could interpret *semyng* as 'furrowing', but this is less probable. It is more likely that in *semyng* we have editorial tampering in a long-text common ancestor with Julian's *semes*, preserved in the short text.

When Julian goes on to describe the lacerations, the

wounds and the bleeding caused by the flagellation, it may be thought that she departs from her customary moderation in describing the physical details of the Passion; but we need to recall the early application in the West of Psalm 128 to Christ in his Passion. Even so, this passage reflects more contemporary enthusiasm for meditating in detail, often gruesome, on the physical sufferings of Christ than do her other descriptions of 'the pains of the Passion'. There is no need to suggest, for the extended reflection on the Precious Blood in the long text, that Julian may have been acquainted with the visions and teachings of Catherine of Siena. Chronology seems to rule this out and, in any case, Catherine was no more an innovator or popularizer of devotion to the Precious Blood than was Margaret Mary Alacoque of Sacred Heart devotions. Demonstrating this, excerpts are given in the introduction to *Showings* and in several footnotes to the text from Latin and English versions of the *Fifteen Oes*, circulating throughout the Western Church in the fourteenth century, and there can be little doubt that Julian's first source of inspiration is Pauline soteriology as expressed in Romans, chapters 5 and 6, and reflected in Hebrews, chapters 8 to 10.

What is most remarkable about this bodily sight and most in favour of its authenticity is the clarity with which Julian distinguishes between a bodily and an imaginative vision, and this is no hindsight, but an account of the vision itself:

> . . .*and I saw it so plentiful that it seemed to me that if it had in fact and in substance been happening there, the bed and everything all around it would have been soaked in blood (pp. 199-200).*

It follows from this observation that her other sights of the bleeding and dying Christ were likewise imaginative. We are reminded of the description of 'a spiritual vision or imaginative' in *The Chastising of God's Children*[4], and of the doubts expressed

---

4. Ed. Bazire and Colledge, 169, 170-171.

by the *Cloud*-author that Martin and Stephen 'saw such things with their bodily eyes'[5].

In her contemplation of the suffering and bleeding Christ, Julian had remarked upon the redeeming power of his sacrifice, signified by the shedding of the blood:

> *For it is most plentiful, as it is most precious, and that through the power of the blessed divinity. And it is of our own nature, and blessedly flows over us by the power of his blessed love.*

John on Patmos had beheld the blood of the Lamb which washes clean and ascends to heaven. In Revelation V, as she still ponders what she sees, the words which she hears, 'With this the fiend is overcome', echo another text from the Apocalypse: 'And that great dragon was cast out, that old serpent who is called the devil and Satan, who seduces the whole world. . .and they overcame him by the blood of the Lamb' (Apocalypse 12.9-11). In the showing which follows, Julian laughs, as the valiant woman who 'will laugh at the latter day' (Proverbs 31.25), 'because he showed that his Passion is the overcoming of the fiend' (p. 201) and because 'I saw that on Judgment Day he will be generally scorned by all who will be saved' (p. 202). With Scripture as her foundation, she synthesizes briefly the teaching of the Western fathers on the devil's impotence, though the striking phrase 'for his power is all locked in God's hands' is surely her own.

A notable addition to the short text is her penetrating theological reflection on how God regards the reprobate, which anticipates the answer, conveyed through the parable of the lord and the servant, to her conundrum, how does God see us in our sin? So she first states that even though there can be no wrath in God, 'it is with power and justice, to the profit of all who will be saved, that he opposes the damned, who in malice and malignity work to frustrate and oppose God's will' (p. 201). This is the first part of her explanation of what she means by the word 'scorn'

---

5. Ed. Hodgson, 106-107.

when she attributes it to God. She then develops the thought by elucidating what 'opposes' signifies in the context. This passage, which is evidently corrupt in the manuscripts, has been rendered into modern English as 'And when I saw our Lord scorn his malice, that was through the fixing of my understanding on him, that is, that this was an interior revelation of his truth, in which his demeanour did not change. For as I see it, this is an attribute of God which must be honoured, and which lasts forever' (p. 202). She seems to be conveying the opinion that God 'looks right through' the reproved who no longer exist for him but are, in the Old Testament phrase, 'blotted out of the book of the living' (Psalm 68.29).

Implicit in the locution in Revelation V, 'With this the fiend is overcome', is the classical teaching of monasticism that the Christian life is a spiritual combat against the world, the flesh and, particularly, the devil. Consequently, the Scriptural theme of Revelation VI is the Pauline hymn, 'If we endure with him, we shall also reign with him' (II Timothy 2.10-13), when the devil 'will see that all the woe and tribulation which he has caused them will be changed into the increase of their eternal joy' (p. 202), and it is largely concerned with a special insight into God's 'familiar love', his gratitude for man's service, and particularly that of dedicated contemplatives. The revelation begins with a locution common to both texts. All God's servants are to be the recipients of his everlasting thanks for their patient endurance, but especially those who have made him the gift of their youth. This ghostly sight is first conveyed by an example which, it seems, was suppressed in the short text because it, too, so resembles the parable of the lord and the servant.

The three aspects of heavenly bliss which are described are common to both texts. What Julian sees as she continues to look at the whole is the applicability of another Pauline text, Romans 8.15-22, where the apostle expresses his confidence that though we are groaning and in travail now, the sufferings of this time are not to be compared with the glory to be revealed in us; and this is because we are co-heirs in Christ. But in the long text particularly she is preoccupied with the Lord's courtesy. She gives the example of a lord rewarding his servant to show the first degree of bliss, and for the second she offers another curial example:

> *If a king thank his subjects, it is a great honour for them; and if he makes this known to all the kingdom, then their honour is much increased (pp. 203-204).*

But it is the addition in the long text to the account of the third degree which is most significant. Though those who as she—we believe—have freely dedicated themselves to the contemplative life in their youth will receive a wonderful reward, it remains true that those spending a single day in the divine service will receive the same gift, the same measure of bliss. This is exactly the teaching of the parable of the labourers in the vineyard, so feelingly and tellingly expounded by Julian's contemporary, the *Pearl*-poet. For though God thanks her with the gift of himself, and shares his knowledge and gratitude with all the blessed, the gift is still unmerited, a 'courtesy'. The very term recalls Pecham's 'he has loved, I say, courteously'; and the vision of this courteous love increases her desire to serve him all her life.

Though the subject matter of Revelation VII—the alternation of spiritual consolation and desolation, the various reasons for the withdrawal of special grace and right conduct in times of dereliction—is commonplace in late patristic and mediaeval spiritual writing, it has its importance in the evolution of Julian's practical experience and later theological reflection. It reveals her response when she is enabled to contemplate the joys of heaven. It associates the heaviness of spiritual desolation with the pains of Christ's Passion. Then, too, it begins to prepare the way for her exposition of the mystery of the Incarnation and its effects on the life and prayer of the Christian.

The variations here between chapters ix and 15 are few, seven in all, none of them consisting of more than a few words; but each change is theologically significant. In the short text Julian had described the vision of God's union with the soul as making her 'powerfully secured without any fear' (p. 139). In the long text this becomes 'without any painful fear', because she has since come to perceive that there is a fear which belongs to the unitive life, in heaven as on earth, the 'reverent dread' of which she will write later. There she will explain that all other fears, even those which are profitable, are also painful.

The two words which she most commonly uses to describe her experience of God's dealing with the soul are 'mind' and 'feeling'. In the short text, she had written of the 'supreme spiritual delight': 'This sensation was so welcome and so dear to me. . .'; but in editing this she seems to have thought it too subjective, and not clearly distinguished from natural feelings of well-being, so that she now writes: 'This sensation was so welcome and so spiritual. . .'.

As her life of prayer developed after the revelations, she received the grace of a progressively deeper contemplative penetration into the mysteries of the Trinity, so that, whereas in the short text she had written '. . .nor did I deserve these sensations of joy; but God gives joy freely as it pleases him. . .' (p. 140), now in the long text she substitutes the more personal 'our Lord'.

Margery Kempe's testimony about Julian's expertise in spiritual guidance is constantly confirmed in the long text, and there is evidence of it here. She had written of the state of spiritual desolation: '. . .every man needs to experience this. . . . And sometimes a man is left to himself for the profit of his soul, and neither the one nor the other is caused by sin'. Now she has come to see that universal statements about the divine action in bestowing or withdrawing contemplative graces are imprudent, so that she qualifies: '. . .some souls profit by experiencing this. . .although [a man's] sin is not always the cause' (p. 205). The additions 'some souls' and 'always' are important; she also gives her reason for the later statement. In the short text it had been: 'For in this time I committed no sin for which I ought to have been left to myself', but in the long text we read: 'For in this time I committed no sin for which I ought to have been left to myself, for it was so sudden'. This is not only the observation of common sense—she had not had the time even for a sinful thought—but also the application of an important canon of spiritual discernment. One should look for possible natural causes or occasions of a state of mind before attributing it to the divine action.

In her reflections at the end of this revelation on the wonderful alternation of joy and sorrow she is solicitous to find the balance, which is hope, between despair and presumption. So she adds, to her earlier observation that pain will be brought to nothing, the qualifying phrase which has so much meaning for her: 'for those who will be saved' (p. 205).

Revelation VII is longer and much more complex than those which precede it, apart from the first; for that Julian had provided a recapitulation and here, too, she concludes the final chapter, 20, with another such summary:

> It is God's will, as I understand it, that we contemplate his blessed Passion in three ways. Firstly, that we contemplate the cruel pain he suffered[6]—this is the first 'way'—with contrition—the second 'way'—and compassion—the third; and our Lord revealed that at this time, and gave me strength and grace to see it (p. 214).

The 'contemplation of the cruel pain', the beginning of this revelation, is a bodily sight, no detail of which Julian spares us. There appear to be two reasons for this intense concentration upon the physical sufferings of the Passion. First, she wishes to show how completely her first prayer was answered, to have recollection of the Passion ('I thought that I wished that I had been at that time with Magdalen and with the others who were Christ's lovers, so that I might have seen with my own eyes the Passion which our Lord suffered for me'—chapter 2, p. 177). The second reason is contained in what is, as the editors have made it, the opening sentence of Revelation IX, chapter 21: 'And I watched with all my might for the moment when Christ

---

6. This rearranges Julian's word order—cf. p. 214—so as to make clear what are her 'three ways'.

would expire, and I expected to see his body quite dead' (p. 214). This, and the allusion in chapter 8 to her 'Doomsday', seem to suggest that she thought that the moment of her own death might coincide with the sight of Christ's. In chapter 16 she sees the effects of his sufferings, and the rest of the bodily sight is concerned with what she calls his greatest bodily pain, the 'deep drying'. She promises us that later she will write of his other, spiritual thirst.

The equivalent 'ghostly sight' which follows this description of Christ's pain is that she herself begins to feel his sufferings, as she had prayed long ago. The long text here may seem to lose some of the clarity and force which the short text has when it cites from the Christological hymn in chapter 2 of Philippians ('But each soul should do as St. Paul says, and feel in himself what is in Christ Jesus'—chapter x, p. 142). She may have decided that Paul's words were not so apposite as she had once thought. He is inviting the Philippians to imitate Christ's humility and obedience, not to experience directly his bodily sufferings. Doubtless she also found it inappropriate to exhort others to share this experience, as she had done, especially since she discovers that she herself can hardly tolerate her participation in his pains.

It is at this point that she becomes aware that her prayer for contrition is being answered in an unforeseen way. She finds herself repenting her one-time aspiration to suffer the same pains as Christ and those who stood by his cross; but she is enabled, through 'reasoning by question and answer', to understand that this pain of Christ which she is now sharing is the purification which she had asked for; it is truly redemptive, because it proceeds from her love for him.

The third way of contemplation, 'with compassion', now begins with chapter 18. First Julian is shown the quality of Mary's compassion for Christ—they were 'so united in love that the greatness of her love was the cause of the greatness of her pain' (p. 210)—and then how those others who were near to him shared in this compassion. She sees this suffering extended to all creatures capable of experiencing pain, because of the 'great unity between Christ and us'. All of them suffered at the time of the Crucifixion, each in his own fashion, including the pagans Pilate and Denis 'of France'; and she concludes this chapter with the reflection:

> *So was our Lord Jesus afflicted for us; and we all stand in this way*
> *of suffering with him, and shall till we come to his bliss (p. 211).*

In chapter 19 she tells how these sights and the accompanying meditation enabled her deliberately to choose the crucified and suffering Saviour as the only fulfillment she desires:

> *. . . for I would rather have remained in that pain until Judgment*
> *Day than have come to heaven any other way than by him (p. 212).*

This deliberate choice enables her to put into psychological and theological perspective her previous feelings of reluctance to share Christ's sufferings. In her experience of such opposition between 'repenting and wilful choice' she seems to have had in mind Christ's own struggle in the garden: 'Father, if it be possible, let this chalice pass', and that of Paul: 'Who will deliver me from the body of this death?' Here, too, she makes for the first time the distinction between the two parts of the soul, a teaching of Augustinian psychology which she will find helpful in the elucidation of the parable of the lord and the servant and of its attendant problems. Further, she is shown that the inward and outward parts are destined, in and through Christ, to be united in eternal blessedness.

With Christ's sufferings still the focus of her continued reflections on contrition and compassion, Julian again considers, in the last chapter of this revelation, Christ's own compassion. She expounds the common theological opinion of her day, that 'the union in him of the divinity gave strength to his humanity to suffer more than all men could' (p. 213), and she explains, in a significant addition to the short text, that the purpose of contemplating the Passion is 'to meditate and come to see. . .what he suffered, and. . .for whom he suffered'. An important point here, she believes, is to consider the mutual compassion between Christ and Mary, because this illumines the ineffable quality of his compassion for all who will be saved. Her contemplation is not merely recollection of an historical event. She had observed earlier, with theological precision, 'I know well that he suffered only once' (chapter 17, p. 209); here she adds that although 'now he has risen again and is no longer capable of suffering. . .yet he suffers with us, as I shall afterwards say', promising the treatment of the divine compassion which will follow in Revelation XIII. In these last lines of Revelation VIII, she intimates that this contemplation of passion and compassion demands the presence and action of the Holy Spirit—'and contemplating all this through his grace'—and that what is true for her is true for all:

> *For when a soul touched by grace contemplates this so, he will truly see that those pains of Christ's Passion surpass all pains, all pains, that is, which will be turned into everlasting joy by the power of Christ's Passion (p. 214).*

The editors here depart from the division into revelations of all the manuscripts and make chapter 21, where the second way of contemplating the Passion is described, the beginning of Revelation IX. Readers are referred to the Introduction and notes of *Showings* for the reasons for this change.

Revelation IX is briefly described by Julian herself as 're-vealed for the joy and the bliss of the Passion' (chapter 23, p. 218). The sudden change from suffering to joy in chapter 21 reveals to her not only our solidarity with Christ in his own human condition during his Passion, but the immediate connexion between the joy and glory of the risen Christ and the glorified Church in heaven. In Revelation VIII her thought was centering on the first part of the Christological hymn of Philippians 2: 'Let that mind be in you. . . . He humbled himself, becoming obedient to death, death on a cross'. Here she recollects the second part of the hymn: 'For this reason God has exalted him', with its corollary in the other hymn in II Timothy 2.12: 'If we endure with him, then we shall also reign with him'.

In chapter 22, following on the bodily sight, the locution 'Are you well satisfied that I suffered for you?' is Julian's way of expressing what appears to be a singular infused grace affecting alike her will and her intellect. 'In response to this my understanding was lifted up into heaven' (p. 216). This seems to describe a 'rapture' in the traditional sense. She had been in the severest bodily and mental anguish, and suddenly she is taken out of herself.

In the long text, as a result of protracted meditation 'with great diligence' on the locution 'If I could suffer more, I should suffer more', with Hebrews 10.10—'in which will we are made holy by the offering, once and for all, of the body of Jesus Christ'—constantly in mind, Julian is able to communicate to us that God's love for the world, the proof of which is the sacrificial death of his Son, is as sure and active and manifest now as it was at the time of the Passion. Every day a glorified Redeemer 'is ready to do the same, if that might be' (p. 217). Modern exegetes can write, on the text of the Apocalypse 'I died, and behold I am alive for evermore', in the same vein:

> *All the mysteries of Jesus's early history, from the cradle to the grave, have been mysteriously endowed in his glorified humanity with a totally new and enduring actuality*[7]

but they say less than Julian does, as she begins, with her understanding of word, of sight and of her own unfolding experience, to develop the insight she receives into the mystery of the Trinity and the divine relationship, in her own person, with all who are to be saved in Christ. She is at one with John, in chapter 15 of his Gospel, and with Hebrews chapter 10 in seeing the revelation and operation of the Trinity as focused particu-

---

7. D. Stanley: 'Contemplation of the Gospels', 430.

larly on the Passion, death and Resurrection of the incarnate Christ. In this suffering all mankind is involved. Because the sight of Christ in his now-glorified humanity is constantly before her inward eye, and his words in her recollection, she is able to write firmly and lucidly, using the ideas and the vocabulary with which Scripture provided her in abundance. With John, as well as with Paul, she can link Passion and Resurrection, earth and heaven in the glory and exaltation of Christ in which we are called to share: 'Between the one and the other all will be a single era; and then all will be brought into joy' (p. 215).

She begins here, too, to develop her teaching on the Holy Spirit, and, as does John himself, she identifies the Spirit with that love which comforts and strengthens. Finally, at the end of the revelation, she offers us a short example which summarizes all the teaching contained:

> *And in this he brought to my mind the qualities of a cheerful giver. Always a cheerful giver pays only little attention to the thing which he is giving, but all his desire and all his intention is to please and comfort the one to whom he is giving it. And if the receiver accept the gift gladly and gratefully, then the courteous giver counts as nothing all his expense and his labour, because of the joy and the delight that he has because he has pleased and comforted the one whom he loves (pp. 219-220),*

a method in which, in the long text, she proves herself so adept. She has stressed the work of the Father and his joy in giving mankind as a gift to his Son; he is the glad giver, and the Son, who receives the gift with that of his own manhood, is he who pays little heed to the value of the gift ('he did not consider equality with God a prize to be coveted'—Philippians 2.6). He receives from the Father, but becomes a courteous giver to the Father, and the Holy Spirit is in the gift, for he is the joy and delight of Father for Son, of Father and Son in us and for us.

The 'bodily sight' of Revelation X has much in common with contemporary representations of the Sacred Heart, and in the Introduction to *Showings* the editors have remarked on Julian's susceptibility to such iconography. Nonetheless, there is a marked difference in tone between this revelation and much of the devotional writing of her own age. It is not the Man of Sorrows whom Julian is shown here, but a joyful, glorified Christ. The Sacred Heart is described as a 'fair and delectable place' (p. 220), a thought which will be repeated in the parable of the lord and the servant. And whereas in the short text she had glossed the locution 'See how I loved you' with

> . . . *as if he had said: My child, if you cannot look on my divinity, see here how I suffered my side to be opened and my heart to be split in two (chapter xiii, p. 146),*

she now understands this sign to mean 'the endless love that was without beginning and is and always shall be'.

This insight into the mystery of the Incarnation, particularly as a corrective to the deficiencies of contemporary devotion, too often betraying both authors and devotees as morbid, neurotic and hysterical, is of sufficient importance to Julian to merit isolation as a separate and integral revelation.

In the closing sight of the 'hard pains' of Christ's sufferings, Julian was shown the compassion of Mary:

> *Christ and she were so united in love that the greatness of her love was the cause of the greatness of her pain (chapter 18, p. 210).*

It is thus logical that the sight of the exalted and glorified yet crucified Christ should end with a showing of Mary sharing her Son's joy. So, in Revelation XI, chapter 25, the bodily sight seems to be extended to the mother who is standing by the Cross. But Julian has already insisted in the short text that this was an intellectual vision:

> *Often times I had prayed for this, and I expected to see her in a bodily likeness; but I did not see her so. And Jesus, saying this, showed me a spiritual vision of her (chapter xiii, p. 147).*

Here in the long text Julian tells why she 'saw her not so': It is far more expedient to see

> *the virtues of her blessed soul, her truth, her wisdom, her love, through which I am taught to know myself and reverently to fear my God (p. 222).*

Julian has no use for sentimentality in her devotion. As she will tell us further on, what Mary exemplifies par excellence is that

> *a man's soul is a creature in God which has the same properties created. . .endless supreme truth, endless supreme wisdom, endless supreme love (chapter 44, p. 256),*

so that it can do what it was made for, perceive God, contemplate him and love him.

In the same revelation, in chapter 25, we have another instance of Julian introducing an 'example' which does not appear in the short version, apparently for the same reason as before, its connection with the parable of the lord and the servant. Indeed, this 'example' seems to be no more than a reference to the matter of chapter 14. There she had written that a king's subjects are more honoured if he makes known to all his realm that he has thanked them. Julian does not now state specifically that this was a part of the revelation introduced by the locution 'Do you wish to see her?' or that the example was shown, as she had written in chapter 14, 'at this time'; and it seems that she is here doing no more than indicating the relevance of an earlier insight also to this revelation.

When Julian had recapitulated, for purposes of reconstruction, her first great revelation (in the long text, chapters 4-9), she made three points with all possible emphasis: That the goodness of God is all, that he is true rest and that there is no rest except in union with him, and that this showing, like all the others, is given to her for the benefit of all who persevere in the knowledge and love of God. These are the themes to which she returns in Revelation XII, which concludes the first part of her book. The first eleven revelations manifest a progressively deeper insight into the Pauline prayer, '. . .to know Christ and the power of his Resurrection and to share in his sufferings by being made like to his death; so may I come to his Resurrection from the dead' (Philippians 3.8-11). So Revelation XII was given as a bodily sight in ghostly likeness, when 'our Lord. . .appeared to me more glorified than I had seen him before' (chapter 26, p. 223). The point is of significance for her. In the short text, she had presented the showing in conjunction with that of Mary, because of the very important observation she makes concerning contemplative graces; now she omits this, probably because she does not wish to restrict her revelations to those vowed to contemplation, and she stresses the new application of the sight of the glorified Christ as Lord and God who is presented to her in the intellectual vision, 'I am he'. It is as Lord and God that he shows himself as he did in the first revelation, 'full of joy, familiar and courteous and blissful and true life'. But now it is in and through the bodily sight in ghostly likeness of the exalted and crucified Christ that she sees afresh and comprehends more deeply that 'where Jesus appears the blessed Trinity is understood' (chapter 4, p. 181):

I am he who is all. I am he whom Holy Church preaches and teaches to you. I am he who showed himself before to you.

But she has still more to see and to learn about the relations of the Trinity and its 'outward operations'. She does not yet know what is comprehended in the word of the triune God, 'I am he'. So she ends the revelation, as she had done in the short text, by recalling that her only purpose in writing at all is so that everyone who will be saved, 'every man. . .according to the grace God gives him in understanding and love', may receive the locution according to Christ's meaning in it.

In the long Revelation XIII, which occupies chapters 27 to 40 of the long text, Julian begins in earnest to give us the fruits of the enlightenment which had come to her in her years of contemplating what she had been shown. The opening sentence, identical in either text:

> *And after this our Lord brought to my mind the longing that I had for him before, and I saw that nothing hindered me but sin, and I saw that this is true of us all in general, and it seemed to me that if there had been no sin, we should all have been pure and as like to our Lord as he created us (p. 224, and cf. chapter xiii, pp. 147-148),*

is so muted that one is hardly aware that this announces a separate revelation, until, after what she deplores as her indiscreet reflection, she writes of 'this vision', and immediately, according to the normal pattern of the revelations, announces a locution: 'Sin is necessary' (in the short text she reports no more, but in the long text she adds: 'but all will be well, and all will be well, and every kind of thing will be well', which serves as first announcement of the theme which will recur throughout this revelation and beyond).

Thus the vision consists of two sights: her longing for God, and the 'ugly sight' (p. 225) of all that is not good. This second sight includes her experience of the sufferings of Christ and of his followers, which she associates with his renunciation in taking on human flesh: 'For we are all in part troubled, and we shall be troubled, following our master Jesus until we are fully purged of our mortal flesh and all our inward affections which are not very good'. It is not that she sees sin itself (she makes the precise theological observation 'for I believe that it has no kind of substance'); she sees all the pain that sin occasioned Christ, and still occasions all who will be saved.

Although this double showing resembles that of Revelation VII, with its alternation of consolation and desolation, here she is anxious to indicate that the desolation caused by the sight of sin 'quickly turned into consolation'; and the chapter ends, in the long text, with what will become the focal point of this revelation, 'an exalted and wonderful mystery, which he will make plain and we shall know in heaven'.

Chapter 28 shows her reflecting on 'how Christ has compassion on us because of sin' (p. 226); but it will only be in the parable of the lord and the servant that we shall find the clarification of her deep understanding of the divine compassion in the mystery of the incarnate Christ. Here she begins to explain how the longing for God with which the vision begins is shown in Christ's compassion, which we are called to share.

At the beginning of the next chapter she seems to be telling us that whenever she reflects upon the 'ugly sight' this alternation of desolation and consolation has been with her; and it would appear from the complete agreement at this point of both texts (pp. 149-150, 228) that she is satisfied with the answer her question invited:

> *He showed that Adam's sin was the greatest harm ever done or ever to be done until the end of the world. . .and that I should contemplate his glorious atonement, for this atoning is more pleasing to the blessed divinity and more honourable for man's salvation, without comparison, than ever Adam's sin was harmful,*

a summary of the contemporary theology of atonement.

In chapter 30, Julian's sight of the divine compassion becomes the sight of Jesus himself, crucified and glorified, in his mystical union with the Church. When she recorded her first version, she was already sufficiently advanced in theology to state clearly that the whole of divine revelation concerns the unity and trinity of God, and the Trinity's 'outward operations', revealed and performed in the incarnate Word, so that any authentic private revelation will do no more than cast a brighter light on this; and in the final text she sees no reason for altering a word of this. Through the reformulation of the locution 'All shall be well' in an explicitly Trinitarian context, she states that the soul's longing for God is a participation in Christ's own longing; and she now gives us the reflection she had promised on his 'ghostly thirst'. She begins with a sight of its fulfillment, everlasting peace and rest (chapter 31, p. 229); and it may be that the meditation which follows in the long text, 'For we know in our faith. . .', is not found in the short text because it depends on her then still undeveloped understanding of the Trinitarian locution in Revelation XII, 'I am he. . .', and of the relationship between Christ and all mankind who will be saved, as this emerges later in the lord-and-servant allegory.

In the examination (in the long text, in chapter 32) of the two forms of the locution of this revelation, 'Every kind of thing will be well' and 'You will see yourself that every kind of thing will be well' (p. 231), Julian shows that the proper object of our contemplation is not the last great work of the Trinity or Judgment Day, but the compassion which is shown in the hiding of that work for our present peace and joy. Spiritual desolation, however, continues to oppress her in this chapter and the next. The doctrines of the faith are

> . . . that many creatures will be damned, such as the angels who fell out of heaven because of pride, who now are devils, and many men upon earth who die out of the faith of Holy Church, that is to say those who are pagans and many who have received baptism and who live unchristian lives and so die out of God's love. All these will be eternally condemned to hell, as Holy Church teaches me to believe (p. 233),

and she continues: 'And all this being so, it seemed to me that it was impossible that every kind of thing should be well, as our Lord revealed at this time'. This is a contrary which reason cannot resolve, and Julian must follow the advice which she gives herself and us in the showing on prayer, and await a better time, a greater grace or a better gift. She recalls that in all her visions of Christ's Passion she saw none of the reproved except the devil himself. She takes this occasion to offer another, far more reasonable theological opinion than that current among the scholastics:

> By this sight I understand that every creature who is of the devil's condition in this life and so dies is no more mentioned before God and

his saints than is the devil, notwithstanding that they belong to the
human race, whether they have been baptized or not (p. 234).

In chapter 34 she further distinguishes between secrets which it
is profitable for us to know in this life, and others, such as
predestination and reprobation, curiosity about which can only
bring disquiet and a troubled conscience. This is her introduction to the general solution of the apparent contradiction: Since
God is Holy Church, its teachings cannot be opposed to authentic revelation.

In chapter 35, Julian is again led to reflect on what she had
already seen in Revelation III: the whole Trinity working in all
things to bring the divine love to fulfullment in every creature,
and that this is possible because of the divine attribute of justice,
which not only is not contradicted by his mercy and compassion
but is complementary to it, bringing good out of evil, and is
subordinated to it, since when all are made perfect in love the
working of divine compassion will cease. Chapter 36, which is
not in the short text, begins with a locution, which may be
rendered in direct speech as 'A deed will be done, and I myself
shall do it, and it will be honorable and wonderful and plentiful,
and it will be done with respect to you, and I myself shall do it'
(p. 238). This represents a more penetrating insight into the
Lord's compassion; it is a sight of the promise of God's fulfillment, and the end is the rest and peace of the eternal Sabbath.
Julian explains clearly that man can do nothing in the order of his
salvation without prevenient and concomitant grace, as the
Council of Orange had defined against 'semi-Pelagianism'; and
in this is the meaning of her phrase, startling to ears not theologically attuned, 'man will do nothing at all but sin' (p. 239). The
firm confidence of her theology here is rooted in her own contemplative experience of purification, active and passive, illumination and union. All this she specifies as she describes the
Lord's compassionate dealings with one who longs for him:

Here you have the matter of meekness, here you have the matter of love, here you have the matter of self-knowledge, here you have the matter of rejoicing in me,

describing purification;

and so long as we are in this life, whenever we in our folly revert to the contemplation of those who are damned, our Lord tenderly teaches us and blessedly calls us,

describing the impulse of grace drawing the soul towards union; and

saying in our souls: Leave me alone, my beloved child, attend to me. I am enough for you, and rejoice in your saviour and your salvation,

describing the soul's illumination. Her immediate comment, 'The soul which is pierced with this by grace will see it and feel it', illumines this entire revelation. She is writing of compunction of heart, from her own experience of visions, sickness and, it would seem, the infused graces which followed the showings; and the reason why so much of this account is original to the long text seems to be that it is integral to all that she has perceived, heard and felt since she recorded the short version. This seems particularly true of the special understanding which she has received concerning miracles; those in the Gospels are preeminently signs of God's compassion.

As Julian explains in chapter 37, the greatest of such signs is that the Lord loves us even while we are in sin. This is a truth which she finds hard to grasp, and she expects it to be so for her fellow Christians. She is anxious to communicate this to them, even though she knows that it will become clear only in the light of the parable. Once again she observes that Revelation XIII consisted of two 'sights', one of the mystery of the divine compassion, the other of the mystery of sin, attending to which she has been assailed by fear and desolation, assuaged only by the final locution of the original showing, 'I protect you very safely' (p. 154).

Then there follows her first reference to the 'godly will', as it is found in all those souls who are to form one soul with the heavenly host, and who have love for one another in Christ. It is this love which is the godly will, which is incorruptible. The theologian whose thought and language appear to be closest to hers is William of St. Thierry in the *Golden Epistle*:

> *For love (*amor*) is a great will towards God, another love (*dilectio*) is a clinging to him or uniting to him, and a third love (*caritas*) is delight in him. Yet the unity of the spirit with God in a man who lifts up his heart towards God is the perfection of his will, when he not only wills God's will, he is not only drawn to God, but in that drawing he is so made perfect that he can will nothing but what God wills. For to will what God wills, this is to be like God; not to be able to will except what God wills, this is to be what God is, for whom willing and being are one and the same. So it is well said that we shall see plainly what he is, when we shall be like him (I John 3.2); that is, we shall be what he himself is.*

This is the 'godly will in the higher part, . . . so good that it cannot ever will any evil, but always good. And therefore we are they whom he loves, and eternally we do what he delights in' (p. 242). William continues: 'And likeness to God is perfection in man, but not to wish to be perfect is to fail'; and Julian concludes chapter 37: 'But all our travail is because love is lacking on our side'.

Readers must be referred to the editors' analysis, in the Introduction of *Showings*, of chapter 38 for the demonstration of the rhetorical dexterity with which Julian there establishes the veracity of the simple but paradoxical statement that 'just as there is indeed a corresponding pain for every sin, just so love gives to the same soul a bliss for every sin' (p. 242). Divine inspiration furnishes her with the 'examples'—Magdalen and the other great penitents—which illustrate her reasoning, and in the last section of the chapter God brings John of Beverley to her mind to drive home the point that the miracles worked through the intercession of such penitent-saints are preeminently tokens of the working of the divine compassion, which in and through Christ continues to bring joy and honour out of sin and shame.

In chapter 39 she sees sin as the scourge of those who will be saved; for it is in our sins that we have the most need of the divine compassion. We experience this compassion in our contemplation of the suffering Christ. Clearly, the Pauline doctrine of reconciliation is in her thought: 'He has reconciled us to himself by Christ. . .for God was indeed in Christ reconciling the world to himself, not imputing to them their sins. . . . For us, he made sin him who knew no sin, that we might be made in him the justice of God' (II Corinthians 5.18-21). Here too, in another addition to the short text, we have a precise summary of the Western teaching on compunction of heart:

> *And also God in his special grace visits whom he will with such great contrition, and also with compassion and true longing for him, that they are suddenly delivered from sin and from pain, and taken up into bliss and made equal with the saints. By contrition we are made clean, by compassion we are made ready, and by true longing for God we are made worthy. These are three means, as I understand, through which all souls come to heaven, those, that is to say, who have been sinners on earth and will be saved (pp. 244-245).*

In a final addition, she once more anticipates the parable, alluding to the lord's compassion for the servant who is shown not only for Christ but also for Adam and every soul who will be saved.

The last chapter, 40, of this revelation establishes a close link between the central locution of the divine compassion, 'I keep you very safely', and Revelation XIV, on prayer, which is to follow. In the short text she had concluded her account of the showing 'for prayer' with a reflection on the sinful soul's unhappy state until God turns to look on her with compassionate love (p. 159). This she has now carefully edited and expanded, so that it introduces and puts into the clear context of our need for prayer the warning against the particular form of 'liberty of the spirit' which she here makes her special concern:

> *But now, because of all this spiritual consolation which has been*
> *described, if any man or woman be moved by folly to say or to think*
> *'If this be true, then it would be well to sin so as to have the greater*
> *reward, or else to think sin less important', beware of this impulse,*
> *for truly, should it come, it is untrue and from the fiend (pp.*
> *246-247).*

On the contrary, sin is to be hated, because God's love teaches us
so; her own contemplative experience confirms this. The whole
revelation ends with a gentle exhortation: The showing of God's
compassion is intended to teach us to love ourselves and our
brethren as he does. This is his endless comforting of us.

In Revelation XIV, with its deceptively simple opening,
'After this our Lord revealed about prayer' (p. 248), Julian is at
last enabled to explain, with an immense wealth of theological
and spiritual detail, that prayer is a living and growing relationship with the triune God in Christ Jesus. In the revelation's first
chapter, 41, there is the locution which, in both texts, is the
nucleus of the whole revelation, 'I am the foundation of your
beseeching'. But in the long text, the reflections upon this
develop in an entirely different way. No longer does Julian
interpret the reasoning which follows, 'First, it is my will. . .',
as a 'serious rebuke' (chapter xix, p. 158) directed at her lack of
trust. Instead, she tells us that the petition is for 'mercy and
grace', and she argues from the question, 'How could it be that
you would not have what you beseech?' that God's goodness is
the cause of our prayer, in the sense in which she is now able to
define the contemplative prayer of petition:

> *Beseeching is a true and gracious, enduring will of the soul, united*
> *and joined to our Lord's will by the sweet, secret operation of the*
> *Holy Spirit (p. 249).*

This definition is Trinitarian. The Father in his righteousness
fastens the will of the soul to the will of the incarnate Son, and
this eternal, creative act is continued in time by the 'sweet, secret
operation', the sending out of the Holy Spirit. Thus the glorified

Christ is the immediate term of the soul's longing, and Julian completes the definition with a homely description of his office as mediator:

> *Our Lord himself is the first receiver of our prayer, as I see it, and he accepts it most thankfully, and greatly rejoicing he sends it up above (p. 249).*

Julian associates herself firmly with the Western tradition, as she links prayer without ceasing with good will. Augustine had written: 'So in that faith and hope and love we pray with continual longing'[8]; and when she writes that thanksgiving belongs to this 'praying continually' (p. 250), one must understand that she is not referring simply to private prayer, but to the 'ceaseless praise' of a contemplative community such as the one to whom the *Ancrene Riwle* is addressed, the eucharistic liturgy, the divine office, the various devotions joined to this 'work of God'. What, perhaps, is special in Julian is the degree to which she sees petition and thanksgiving integrated in the one contemplative process:

> *Thanksgiving also belongs to prayer. Thanksgiving is a true inward acknowledgment, we applying ourselves with great reverence and loving fear and with all our powers to the work that our Lord moved us to, rejoicing and giving thanks inwardly. And sometimes the soul is so full of this that it breaks out in words and says: Good Lord, great thanks, blessed may you be. And sometimes the heart is dry and feels nothing, or else, by the temptation of our enemy, reason and grace drive the soul to implore our Lord with words, recounting his blessed Passion and his great goodness. And so the power of our Lord's word enters the soul and enlivens the heart and it begins by his grace faithful exercise, and makes the soul to pray most blessedly, and truly to rejoice in our Lord. This is a most loving thanksgiving in his sight (p. 250).*

---

8. Letter 130.

All is seen as dependent on the power of the Lord's word, alive, penetrating and quickening.

In chapter 42 Julian begins to explore the nature of this relationship, the true expression of which is contemplative prayer. To do so, she has recourse to current philosophical doctrine on causality. God is the efficient cause of the relationship, and of every true expression of it, 'by his goodness'; God is the highest good, and all desired perfections flow from him as from the first cause[9]. Next is stated the form and the quality of our response: 'Man inheres in God', Thomas had written, 'in whom alone true happiness consists'[10]. Thirdly, the actuality of the relationship is located in God as the final and exemplary cause, 'to be united and like to our Lord in all things' (p. 251). As Thomas expresses this, 'In man is found a certain likeness to God which is taken from God as from the exemplar'[11]. Finally, Julian again stresses that it is the triune God to whom man is united and assimilated:

> . . . and he wishes to help us, and he will make it so, as he says himself, blessed may he be (p. 251),

where 'help' is for the Holy Spirit, 'make' is for the Father and 'says' is for the Son, the Word made flesh.

Then Julian considers in more detail the quality and shape of our response: because of faith and grace it can in some mysterious way be 'generous', matching to some degree divine liberality and generosity; and though our sight of this is often severely limited, he is the sure object of the prayer of hope. Her own trust is so generous that she begins to catch a glimpse of the Lord who is visiting her with mercy and grace, communicating his very being to her:

---

9. Thomas Aquinas, *Summa theologiae* I.6.2 *in corp.*

10. *Ibid.*, I.82.2 *in corp.*

11. *Ibid.*, I.93.4 *in corp.*

*He wants us to have true knowledge in himself that he is being; and
in this knowledge he wants our understanding to be founded, with
all our powers and all our purpose and all our intention (p. 251).*

She holds with Thomas Aquinas that God's self-knowledge is
his being[12], and that in contemplation we are drawn to share in
this knowing. All the divine activity, or all of it which is revealed
to us in Christ, has as its term this unitive relationship which is
called prayer:

*Behold and see that I have done all this before your prayer, and now
you are, and you pray to me.*

Prayer is on our part the simple realization and acknowledge-
ment that God is for us and that we are for God. But Julian still
retains the understanding, inherited from monastic tradition,
that every human happiness is a participation in divine
beatitude, and so both contemplative and eschatological. So she
offers us another definition:

*Prayer is a right understanding of that fulness of joy which is to
come, with true longing and trust. The savouring or seeing of our
bliss, to which we are ordained, by nature makes us to long; true
understanding and love, with a sweet recollection in our savour, by
grace makes us to trust.*

This is a reminder that she is also no stranger to the doctrine of
the spiritual senses, particularly the sense of taste, as developed
by Cistercian spiritual writers. Her final description of prayer
has much in common with William of St. Thierry's exegesis of
John 17.3: 'This is, he says, eternal life, that they may know
thee. . . . Blessed is the knowledge in which eternal life is
contained. This life is from that taste, for to taste is to know'[13].

In chapter 43 Julian amplifies her teaching in the first

---

12. *Ibid.*, I.14.4.
13. *De natura amoris* X 31 (PL 184 399).

62

revelation that contemplative prayer for us must be seeking, suffering and trusting under the prompting of the Holy Spirit. To pray is to acknowledge that we need God so as to attain to union with him in knowledge and love; but it is also witnessing to him that through his grace we desire to have him as he desires to have us. For Julian, as for Bernard, God is a God moving his creatures because he desires them[14], and the movement brings peace and consolation, 'it eases the conscience and fits man for grace' (p. 253). We become partners, first in desire and then in fact; we share God's activity, and all this is prayer:

And so he teaches us to pray and have firm trust that we shall have it; for he beholds us in love, and wants to make us partners in his good will and work (p. 253).

Implicit in this understanding is Julian's previous insight of herself at prayer: 'I saw him and I sought him, I had him and I lacked him' (chapter 10, p. 193). What frustrates his desire and ours is 'because we are failing and unfit for Jesus' (p. 254). So prayer in times of desolation is equally prayer for union and a response to grace, which itself implies the divine presence: 'Our Lord God is following us, helping our desire'. All of this belongs to the contemplative exegesis of the Canticle of Canticles, which was Bernard's speciality; and for him 'you would not seek me, had you not already found me' is a principle of unitive prayer.

New that Julian has shown the contemplative process as the consummate point of union in the divine presence, she can demonstrate how this happens in practice in the prayer of the Gospel prototype, 'our Lady St. Mary' (p. 256). So chapter 44 begins with a proleptic allusion to man as the servant in the parable, the son who 'always works the Father's will and to his glory, continually, without ceasing', and how this 'working' (the force and content of the word will not be lost on any reader of the *Cloud*) is achieved. Julian sees Mary's contemplation as an intel-

---

14. See Dumontier, *S. Bernard et la Bible*, 40-43.

lectual and affective 'sight' of the mutual presence and relationship of the divine persons in her soul. The truth which is the Father sees God who is the Son, the wisdom which is the Son beholds God who is the Father, and the Spirit who is love is endlessly proceeding from this mutual contemplation. And yet, mysteriously, 'all are of God's making', because the Son who is wisdom is at the same time a human being who beholds, is given the power to contemplate, as well as seeing divinely; his soul is 'a creature in God', possessing by participation these same properties of truth, wisdom and love. So Julian now sees in Mary's contemplative prayer the analogue of the divine processions and relationships, in which the creature truly knows himself as made and existing now forever ('always it does what it was created for') out of the divine creative love, but also for the love with which God loves him endlessly.

It is true that man, in his creation and his immortal existence, is assimilated to God in his substance, but it is equally true that man in this life often loses this likeness through sin. Now, in chapter 45, Julian begins to reflect on the apparent incompatibility of these two truths and their consequences in man's life of prayer. God's knowledge and judgment of us is 'in our natural substance' (p. 256), that is, in our relationship to him as Father, through the Son, in the Holy Spirit:

> It is a great understanding to see and know inwardly that God, who is our creator, dwells in our soul, and it is a far greater understanding to see and know inwardly that our soul, which is created, dwells in God in substance, of which substance, through God, we are what we are (chapter 54, p. 285).

But there is another knowledge and judgment which is only partial, one which does not see this unchangeable substance, except insofar as it is reflected in man's visible actions, which involve his changeable sensuality. It is the work of God's mercy and grace, with our cooperation (the mutual activity which Julian has called prayer), so that man becomes like to God in condition as well as in substance—what Walter Hilton calls 'reforming in faith'. However, throughout the whole revelations, all that Julian has seen is God knowing and approving us in our substantial relationship with him (which she will come to see, through the parable, as our relationship in Christ). But the teaching Church which proclaims Christ's perfection is also the learning Church, the body of Christ not yet completed which must acknowledge its own sinfulness; that is, in that condition it is incapable of being incorporated into God's righteousness. It would seem that it was precisely at this point that Julian was shown the parable:

> *This then was my desire, that I might see in God in what way the judgment of Holy Church here on earth is true in his sight, and how it pertains to me to know it truly, whereby they might both be reconciled as might be glory to God and the right way for me. And to all this I never had any other answer than a wonderful example of a lord and a servant, as I shall tell later, and that was very mysteriously revealed (p. 257).*

When finally understood, the parable would show her how God reconciles the apparently irreconcilable, and, what is more to the point, manifests that sinful man is called to contemplative prayer. As yet, however, she cannot at all see its relevance; she can only reiterate that God's word and the Church's teaching alike must contain all that is relevant to salvation.

When Julian writes, at the beginning of chapter 46, that

> *when we know and see, truly and clearly, what our self is, then we shall truly and clearly see and know our Lord God in the fulness of joy (p. 258),*

she is not simply dealing with the eschatological character of all contemplative prayer, or giving voice to her own desire 'to be dissolved and to be with Christ'; she is reflecting as a monastic theologian on the nature of man. He can only know and love himself truly in the fulness of his knowledge and love of the incarnate, glorified Christ. So William of St. Thierry teaches that the ultimate object of Christian contemplation is not only God, nor is it the self, '. . . when in the embrace and the kiss of the Father and the Son the soul is blessedly aware that in some way it finds itself the mean, when in a way that cannot be told or thought the man of God is made worthy to become, not God, but still what God is, man becoming by grace what God is by nature'[15]. However, Julian is here at pains to insist (and this is another insight which flows from her reflection on the parable) that through Christ and his Spirit there is interaction between substance and sensuality, which leads to the intensification of this contemplative knowledge of self:

> *We may have knowledge of ourselves in this life by the continuing help and power of our high nature, in which knowledge we may increase and grow by the furthering and help of mercy and grace.*

And if the woe and pain brought by sin constitute an obstacle to the communication of wisdom and truth by the grace of contemplation, this is still communicated in the doctrines of Holy Church by the gift of faith. In this second kind of contemplation of truth Julian seems to assert that there is room for error, at least so far as the conclusions to be drawn from such truth are concerned:

> *And so in all this contemplation it seemed to me that it was necessary to see and to know that we are sinners and commit many evil deeds which we ought to forsake, and leave many good deeds undone which we ought to do, so that we deserve pain, blame and wrath.*

'It seemed to me' advances this as no more than her own opinion, which she then proceeds to refute. Her conclusion is now that in her prayerful relationships with the Lord she needs to wait for him to express himself more clearly or to prepare her to receive

---

15. *The Golden Epistle.*

his communication. Meanwhile, she exercises herself in both beholdings, the wonder of contemplation and the childlike submission to the truths of faith as proclaimed by the Church.

In chapter 47 she begins as a preparation for her full account of the parable, against the background of twenty years of contemplative reflection on this 'showing for prayer', to tell us how she now 'saw and understood the operation of mercy' (p. 260). She begins with an examination of her own feelings and reactions in times of desolation. She couches her description of this in terms of that 'unlikeness' which is contrary to the Trinitarian appropriations, power, wisdom and goodness. The powerlessness and ignorance, she observes, are in the self; but the will is 'overpowered'. So we see that she is writing not merely of her own experience of such desolation, but of all that she has seen and understood concerning the will of the servant in his falling. Here, as there, it is the 'godly will' with which she deals:

> This man was injured in his powers and made most feeble, and in his understanding he was amazed, because he was diverted from looking on his lord, but his will was preserved in God's sight. I saw the lord commend and approve him for his will, but he himself was blinded and hindered from knowing this will (chapter 51, p. 270).

In the desolation she also perceives the hidden working of this godly will, in the 'great desire which the soul has to see God'. So she is able, as were Bernard and Richard of St. Victor before her, to identify the various affections in which her interior reactions originate, and the quality of the discretion to which she has attained through her own experience, not merely of the alternation of consolation and desolation, but of the coexistence of desolation and consolation, a theme much more rare in spiritual literature.

This interior knowledge of 'the opposition that is in ourselves', the confrontation between rejoicing, desire and true hope, and mourning and dread, brings her in chapter 48 to reflect on the predominantly passive nature of contemplative prayer. There is no such opposition in the good Lord, whom she has seen as the initiator and also as the term of all human spiritual endeavour. We can no longer foist off our own inner contradictions on the God 'who is endless life dwelling in our soul' (p. 261). So she is able to describe human wrath as the substance of man's unlikeness to the Trinity:

> . . . *for wrath is nothing else but a perversity and an opposition to peace and to love. And it comes from a lack of power or a lack of wisdom or a lack of goodness, and this lack is not in God, but it is on our side.*

Far from calling down divine anger, it invites that mercy which is

> *a sweet, gracious operation in love, mingled with plentiful pity, for mercy works, protecting us, and mercy works, turning everything to good for us.*

Julian has no wish, however, to minimize the pain of the contemplative experience. It involves her in the daily dying of which Paul writes in II Corinthians. Nonetheless, with Julian as with Paul, an optimistic note predominates. Here she begins to treat of the Trinitarian processions, and of their interaction in the working out of man's total salvation. Her reflection on this constant Trinitarian concern and care for the work of the divine hands leads her now to anticipate her teaching on motherhood as a divine attribute, and to introduce for the first time her own coined word for the highly technical *perichoresis, circumincessio,* 'spredyng abrode', 'distributing', as referring to the interrelationship of Son and Spirit indwelling in man:

> *Mercy is a pitiful property which belongs to motherhood in tender love; and grace is an honourable property which belongs to royal dominion in the same love. Mercy works, protecting, enduring, vivifying and healing, and it is all of the tenderness of love; and grace works with mercy, raising, rewarding, endlessly exceeding*

what our love and labour deserve, distributing and displaying the vast plenty and generosity of God's royal dominion in his wonderful courtesy.

She will have much more to write, in the light of her coming exposition of the parable, on the Trinitarian mystery; but few theologians of her time or since her time have written with such clarity and concision, such simplicity and courtesy of this high mystery. No less a thinker than Karl Rahner has recently insisted that the great theological trap, which by no means all the scholastics or their precursors were able to avoid in writing on the Trinity, is to attempt to speculate in the abstract on the unity and distinction of the persons, prescinding from the data of revelation of the divine economy, the triune God concerned eternally with and for man's salvation, manifested in the existence of the incarnate Christ[16]. Julian was not so trapped, as she wrote of the

property of the blessed love which we shall know in God, which we might never have known without woe preceding it (p. 263).

In chapter 49 she continues to share her reflections on the illumination which she has received concerning divine mercy, grace and love, following her experience of purification; but here the prayer is not merely passive—she is 'contemplating with great diligence' (p. 263). The first part of the chapter consists of two syllogistic arguments with identical conclusions: There is no wrath in God, but only endless goodness and friendship. The immediate object of this consideration appears to be that the illumination is inevitably leading to contemplative union, for she confirms her statement that wrath in God is an impossibility by a reference to 'the soul which by God's special grace sees so much of his great and wonderful goodness as that we are endlessly united to him in love', and manifestly she herself is that

---

16. *The Trinity*, 19.

soul. The divine goodness is present to her in the person of the risen and glorified Christ:

> *I saw most truly that where our Lord appears, peace is received and wrath has no place (p. 264).*

In the risen and glorified Christ are the Father and the Spirit, are endless might and endless goodness as well as endless wisdom. She develops here the traditional teaching that the God who is in some way consciously present to us in consolation is equally present in the darkness of the contemplative's desolation, and that this is the experience of our sinful nature, a presence which is manifest as soon as we perceive our need for his forgiveness:

> *That same endless goodness constantly draws into us a peace, opposing our wrath and our perverse falling, and makes us see our need with true fear, and urgently to beseech God that we may have forgiveness, desiring (which is a grace) our salvation. For we cannot be blessedly saved until we are truly in peace and love, for that is our salvation.*

She concludes by describing, now in the context of the Western tradition's anagogical interpretation of 'Jerusalem' as the symbol of everlasting peace, how the heavenly fulfillment will mean that we shall be as pleased with ourselves and our fellow Christians as we shall be with God and with all his works.

Julian has already indicated in the long series of contemplative insights and reflections upon them, which are introduced in Revelation XIII by the locution 'Sin is necessary', that compunction of heart is a virtue which is essential to contemplative life and prayer. The constant tradition, in the East as in the West, is that shame and sorrow for sin are linked with a proper fear of the divine retribution. So Julian here writes that 'the blame of our sins continually hangs upon us, from the first man until the time that we come up into heaven' (chapter 50, p. 266). Yet it is equally true that God guards, watches over and protects his own, no matter what man's judgment may be. The clarity with which Julian sees both judgments only intensifies her anxiety; as she states her dilemma, she is not dismissing it, but merely sharpening its horns. This is no problem in logic, but a real cause of suffering to many a good and simple contemplative; and she is no longer, as in the short text, expounding with lyrical intensity a philosophical conundrum—'O, wretched sin, what are you?' (chapter xxiii, p. 166). What she does here is to formulate a simple petition, prefaced by an ejaculation:

> *Ah, Lord Jesus, king of bliss, how shall I be comforted, who will tell me and teach me what I need to know, if I cannot at this time see it in you? (p. 267).*

When she protests that what she is asking for is 'so humble a thing', we may justly suspect her of art, especially when we perceive how deeply complex is the simple-seeming lord-and-servant parable. Were it not that for twenty years she persevered in prayer, and preserved her confident, childlike expectation that in the end divine help would be given to her, she might well have been hoist with her own petard. What is wholly admirable is that she was able to make a coherent whole of the short text and yet in it to suppress any reference to her prayer for relief and to the showing, still at that time dark, mysterious, troubling, which had been given in answer to the prayer.

Some years ago it was indicated[17] that the servant in chapter 51's parable is none other than the 'Suffering Servant of God', as he (and his Lord) are depicted in the 'servant-songs' of Isaias. Furthermore, Julian's first reflection upon him identifies him with Adam, with Adam's friendship with God and with his fall, although she hastens to add that the servant is not wholly identifiable with the historical Adam, that is with the Genesis narrative. All this accords well with a fundamental principle of mediaeval Scriptural commentary, that the Old Testament has to be 'opened', examined, so that the incarnate Word can be

---

17. Walsh, *Revelations*, 31-32.

found. Julian's parable shows that in her times the tradition still prevailed. We may take it that for her the literal sense which builds the parable's foundation is contained in the first chapter of Genesis, and is also adumbrated in the Isaian prophecies. She is well aware, as she constructs chapter 51, that she is embarking upon the use of Scriptural allegory, in which words and their outward meanings are there to lead us to hidden senses. It cannot be accidental that in writing of the revelation of the parable she should use the adverb 'very mysteriously' (p. 267), or that the later remark, 'twenty years after the time of the revelation except for three months, I received an inward instruction' (p. 270) should use the epithets 'mysterious' and 'unimportant':

> *You ought to take heed to all the attributes, divine and human, which were revealed in the example, though this may seem to you mysterious and unimportant (p. 270).*

And Julian writes, after the allegory's first showing:

> *. . . for the complete understanding of that wonderful example was not at that time given to me. The secrets of the revelation were deeply hidden in this mysterious example (p. 269).*

The reality hidden in God is revealed to individual men at the moment when it is realized in Christ, but only insofar as it is addressed to each individual man. Bernard writes: 'For there are those to whom Christ is not yet born'[18], and, elsewhere: 'God spoke once, but his speech is continual and perpetual'[19]. This mystery of Christ is inseparable also from the mystery of the Church. Augustine had written: 'The whole mystery of all the Scriptures confesses Christ and the Church'[20]. Thus, as soon as Julian has understood that the lord of the parable is God, she also understands that the servant

---

18. *Sermones de diversis*, 44.
19. *Ibid.*, 5.
20. *Enarratio in Psalmum* 79.

INTRODUCTION

*. . . was shown for Adam, that is to say, one man was shown at
that time and his fall, so as to make it understood how God regards
all men and their falling. For in the sight of God all men are one
man, and one man is all men (p. 270),*

'all mankind', as she will write later, 'which will be saved by the
sweet Incarnation and the Passion of Christ' (p. 276). Finally,
allegory has a doctrinal quality. Since the parable's central
object is the divinity of the incarnate Word—and it is precisely
thus that in the end it unfolds for Julian—it presupposes faith.
This knowledge, mysterious and hidden, of the whole Christ
can be revealed only to the internal eyes of the soul, the eyes of
faith illumined by the Gospel. Julian, through the constant
contemplation of her revelations, it convinced that there is no
discord between them and the common faith of the Church, and
that

*I have instruction by which I ought to believe and trust that our
Lord God, out of the same goodness and for the same purpose as he
revealed it, by the same goodness and for the same purpose will make
it clear to us when it is his will (pp. 269-270).*

As Gregory had written, allegory not only presupposes faith but
builds it up[21].

Julian, in her first reflections on what she was shown 'about
prayer', began by considering how she and we should conduct
ourselves in all that concerns our relationship with God. This
indicates what is the parable's third, tropological sense. The
Word is always addressed to us, and to how we live in its light.
In fact, every grace for which Julian ever asked, including the
bodily sickness, was so that she might live more to God's glory.
Through the tropological sense the mystery of Christ,
prefigured by the allegory, is made real and actual in the Christian soul; and this is an interiorization which takes place in the

---

21. *Homiliarium in Evangelia II*, Sermon 40; see H. de Lubac, *Exégèse médiévale* 2 530.

73

present moment. So Julian from the start recounts the actions of the lord and the servant in the present tense: 'A lord who has a servant. . .the lord sits. . .the servant stands. . .dashes. . .runs . . .falls'. Julian is writing in the tradition of the monastic or contemplative development of the tropological sense, as she extracts the various virtues of the lord and the servant from their general appearance and demeanour. Of the lord, for example, she writes:

> *The blueness of the clothing signifies his steadfastness, the brownness of his fair face with the lovely blackness of the eyes was most suitable to indicate his holy solemnity, the amplitude, billowing splendidly all about him, signifies that he has enclosed within himself all heavens and all endless joy and bliss (p. 272).*

At the same time, she avoids the tendency among monastic exegetes to dismiss all other forms of spiritual living but their own. In editing the long text, she deliberately suppresses every indication in the short text that she may be addressing herself only to those who are cloistered. What she is able to draw from the parable is that

> *. . . so has our good Lord Jesus taken upon him all our blame; and therefore our Father may not, does not wish to assign more blame to us than to his own beloved Son Jesus Christ (p. 275).*

Though she understands well and appreciates the mystical tropology which is the renewed experience of the interiorized savour and joy of the allegory, she is never guilty of emphasizing a personal interior life to the detriment of the social and eschatological elements of Christian spirituality. In the last analysis, as the S2 (*see* footnote 13, p. 141) scribe insists, these revelations 'of the unutterable love of God in Jesus Christ' were 'vouchsafed. . .to all his dear friends and lovers', and not only to cloistered contemplatives.

Julian is very much at home with the fourth, anagogical sense of Scripture, which for so many of the Fathers expresses the whole of the Christian mystery, and, as such, absorbs the allegorical and tropological senses and makes the synthesis of the 'spiritual or fuller sense'. So much of her contemplation throughout the revelations (and notably in the first, which sets the tone and temper of the rest) is anagogical; it could with justice be described as the meeting place of her developing understanding of Scripture and of the infused contemplative graces bestowed on her. She often renders the word itself, *anagoge*, *subvectio*, *elevatio*, in her English. She writes of a 'direction of my understanding towards the lord' (p. 268), 'now my understanding was led back to the first' (*ibid.*,), 'our good Lord led my understanding on to the end of what was to be seen and shown' (p. 269); and much earlier she writes of a 'bodily example', very reminiscent of the lord-and-servant parable, that it 'was shown, so exalted that this man's heart could be ravished and he could almost forget his own existence in the joy' (p. 188). Yet perhaps the most anagogical of all Julian's experiences was Revelation IX, when, like Paul's (II Corinthians 12.2), her understanding was lifted up to where she saw three heavens (chapter 22, p. 216). It is to this experience, and its link with her sight of the suffering Christ, that she reverts as she contemplates the parable, an anagogy which is both doctrinal and contemplative, echoing Gregory's classical statement: 'And that same city which is Holy Church, which will reign in heaven, still labours upon earth'[22]:

> For . . . all mankind which will be saved appeared in Jesus (p. 276).

Here we have an expression of the whole Christian mystery in which the anagogical sense embraces the allegorical and the tropological. A similar 'ascent of the mind' through the three spiritual senses is equally evident in her progressive consideration of the place where the lord sits and of the ravine where the

---

22. *In Ezechielem* II 1.

servant lay after his fall. The ravine was 'narrow and comfortless and distressful' (p. 268). The place where the lord was seated was 'unadorned, on the ground, barren and waste, alone in the wilderness' (p. 271). Later this landscape becomes the scene of the servant's toil as a gardener, 'digging and ditching and sweating and turning the soil over and over' (p. 273), the place where is the treasure which the lord loved; and finally it becomes the city of God, the city of rest and peace which is at once man's soul, redeemed and perfected, and the New Jerusalem, the bride of Christ:

> *Now the spouse, God's son, is at peace with his beloved wife, who is the fair maiden of endless joy. Now the Son, true God and true man, sits in his city in rest and in peace, which his Father has prepared for him by his endless purpose, and the Father in the Son, and the Holy Spirit in the Father and in the Son (p. 278).*

Bede had written that 'allegory is when Christ's presence and his Church's sacraments are signified by words or things which are mysterious'[23]. Throughout her final investigation of the parable, Julian is seeking and finding, in its 'words and things', the presence of the incarnate Word in his suffering past, 'in the days of his flesh' (Hebrews 5.7), in his glorified present and in his mystical body the Church: 'He is the head, and we are his members' (p. 276). What Julian has achieved in this chapter through the contemplation of the parable against the background of the whole sequence of the revelations is a united spiritual exegesis in which the three senses, allegory, tropology and anagogy, are constantly and easily identifiable but, nonetheless, inextricable. It is Paul who is the father of such exegesis, and it appears to be from her study of the Pauline letters in the Vulgate (there are at least thirty such allusions in chapter 51 alone) that she has chiefly acquired her exegetical skill, based on her understanding of revelation (whether this be Scripture and

---

23. *De tabernaculo et vasis ejus* I 6.

tradition or her own contemplative graces) and of the nature of Christ's Church.

The opening paragraph of chapter 52:

> *And so I saw that God rejoices that he is our Father, and God rejoices that he is our Mother, and God rejoices that he is our true spouse, and that our soul is his beloved wife. And Christ rejoices that he is our brother, and Jesus rejoices that he is our saviour (p. 279)*

appears to be the peak of her contemplation of the parable, her beholding and sharing in the joy of the Trinity in their own divine activity, which terminates in the incarnate Word, the glorified and risen Christ in his relationship with the Church in glory. This is a vision similar to that granted to John on Patmos of the heavenly liturgy, but in addition Julian's sight has comprehended the various aspects of God's relationship in Christ with mankind, the origins of her 'five joys': Father/Son, mother/child, husband/wife, brother/sister, Redeemer/redeemed.

The chapter proper begins with a renewed reflection on this last relationship, of Christ with us as our saviour. The working out of this salvation involves us, as it did him, in 'a marvellous mixture of both well-being and woe' (p. 279). She bases this on her understanding of the relations between the first Adam, natural parent of the human race, and the second Adam, the race's spiritual parent, and of the participation of all the children in the life of both parents. Towards the end of this demonstration, Julian makes it clear that we still have, as the chief object of our attention, unitive prayer—the mercy and grace which work in us when God 'in his goodness opens the eye of our understanding' demand from us a 'holy act of assent to God which we make when we feel him, truly willing with all our heart to be with him, and with all our soul and with all our might'—a Trinitarian allusion which is also a tropological exegesis of the great commandment, 'You must love the Lord your God with

your whole heart and your whole soul and with all your might'
(Luke 10.27).

Julian then elaborates on what she had stated at the beginning of this revelation to be the second condition for unitive
prayer, 'confident trust' (p. 248). The foundation of this trust is
in Christ's two natures and his two-fold relationship with us in
his divinity and glorified humanity. All the children of Adam
are even now by the power of Christ's Passion and death being
raised up. Our falling with Adam is real and sorrowful enough,
but the cause of our deepest sorrow is 'because our sin is the
cause of Christ's pains' (p. 280). It is the sorrow of the contemplative, which leads to the 'sweet touching of grace' which may
readily be experienced in the sacrament of penance.

The showing of the parable has also enabled her to reconcile
the apparently contradictory judgments which earlier she had
seen as threatening a conflict between her revelations and the
teachings of the Church. The solution lies 'in the double demeanour with which the lord saw his beloved servant falling' (p.
281). The Church teaches that we should accuse ourselves, both
sacramentally and in our private prayer, to a Lord who is loving
and merciful; and this she now sees, 'shown in the outward
demeanour, and in this showing I saw two parts' (p. 282). What
is more, the second, outward judgment, 'the meek self-
accusation which our good Lord asks from us', is itself a grace:

> . . .he himself works where it is, and this is the lower part of man's
> life. . .for the life and the power that we have in the lower part is
> from the higher, and it comes down to us from the kind love of the
> self, by grace.

In chapter 37, at the beginning of Revelation XIII dealing
with the divine compassion, Julian had already been writing in
the light of the parable. There, writing of what she here in
chapter 53 calls the 'godly will which never assented to sin nor
ever will' (p. 283), she had taken it for granted that her readers
would be familiar with the principles of Augustinian psychol-

ogy which are the point of departure for all her teaching on the Trinity in its 'outward workings'. Now she can repeat verbatim and with assurance what she has already written, and she can add that this is the partial answer to her question: How can God love us in our sin? What she has seen in the parable, what she is now contemplating, is the good will which is God's first gift in the creation of the human soul of his servant, Christ, who is every man who will be saved, a creation which is participation in the divine being. Furthermore, she now sees that this teaching is no novelty in her showings, but belongs, by God's will, to the faith and belief of the Church:

> *Therefore our Lord wants us to know it in our faith and our belief, and particularly and truly that we have all this blessed will whole and safe in our Lord Jesus Christ, because every nature with which heaven will be filled has of necessity and of God's rightfulness to be so joined and united in him that in it a substance was kept which could never and should never be parted from him, and that through his own good will in his endless prescient purpose.*

Her contemplation here is in the fullest sense anagogical: She is seeing Christ not only in his fall into the maiden's womb and in the pains of his Passion, but in his union with the blessed in glory, now and to the end of time.

As Julian, still pondering the parable, penetrates further into the mystery of the incarnate Christ, speculating about the divine and human origins of the servant, she is, as very often, close to Paul and his Trinitarian teaching in the eighth chapter of Romans. Though it suits her here to translate into her own English the language of the schools, when she describes God as 'substantial uncreated nature' (p. 284), and to insist with Bede that when we speak of 'creation from nothing' we mean the 'inspiring' of the soul, her point is ultimately Pauline: There is nothing between man's soul and God, because 'nothing can separate us, neither now nor in the time to come, from the love of God which is ours in Christ Jesus' (Romans 8.38-39):

In this endless love we are led and protected by God, and we never shall be lost; for he wants us to know that the soul is a life, which life of his goodness and his grace will last in heaven without end, loving him, thanking him, praising him (p. 284).

As Julian continues her reflection in chapter 54, she seems especially aware of Johannine teaching. 'The Word was with God from the beginning. . .the Word was made flesh. . . . To everyone who received him, he gave the power to be the children of God' (John 1.1-12). Again she is concerned, by means of the tropological and anagogical interpretation of Scripture, to insist on the unity between the Church's faith and what she sees in her contemplation. Like the apostle, she is telling of what she has seen: 'What we have seen and heard we are telling you, that you may also have this union. . .with the Father and with his Son Jesus Christ. . .and we write this so that you may rejoice, and that your joy may be full' (I John 1.3-4). So she describes the mutual indwelling not, as do so many of her contemporaries, with respect to transforming union, but by oblique reference to John chapter 17, where Christ is praying for all believers, 'that they may be one, as thou, Father, in me and I in thee'. The sight which accompanies this belief is indeed 'full of mysteries'; and so, with a theologian's care, she insists that though

I saw no difference between God and our substance, but, as it were, all God; and still my understanding accepted that our substance is in God, that is to say that God is God, and our substance is a creature in God (p. 285).

But aware that those for whom she is writing may have too limited a view of the faith of Holy Church in this doctrine, she also stresses the tropological sense of all these Johannine texts: Love leads, and the gift of indwelling is equally the gift of unitive love. But it is faith which gives understanding of this:

. . . for it is nothing else than right understanding with true belief and certain trust in our being, that we are in God and he in us, which we do not see.

This is a power received when Christ becomes incarnate, when our sensual nature is linked with our substance, that substance in God which becomes ours and becomes human when Christ becomes human by the power of the Spirit in the womb of the virgin. She sees faith as the form of all man's knowing and loving, by means of which we believe, hope and love what we do not see.

So far, Julian has related the mutual indwelling which she has come to see contemplatively in the relationship between the lord and the servant with the Trinitarian teaching of John and Paul, as interpreted allegorically and tropologically by traditional commentators. Now, in chapter 55, she turns again to Christ as she saw him in the ninth revelation, as leading us where we are to go, that is, to the anagogical meaning of her showings. Hope is the virtue of anagogical contemplation, just as it is the prerequisite for Julian's unitive prayer. It is the virtue which flows from our incorporation into Christ, and it becomes operative in the first moment of our separate existence:

> *And when our soul is breathed into our body, in which we are made capable of sensation, at once mercy and grace begin to work, having care of us and protecting us with pity and love, in which operation the Holy Spirit forms in our faith the hope that we shall return up above to our substance (pp. 286-287).*

It is, however, an existence in Christ, as is seen in the sign of its inception, 'at once mercy and grace begin to work', in that baptism in which the formal cause is the Holy Spirit—'in which operation the Holy Spirit forms in our faith the hope . . .' She also sees Christ in relation to his Mystical Body as life, and suggests that the instant of the divine presence is also the instant of union between soul and body:

> *. . . for in the same instant in which our soul is made capable of sensation, in that same instant exists the city of God, ordained for him from without beginning.*

Again she reverts to the ecclesial implications in her contemplation of the lord and the servant, as she refers to the divine gift to man of growth, and alludes to Christ's own human growth:

> *All the gifts which God can give to the creature he has given to his Son Jesus for us, which gifts he, dwelling in us, has enclosed in him until the time that we are fully grown, our soul together with our body and our body together with our soul (p. 287).*

It is here, as she reflects with William of St. Thierry on 'image and likeness', that she offers us a definition of her understanding of this aspect of the parable:

> *This sight was sweet and wonderful to contemplate, peaceful and restful, secure and delectable.*

Perhaps in this reflection on the union of soul and body in Christ incarnate and in his brethren she begins to see more clearly what before she had simply stated as a fact, mankind's need of the redemptive activity of the whole Trinity in Christ.

In the parable the final object of revelation is Christ and the Father in the unity of the Spirit working out man's salvation. As chapter 56 begins, she is thinking of Colossians 3.3: It is only when we are risen with Christ that we shall see ourselves in him. So she returns to her teaching on that desire for God which leads us to seek the hidden treasure which is the life of union with him. She accepts that we can know only the nature of body, soul and spirit and how they are conjoined insofar as we are shown 'from whence the servant came'. So she examines again the whole course of the parable. In the sixteenth revelation she will write more of the process of assimilation to Christ, which is our becoming 'holy in this holiness' (p. 284). Meanwhile, like Paul, we must share Christ's Passion if we are to enter the depths of his charity.

She writes that 'I had a partial touching' (p. 289 and note 267). Here she reinforces what she has just been expounding by reference to her own experience. The dynamic relationships of the persons of the Trinity can be 'felt' in us when God wishes to 'touch' us, that is, to make us aware of such activity in a way which transcends our normal intellectual and affective processes, because of our existential participation in the divine life. At the same time, the activity can be known and is known only because it is revealed in the mystery of the incarnate Word. Mercy and grace (Son and Spirit) eternally flowing from substantial kindness (Father, and also the triune God) complete their 'sending outward' (the Son is sent by the Father, the Spirit by both Father and Son) by returning man in Christ to his source:

> From this substantial nature spring mercy and grace, and penetrate us, accomplishing everything for the fulfillment of our joy (p. 290).

She shows art and skill and she indicates her multiple triadic terminology by the singular pronoun 'this':

> This is three properties in one goodness, and where one operates all operate in the things which now pertain to us.

Her knowledge of the Trinitarian operations and attributes is theological, but it is also contemplative, a beginning, growing knowledge in love of the three persons:

> God wants us to understand, desiring with all our heart and all our strength to have knowledge of them, always more and more until the time that we are fulfilled; for to know them fully and to see them clearly is nothing else than endless joy and bliss, which we shall have in heaven, which God wants us to begin here in knowledge of his love.

The 'touch', however, is not merely in our reason or the higher part of our nature, though it has there its ground. It is in our sensuality, which Christ has taken. His Incarnation and glorification through Passion and death constitute a second creation for mankind. All this Julian sees as the manner and the order of human endowment, that is, of all those who are destined for final fulfillment by the working of the Trinity through 'nature, mercy and grace'.

In Revelation XVI Julian will show that the Trinity 'made man's soul as beautiful, as good, as precious a creature as it could make' (p. 314). Here in chapter 57 she states why this is so: Because our (that is, Christ's) human substance is a participation in God's substance, the Father's will is fulfilled in the will of his creature, of Christ and all who will be saved in him. This salvation, she insists, is the restoration and the fulfillment of man's sensual soul, which, by virtue of its substance, participates in the endowment of his substantial spirit, but through the operation of mercy and grace. So faith is described as our participation in and reception of the Word made flesh, who 'for love made mankind, and for the same love he himself wanted to become man' (p. 291). The relationship, by gift, is instantaneously mutual. On our side, it is a knowledge which has its impact on the lower part of our life which Christ has assumed. In him, every mode of his human relationship with his Father is available to us—the reflection of God's life by humankind as he prepares it to receive the Son, the power which Christ as man receives from the Father and shares with his Church, that power in which we receive the Spirit. Again, Julian is contemplating the servant's origins, 'from whence he came', so that her mind is logically led to that maiden who is the human origin by the power of the Spirit of Christ's sensual life. She catches exactly the mystical tropology in monastic exegesis of the twelfth century, especially in the Mariological commentaries on the Canticle of Canticles. The union of the Word with all human nature was achieved in Mary's womb, so that she is to be found at the heart of the mystery of the Church. But Julian also takes the occasion here (following, apparently, Augustine) to observe that it is Christ who is Mary's spiritual mother, not Mary Christ's.

In chapter 58 Julian presents us with a synthesis of all that she has learned by reflecting not only on the parable but also on Revelations I, IX and XI as she now understands them in the parable's light as they deal with the mysteries of Trinity and Incarnation. She sees all mankind in its relationship to Christ, expressing the view of all mediaeval theologians who are in the authentic tradition of Origen and Gregory about the union between him and his Church, seen at once as 'fighting and conquering'. It is thus that in our making we are destined now and everlastingly to share in Christ's own will:

> *This is the work which is constantly performed in every soul which will be saved, and this is the godly will mentioned before (p. 293).*

Again she rehearses the various characteristics of this relationship with God, one and three; but she differs in emphasis from Cistercian and Victorine spiritual writers, as too from her contemporaries Hilton, the *Cloud*-author and the English translator of Suso's *Horologium*. The Church for her is the virginal wife of God the Trinity, in the Trinity's union with the incarnate Christ. We may, if we wish, follow other writers of the fourteenth century in applying this teaching to the relationship of Christ with the individual soul in the transforming union, the 'spiritual marriage'; but Julian, though her language can closely resemble theirs ('I love you and you love me, and our love will never divide in two', p. 293), never makes this application.

Here, in writing of the creative activity of the Trinity, the 'creating nature', she carefully lays down the principles which she will follow when she comes to deal with the 'Motherhood of God' and the incarnate Christ. To explain the matter as clearly as she has seen it, she constructs a rhetorical argument which begins from what she had seen in the parable of Christ's 'preexistence': there, the Son stands before the Father (p. 275), his 'rushing away was the divinity' (p. 277), he was 'saying in intention: See, my dear Father, I stand before you' (pp. 275-276), he 'stands before his lord, respectfully, ready to do his lord's will' (p. 267) and 'has now become our Mother sensually' (p. 294). From this she reasons that 'we are double by God's creating, that is to say substantial and sensual'. To support this she appeals to the Son's two natures: He 'is our Mother in nature in our substantial creation, in whom we are founded and rooted, and he is our Mother of mercy in taking our sensuality'; and she embellishes her argument by rehearsing the way in which this mercy works through Passion, death and Resurrection, thus keeping our 'parts undivided' and uniting us to our substance, the triune God. She goes on to summarize what she has seen in contemplative prayer concerning the operation of the Holy Spirit, the working of that grace which belongs to the 'royal lordship', elucidating what she had called 'rewarding' by defining it here as 'a gift for his confidence'. She ends the chapter with a characteristic anagogical contemplation: The purpose of the divine Trinitarian operation in the Incarnation is that all who are to be saved should be

> *gloriously brought up into heaven, and blessedly united to our substance, increased in riches and nobility by all the power of Christ and by the grace and operation of the Holy Spirit (p. 295),*

as Cassiodorus had written of the Church's ultimate reality: 'The gathering of all faithful saints is one soul and one heart, the bride of Christ, the Jerusalem of the life to come'[24].

Julian devotes the last chapters, 59 to 63, of Revelation XIV to setting out, in as clear and orderly a fashion as possible, the fruits of all that she has seen and heard concerning the second person of the Trinity, the 'mid person' who never appears to her understanding except in his relationship to Father and to Spirit. There is now a serenity in her vision of Jesus. She sees in him every man who will be saved, enriched by his wisdom and knowledge, built up in him who is the firm hope of heavenly glory, for all the fulness of the divine substance is incorporated in his glorified humanity: 'In him bodily there dwells the whole fulness of the divinity' (Colossians 2.9). As does Paul, she sees

---

24. De Lubac, *Exégèse médiévale* 2 515 and note 5.

Christ as God's principle and instrument of goodness, opposing all the evil and wickedness in the sinful world of man. This is the starting point in chapter 59 for her magisterial teaching on the motherhood of God, teaching which stands as a unique theological achievement in the Church's spiritual traditions.

When André Cabassut wrote of this as 'a little-known mediaeval devotion', his title probably indicated no more than that it is little known to 20th-century students of spirituality; he was himself able to show that it was well known in the 13th century to devotees of Francis of Assisi and to the many in the 17th century who read Benet Canfield; the present editors demonstrate in *Showings* that the devotion was well established in the *Ancrene Riwle*, in Mechtild of Hackborn's *Book of Special Grace* and in *The Chastising of God's Children*. Of special importance is the allusion to it in Anselm's 'Prayer to St. Paul':

> But you, too, good Jesus, are not you also a mother? Is not he a mother who like a hen gathers his chicks beneath his wings? Truly, Lord, you are a mother too. . . .

It seems certain that the source for this notion in Anselm is Augustine's comment on Psalm 101.7, 'I am made like to the pelican in the desert', where he writes that 'Christ exercises fatherly authority and maternal love', making the same comparison as Anselm, 'just as Paul is also father and mother. . .through his gospel-preaching'. Yet elsewhere we may suspect in Augustine a reluctance, Western rather than of the East, to assign to the eternal Son a feminine, creative role. In Julian there is no such hesitance, and what in her Western precursors is little more than devotional hyperbole is, for her, a sober expression of revealed truth.

For her, the most exalted of her revelations had been the twelfth, where our Lord had shown himself more glorified than she had seen him before. Accompanying this rarified intellectual vision of the heavenly Christ had been the locution 'I am he', which she often heard repeated. She implies there that her inability to comprehend the singular number of the words 'I am it', which were 'in the highest', had to do with unity and Trinity. Now, through her understanding of the Trinitarian relationships in the light of the parable, she is able to offer a truly evangelical interpretation of the great revelation of the name of God, 'I am who am' (Exodus 3.14). If the qualities of human fatherhood are the vestiges in creation appropriated to the first person, as Paul had taught (Ephesians 3.14-15), then equally the qualities of motherhood should be appropriated to the second person, whilst the fecundity of this knowledge and love in the 'divine creating nature' is rightly appropriated to the third person.

In her final version of the first revelation, Julian repeats several times that God is all that is good. So here she writes of the unity of God, 'I am he, the great supreme goodness of every kind of thing' (p. 296). This is the substantial ground in which we participate by the eternal decree of the Trinity, the divine nature, his being, which is communicated to us in the second person who is first our Mother, equal to the Father, and then in the Incarnation 'our true Mother in grace by his taking our created nature' (p. 296) and, finally, he is our saviour through 'motherhood at work', in which, in the Godhead, he is equal to the Spirit, who confirms the motherhood's working. Here she reminds us that this entire revelation is still 'about prayer'. Our response to the knowledge of our existence and growth in the Trinity is

> to love our God in whom we have our being, reverently thanking and praising him for our creation, mightily praying to our Mother for mercy and pity, and to our Lord the Holy Spirit for help and grace.

Here also she mentions the godly (or, more probably here, 'goodly') will for the last time:

All the lovely works and all the sweet loving offices of beloved motherhood are appropriated to the second person, for in him we have this 'goodly' will, whole and safe forever, both in nature and in grace, from his own goodness proper to him.

As one of the present editors indicated several years ago[25], Dom Roger Hudleston was right in linking Julian's teaching with that of William of St. Thierry, but was wrong in dismissing it as unorthodox. Hudleston's opinion continues to be repeated: 'This is wishful thinking and not the teaching of the Church'[26]. Her own visions and contemplations coincide with William's teaching in the *Aenigma fidei*: It is inconceivable that in the predestined, those who will be saved, the good will of God in Christ should be absent or extinguished, for that would be a sign that they are among the reproved, of whom, we recall, Julian saw none except the devil himself. It now appears likely, in view of her closeness to William's teaching, and of such considered statements as:

God is closer to us than our own soul, for he is the foundation on which our soul stands, and he is the mean which keeps the substance and the sensuality together, so that they will never separate (pp. 288-289),

that she was as well aware as was the *Cloud*-author in his teaching on the sovereign point of the spirit[27] that, affectively as well as morally, the 'spark of the loving soul' will never be extinguished in the minds and hearts of the predestined. And for Julian, as for monastic theologians in general, the very movement towards repentance is the sign of his continuing and permanent presence, 'from his own goodness proper to him'. The text employed by both William and by Hugh of St. Victor, discussing this matter,

---

25. Walsh, *Revelations* 37-40.
26. C. Wolters, *Julian of Norwich*, Introduction, 37.
27. P. Hodgson, *Cloud*, 18.

is I John 3.9: 'Whoever is born of God does not sin'. To 'be born of' refers properly to the mother:

> . . . *it cannot truly be said of anyone or to anyone except of him and to him who is the true Mother of life and of all things. To the property of motherhood belong nature, love, wisdom and knowledge, and this is God (p. 299).*

To conclude this chapter 59, Julian classifies the Trinitarian modes of the divine motherhood as she has become aware of it; and in this same context she again uses the word which she had previously coined to translate *circumincessio*, 'forth spredyng', this time in the Pauline reference to the Christian's interior knowledge of the expansion of the divine love in Christ (Ephesians 3.18-19) in his own spirit. This is the working of the motherhood of God in creation, redemption and glorification, which is the content of these last four chapters of Revelation XIV.

In chapter 60 she recalls how in Revelation I she was shown Mary in the mystery of the Annunciation, and she implies that Mary's own contemplation of her God in her acceptance of motherhood is a reflection of Christ's own service in the mystery of the Incarnation, as this was shown to her in the parable. He served when he 'arrayed and prepared himself in this humble place, all ready in our poor flesh' (p. 297); and she goes on to show that the mothering which Jesus received from Mary is derived from his own:

> *The mother's service is nearest, readiest and surest; nearest because it is most natural, readiest because it is most loving, and surest because it is truest. No one ever might or could perform this office fully, except only him.*

'He is our Mother in nature by the operation of grace in the lower part' Julian writes at the end of chapter 60, and it is in this way that she is found to be at one with so many of her contemporaries who share her devotion to Christ the Mother without necessarily being capable of the care with which she develops her theology. Of them all (Mechtild of Hackborn, William Flete, Bridget of Sweden and Catherine of Siena, among others), Julian is the only one who bases her devotional expression on a firm theological and contemplative understanding:

> . . . *he kindles our understanding, he prepares our ways, he eases our conscience, he comforts our soul, he illumines our heart and gives us partial knowledge and love of his blessed divinity, with gracious memory of his sweet humanity and his blessed Passion, with courteous wonder over his great surpassing goodness, and makes us to love everything which he loves for love of him, and to be well satisfied with him and with all his works. And when we fall, quickly he raises us up with his loving embrace and his gracious touch (chapter 61, pp. 299-300).*

It is only thus that Christ our Mother 'may sometimes suffer the child to fall' (p. 300), but he 'may never suffer us who are his children to perish', for that would contradict the very nature of the Godhead.

In chapter 62, as she draws to the end of her final redaction of Revelation XIV, Julian returns to the three chief lessons of the parable. First the servant was shown for Adam in his falling, secondly the servant was shown for God's Son with his power, wisdom and goodness, and thirdly it was shown that Jesus is our keeper in our time of falling. This summary reflection leads to another of wider scope. Behind the parable of the lord and the servant is the revelation of the being and working of God, one and three, the concept of all creation as emanation from and return to the divine being, firmly based on Scripture, and the return is perceived as salvation through grace:

> *And all natures which he has made to flow out of him to work his will, they will be restored and brought back into him by the salvation of man by the operation of grace (pp. 302-303).*

Here she sees, it would seem, through the eyes of William of St. Thierry (himself indebted to Gregory of Nyssa) in his 'Of the

Body's Nature and the Soul's'. All created things find their integration in the creature man, whose royalty is a participation in God's sovereign being. This man is, of course, Christ, who is also God; to him we are all fastened by nature and grace: 'We are all bound to God by nature, and we are bound to God by grace'. This is the quality and extent of his motherhood: All is known in him, and he in us. It is one of Julian's extraordinary gifts that she is able to take up the phrase 'know thyself', with all its mediaeval philosophical and theological implications, and express it in devotional language.

Early in this revelation Julian had written:

Prayer unites the soul to God, for though the soul may be always like God in nature and in substance restored by grace, it is often unlike him in condition, through sin on man's part (p. 253).

Now in the last chapter, 63, she returns to the point of union and disunion, with a variation on the words she has used in chapter 59 to describe goodness (with mercy and grace) and wickedness as adversaries. Here the antagonists are nature and sin. 'Nature' here stands for 'all natures which he has made to flow out of him to work his will', and 'grace' again is the restorative, now seen also as destructive of all that prevents the return to God. She seems to be making the point that sin is not merely transgression of a divine commandment; its malice consists in its being against human nature:

For [sin] is in opposition to our fair nature; for as truly as sin is unclean, so truly is sin unnatural (chapter 63, p. 304).

But it is the loving soul that will see this malice, and it will tend to be overcome by its burden. Again Julian moves with dexterity from what appears to be abstract theological speculation into 'Franciscan' devotional language as she counsels us to have recourse in such a dilemma

to our beloved Mother, and he will sprinkle us all with his precious blood, and make our soul most safe and most mild.

Alternation between meditative reflection and devotion is the pattern of this chapter, in a last recapitulation in its Trinitarian relations and its Christological operation which is followed by a pictorial image of this theological statement: The chief virtue of a child is true trust, which is the golden mean between despair and presumption:

> For the child does not naturally despair of the mother's love, the child does not naturally rely upon itself (p. 304).

The chapter ends with the anagogical contemplation of this child with its parents in eternity:

> And then will the bliss of our motherhood in Christ be to begin anew in the joys of our Father, God, which new beginning will last, newly beginning without end.

At the end of her account of the fifteenth showing in her short text, Julian had written: 'And here came the end of all that our Lord revealed to me on that day' (p. 162). In this long text's version of Revelation XV, she is more exact in her recollection:

> . . . of these fifteen revelations, the first began early in the morning, about the hour of four, and it lasted, revealing them in a determined order, most lovely and calm, each following the other, until it was three o'clock in the afternoon or later (pp. 309-310).

The statement is not without its psychological significance. Though she knew that she was the object of a direct supernatural intervention, it cannot be doubted that twelve hours of intense concentration, coupled with the alternation of spiritual consolation and desolation culminating in the mental perplexity which accompanied the showing of the parable, must have greatly taxed her mentally and physically. All this appears to be part of 'the woe that there is here' (p. 305), to which she alludes at the beginning of this revelation. It is noteworthy, too, that when she reports the locution which is the substance of the long text,

Suddenly you will be taken out of all your pain, all your sickness,
all your unrest and all your woe,

there is the phrase 'all your sickness', which is not found in the
corresponding short text.

The locution, which is an answer to her present prayer in
which she experiences once again the mingling of joy and woe, is
heavy with Scriptural allusions; and perhaps the most significant among them is the implied reference to the vision of
heaven in the Apocalypse, God's dwelling among men, when
there will be no more weeping or mourning. This is also the text
which she seems to have had in mind as the account of the
revelation begins and she writes of the 'new beginning without
end'.

Thus far in this revelation there has been almost verbatim
agreement with the short text. Now, however, Julian adds a
short parabolic picture, which, though it is an 'example' in the
strict sense, is introduced by the rubric 'And in this time I saw'
(p. 306). In other words, this belongs to the objective content of
the revelations, so that once again the question arises, why was it
suppressed in the short text? Several reasons suggest themselves. Firstly, this vision of a body 'which appeared oppressive
and fearsome and without shape and form, as if it were a
devouring pit of stinking mud' forces Julian out of her normal
delicacy and restraint. Secondly, her feeling about this is much
the same as when in Revelation II she had described the face of
the dying Christ. There she had written:

This second revelation was so humble and so small and so simple that
my spirit was greatly distressed as I contemplated it, mourning,
fearing, longing; for sometimes I was fearful of whether it was a
revelation (p. 194).

Considering this similar showing 'in bodily likeness', she may
have wondered whether it was merely the product of an imagination affected by pain, sickness and desolation. Thirdly, as

with her great 'example', the parable, she may have been unsure at the time when she wrote down the short text of the techniques of Scriptural interpretation which she had needed another twenty years to master. So now she explains the details of this 'example', and how it helps, by its sharpness of contraries, to lead to contemplation of 'the glory that is to come', which reveals once more the Lord's merciful compassion in his preservation of us and his promises to us.

The similarity between the bodily sight, gruesome in detail, in this revelation and the face of the dying Christ which reminded her of the Vernicle in Rome in Revelation II has already been remarked. The resemblance does not cease there. She had also written of the 'two activities which can be seen in this vision: one is seeking, the other is contemplating' (p. 196). Of this seeking, she had added:

> *It is God's will that we receive three things from him as gifts as we seek. The first is that we seek willingly and diligently without sloth, as that may be with his grace, joyfully and happily, without unreasonable depression and useless sorrow. The second is that we wait for him steadfastly, out of love for him, without grumbling and contending against him, to the end of our lives, for that will last only for a time. The third is that we have great trust in him, out of complete and true faith, for it is his will that we know that he will appear, suddenly and blessedly, to all his lovers (p. 196).*

When rightly understood, during the time that God wishes us to wait for his coming in hope, this is as good as contemplating. This teaching is now confirmed, in the long-text version of Revelation XV, by the locution and the vision of the example which accompanies it. The trust in his promise is the spiritual energy of contemplative reflection on the evangelical word: 'I am the resurrection and the life; he who believes in me, though he be dead, will live' (John 11.25), particularly in those times when, as the great spiritual masters of the West consistently teach, contemplative vision fades and the human frame feels the weight of its weakness:

. . . when we fall back into ourselves, through depression and spiritual blindness and our experience of spiritual and bodily pains, because of our frailty (p. 307).

Her reflection continues in chapter 65 with a conclusion which is implicit in her aphorism 'seeking is as good as contemplating':

For he wants us to pay true heed to this, that we are as certain in our hope to have the bliss of heaven whilst we are here as we shall be certain of it when we are there (p. 308).

Her use of the words 'here' and 'there' is a clear indication of how much at home she feels herself in the spiritual traditions of the 12th century. A key text for the understanding of this vocabulary is a passage from Caesarius of Arles: 'Our saviour has gone up to heaven; therefore let us not be troubled upon earth; let our minds be there, and here let there be rest. Meanwhile, let us go up with Christ in our hearts; and when the promised day will come, our bodies too will follow him'[28]. The various points made by Julian all accord with this tradition: As one is mindful of the blessings to come, one has joy in the Holy Spirit; one must suffer present tribulation patiently; one must persevere in the prayer of petition; through the illumination of the Word one must believe steadfastly in the divine promises; and, as Augustine writes of the Mystical Body: 'Be my members, if you wish to ascend into heaven. . . . Meanwhile, let us find strength in this, in this let us pour forth fervent prayers'[29]. It is this last point which Julian develops in her own way, by referring to her final statement on God's motherhood, on the contemplative disposition of a child of God, that total trust of which the elements are love, joy, reverence and humility:

And always, the more delight and joy that we accept from this certainty, with reverence and humility, the more pleasing it is to

---

28. Chatillon, 'Hic, ibi, interim', p. 194 n. 1.
29. Sermon 263, 'Of the Ascension of the Lord'.

*God. For as it was revealed, this reverence which I mean is a holy
courteous fear of our Lord to which humility is joined; and that is
that a creature should see the Lord marvellously great, and herself
marvellously little (p. 308).*

Now Julian, as she comes to the end of Revelation XV in
the long text, is looking both ahead and backwards to her experiential fear of the evil one, and she wants, for her readers' sake as
well as her own, to place the matter in perspective. There is only
one true fear, as she will tell us later, and that is the 'lovely dread'
which dwells in brotherhood with the divine love poured out in
our hearts. At this point, it may be, she wishes to prepare her
readers to share her own fearful experience. So she uses all her
rhetorical skill to make the point that all diabolic fears have a
hallucinatory and transitory quality, no matter how much they
may move us and confuse us. They are a part of our normal
experience of inadequacy and suffering, which 'let us, as soon as
we may, pass it over lightly' (p. 309).

So Julian concludes the first part of her showings; the first
fifteen revelations divide themselves, both chronologically and
psychologically, from the last. And here she reminds us that the
assurance which God's gift of hope confers is very much hers, as
she reflects at this point on the graces which she has received in
more than twenty years.

Revelation XVI begins with an account of the events in the
interval between the first fifteen showings and this last. She was
visited by a religious, whom she took into her confidence, telling
him that the crucifix before her had seemed to bleed, and that
she was inclined to consider this a hallucination. The seriousness with which he heard her story, and his amusement at her
lack of confidence, brought her to contrition for her own disbe-
lief; and then she fell asleep. During the night she experienced
the terrifying dream in which the devil was on the point of
choking her. The nightmare's horror woke her, and as she was
lying there, in 'great rest and peace, without sickness of body or
fear of conscience' (p. 312), the sixteenth revelation, as she

describes it in chapter 68, began. It moves through all her previous classification of her sights, and it is succeeded by a locution:

> *Our Lord very humbly revealed words to me, without voice and without opening of lips, just as he had done before, and said very sweetly: Know it well, it was no hallucination which you saw today, but accept and believe it and hold firmly to it, and comfort yourself with it and trust in it, and you will not be overcome. These last words were said to me to teach me perfect certainty that it is our Lord Jesus who revealed everything to me; and just as in the first words which our Lord revealed, alluding to his blessed Passion: With this the fiend is overcome, just so he said with perfect fidelity, alluding to us all: You will not be overcome (pp. 314-315).*

Above all else this shows Julian's grasp of the teaching, specifically Johannine, on the victory achieved by the Passion in the struggle against evil. 'Now', says Christ as he goes to the Passion, 'the prince of the world will be cast out' (John 12.31); 'now the prince of this world comes . . .' (*ibid.* 14.30); 'in this world you will have distress, but have confidence; I have overcome the world' (*ibid.* 16.33). This is exactly her point as she reflects in her final locution:

> *He did not say: You will not be troubled, you will not be belaboured, you will not be disquieted; but he said: You will not be overcome (p. 315).*

Secondly, John teaches that those who have true faith in Jesus as Son of God participate in the power of his Passion and overcome the world: 'This is the victory which overcomes the world, our faith' (I John 5.4). For Julian, those who will be saved possess this faith; they are born of God, who is their Father and Mother:

> *Our faith is a light, naturally coming from our endless day, which is our Father, God, in which light our Mother, Christ, and our*

good Lord the Holy Spirit lead us in this passing life (chapter 83, p. 340).

This is why she agonizes so greatly over her momentary lapse of faith, and treats it with such seriousness. It is on 'the children of unbelief' that 'the prince of the power of air' is at work (Ephesians 2.2).

Finally, the verb 'to overcome' has a special application to those who overcome the devil by the supreme witness of their lives (cf. Apocalypse 5.5, 7.14, 12.11). So she, who had asked for the grace of suffering with the dying Christ and of a sickness which might seem as if mortal, desired to share this combat, 'every fear and temptation from devils' (p. 178).

In Revelation V, Julian had written that she was shown the devil's total impotence (p. 201). Her language there, in chapter 13, resembles that of Paul in his letter to the Colossians: '. . . despoiling the principalities and powers, he has confidently exposed them in open showing, triumphing over them in himself' (that is, on the Cross—Colossians 2.15). And when she writes of the devil's malice and wrath and sore travail, she has in mind John's imagery: '. . . the devil has come down to you, having great wrath, knowing that he has but a short time' (Apocalypse 12.12).

Thus Julian's belief in the devil is firmly rooted in Scripture; and when she insists that temptations against faith and hope come from him, she is merely echoing John and Paul in their cosmic visions of the struggle between death and life, light and darkness, good and evil. When she describes her nightmare and the temptations which she endured after the sixteenth revelation, Julian can still betray the agitation which she then suffered; but, apart from this, all that she writes on the theology of the devil and temptation is of impeccable orthodoxy and is a model of restraint. She shows none of the self-consciousness, so common in her time, of those who, considering themselves chosen souls, expect frequently to be harassed by the fiend. On the contrary, she is concerned to minimize the role of demonic activity in the life of the contemplative. It is remarkable that although the revelations show her so concerned with the enigma of sin and damnation, no mention is made of the sin of the angels. She can personify wrath (chapter 49, p. 264) without mentioning the evil spirit; and in her account of Adam's fall, in the parable, and of the Harrowing of Hell, there is no mention of Satan or of devils. Though in times of sickness or depression fear of the fiend seems to have been prominent in her consciousness, that fear is elsewhere merely catalogued with all the other 'doubtful dreads'; and she can write with serenity that fear of ghostly enemies is profitable, along with dread of pain and bodily death, as a point of entry into contrition:

> . . . for anyone fast asleep in sin is not for that time able to receive the gentle strength of the Holy Spirit, until he has accepted this fear of pain from bodily death and from spiritual enemies (p. 324).

And in the long text she is content to suppress the short text's gloss on II Corinthians 11, when she had proferred her advice on dealing with 'doubtful dread', presumably because she herself had never seen the devil so disguised.

Revelation XVI, Julian tells us, is 'a conclusion and confirmation to all the fifteen' (p. 310). It is also the climax of what may be called her mystical experience. She indicates clearly that it 'was shown . . . by ghostly sight' when she writes: 'And then our good Lord opened my spiritual eye, and showed me my soul. . .' (chapter 68, p. 312). At first glance the revelation appears to be simply a bodily sight, an imaginative vision of Jesus dressed as a king and seated on a throne. Julian, however, is trying to find words and images to express what for her is ineffable: '. . . about the spiritual vision, I have told a part, but I can never tell it in full' (chapter 73, p. 322). So she uses the phrase 'as it were', and writes of Jesus as 'splendidly clad in honours' (p. 313). She also substitutes in the long text 'I understood that it is a fine city' for the short text's 'it seemed to me as if it were a fine city' (chapter xxii, p. 163), presumably in order to make it plain that she is seeking to describe the special insight into the mystery which was granted to her.

In chapter 52 of the long text she has already neatly summarized what her revelations and the faith of the Church teach her about the divine presence, that relationship which must find its human expression in unitive prayer:

> *He wants us to trust that he is constantly with us, and that in three ways. He is with us in heaven, true man in his own person, drawing us up. . .and he is with us on earth, leading us. . .and he is with us in our soul, endlessly dwelling, ruling and guarding. . .*
> *(p. 280).*

It is with this third mode of presence that this final revelation concerns itself. It is indeed a 'conclusion and confirmation' in that it depends for its understanding upon her careful and informed elaboration of the mysteries of the Trinity and the Incarnation. It has recently been observed that the richest context for theological reflection on the mystery of the indwelling is the doctrine of the Trinity, particularly with regard to 'missions' and 'processions'[30]. This is why the sixteenth revelation, in the long text, changes character dramatically, to show Julian contemplating the delight of the Trinity as the Word is made flesh, its 'home of homes and his everlasting dwelling' (chapter 68, p. 313). This is surely an echo of Wisdom's words: 'I was with him forming all things, and was delighted every day. . .and my delights were to be with the children of men' (Proverbs 8.30-31). 'And in this', Julian writes, 'he revealed the delight that he has in the creation of man's soul; for as well as the Father could create a creature and as well as the Son could create a creature, so well did the Holy Spirit want man's spirit to be created, and so it was done'. Plainly, just as the prologue to John's Gospel is full of allusion to the Genesis creation narrative, so here Julian, treating ostensibly of the creation of humankind on the sixth day, is

---

30. R. Moretti: 'Inhabitation' (*Dictionnaire de Spiritualité* 7 1745).

developing and relating three themes: man's creation, God's delight in his creation, and the Trinity's delight in the Incarnation, as she alludes to Genesis, to the sapiential books and to John's prologue. 'And so it was done'; 'and so it was made'; 'and the Word was made flesh'. In the short text, Julian seems to have restricted herself to considering the mystery merely as union, in the fulfillment of knowledge and love. But now, as well as expressing her delight in all that is static in the relevation—

And it was a singular joy and bliss to me that I saw him sitting, for the truth of sitting revealed to me endless dwelling (p. 314)—

she is able to use an 'example' which was provided at the time of the showing but had been suppressed in the short text: 'And [the Trinity] wants our hearts to be powerfully lifted above the depths of the earth and all empty sorrows, and to rejoice in it'.

The locution which follows this example becomes a confirmation of all that faith and grace have taught her in the twenty years which she had devoted to the love of learning, and the desire for that God who has revealed himself in Christ to all who will be saved from all harm and for all bliss, through Christ:

Just so he said. . .with perfect fidelity, alluding to us all: You will not be overcome (p. 315).

The short text at this point shows her still in the sort of trouble and distress which, the locution had indicated, might be her lot:

He did not say: You will not be assailed, you will not be belaboured, you will not be disquieted, but he said: You will not be overcome (chapter xxii, p. 165).

There she had apostrophized sin, because she was experiencing the sorrows of the contemplative, the heavy burden of herself, but also because the revelations are at an end and she has not yet seen 'this truth in you, who are my God, my maker in whom I desire to see all truth' (chapter 50, p. 266). So she had ended the apostrophe with an ejaculatory prayer against the evil one: God protects us all from you. 'Amen, for love of him' (p. 166). Now her life of prayer and study enables her to see matters quite differently. She is well content that the sight should have passed; faith has sought and brought understanding of the living truth: 'It is faith which preserves the blessed revelation through God's own good will and his grace' (pp. 316-317). So, in the long text, she recalls that with the final locution which followed her lapse of faith and her first temptations, 'he revealed it all again in my soul, more completely in the blessed light of his precious love' (p. 317). God in his mystery has become the light of her life; and this is faith, as she will write when she brings her book to a close:

> Our faith is a light, naturally coming from our endless day, which is our Father, God, in which light our Mother, Christ, and our good Lord the Holy Spirit lead us in this passing life (chapter 83, p. 340).

In chapter 71 Julian continues her protracted reflection on the final locution and on what it teaches about the relationship between her revelations and the faith. Its power is weakened and its content is obscured, because we see now only 'through a glass in a dark manner . . . in part' (I Corinthians 13.12, a text she clearly has in mind), and also because of the hostile presence of evil in ourselves and in our world, 'our spiritual enemies, internal and external' (p. 318). She goes on to add:

> And therefore our precious lover helps us with spiritual light and true teaching, in various ways, from within and from without, by which we may know him.

The 'spiritual enemies' at least include evil spirits, but she has nothing to say of the activities of good spirits. She will tell us later that 'I believe and understand the ministration of holy angels, as scholars tell, but it was not revealed to me' (p. 336).

Here she writes: 'However he teaches us, he wants us to perceive him'; and he had taught her that he is the Trinity, that he is he whom Holy Church preached and taught her. So it is that for her the contemplative faith and vision reflect one another, until faith receives the reward it deserves.

This working of faith and grace she now connects with God's three demeanours: his revelation of himself in the suffering and dying incarnate Word (Revelations I, II, V and VIII), in the lord looking on his servant in his falling, and, finally, the joyful face of the glorified Christ which she first saw in Revelation IX. In this life, the first two are 'usual aspects' (p. 319); the third is known only through infused contemplative grace.

In chapter 72 she appears to be reviewing what she had written at this point in the short text, the apostrophe to sin, and she now feels able to confront the problem—'how I saw that sin is deadly in creatures who ought not to die for sin but live in the joy of God without end' (p. 319). She is in the first place writing of the penitent-saints whom she had seen in the great revelation of divine compassion (chapter 38), and of those like them. She has in mind the text 'The souls of the just are in the hands of the Lord, and the torments of death will not touch them. . .they seemed to die. . .but they are at peace' (Wisdom 3.1-4); and this is the same 'opposition of contraries' as she herself is using throughout this chapter:

> . . .always, the more clearly that the soul sees the blessed face by the grace of loving, the more it longs to see it in fulness, that is to say in God's own likeness. . .for in that precious sight no woe can remain, no well-being can be lacking.

She seems to be praying even as she writes; the sorrow which flows from her own sinfulness, as that which prevents her from seeing God's face, becomes the spiritual weeping which is the gift of tears:

> Still we should never cease to mourn and to weep in the spirit,

because, that is, of our painful longing, until we might see our Creator's fair blessed face (p. 321);

and she refers again to Revelation XII, when she saw him in his glory, and was first taught that our soul will never be at peace or rest until it comes into him who is the fulness of joy and true life. So at last she considers that the question she posed in chapter 50 has been placed in its entire context and thoroughly elucidated, not only in the showings and all that she has been taught, but also through her continuing prayer of faith.

One task remains, to try in a practical way to expound all that she has learned, for the sake of those who 'for the love of God hate sin and dispose themselves to do God's will' (p. 322). At this point in the short text she had first given a general description of wretchedness, seeming in fact to be addressing those who love God and hate sin but yet sometimes fall into the sin they hate 'through frailty or ignorance'. In the long text she abides by what God has shown her of sins in particular. 'Impatience or sloth. . .despair or doubtful fear' are part of such frailty and ignorance. She repeats here what she had written earlier. God had given her a general sight of sin, of 'all that is not good'; and she adds 'but he showed no sins in particular but these two'—that is, impatience or despair. Impatience, 'grudging', is for her serious, because she sees it as a refusal to imitate Christ's own meekness and patience. She makes oblique allusion, in the Trinitarian context which she has so long and lovingly pondered, to 'doubtful fear', which is to refuse to share in faith the life of the Trinity, to refuse the Spirit who is the love between Father and Son; 'that he is all love and wishes to do everything, there we fail' (p. 323). She has now come to see that she is one with her brethren in their sin; 'doubtful fear' is for her synonymous with the guilt she feels because

we do not keep our promise or keep the purity which God has established us in, but often fall into so much wretchedness that it is shameful to say it.

Such guilt can often masquerade as humility, a fault to which religious are traditionally prone; but there is only one true humility, that of God, revealed in the incarnate Word, coming to us out of love to share with us his Father's strength and his own wisdom:

> *For love makes power and wisdom very humble to us; for just as by God's courtesy he forgets our sin from the time that we repent, just so does he wish us to forget our sin with regard to our unreasonable depression and our doubtful fears.*

So Julian offers us her exegesis of Paul's 'oppositions' in I Corinthians 1.25: 'For the foolishness of God is wiser than men, and the weakness of God is stronger than men'.

Chapter 74, which treats of love and fear, shows us two different aspects of her ability as theologian. First she deliberately uses Scriptural and patristic allusions to draw the necessary distinctions between the schoolmen's 'fear in the beginning', 'abjectly servile fear', and 'filial' or 'chaste fear'. But then, basing her thought on I John 4.18, and, perhaps, Augustine's exegesis of this, she uses all her rhetorical and lyrical skills to describe how reverent fear can come to mean that experiential knowledge of the triune God granted to his chosen as a foretaste of the vision of the blessed, that special awareness of the fulfillment, now in time, of the promise of divine indwelling: 'We shall come to him and make our home with him' (John 14.21, 23). She is also, however, describing the process of purification which demands a progressive self-discernment. She has recourse to the mother-and-child image, but with all the weight of her teaching on God's motherhood to give it substance, as she appeals to God's everlasting goodness and uses the Scriptural verb 'cleave'. It is Paul who sums up the whole tradition of God's loving commerce with his people as he writes: 'He who cleaves to the Lord is one spirit with him' (I Corinthians 6.17). And Julian's chapter ends with a refutation, beautifully composed and expressed, of Peter Abelard's condemned proposition, 'That even chaste fear will be excluded from the life to come':

For the natural attribute of fear which we have in this life by the grace-giving operation of the Holy Spirit will be the same in heaven before God, gentle, courteous, most sweet; and thus in love we shall be familiar and close to God, and in fear we shall be gentle and courteous to God, and both the same, in the same way (p. 325).

Chapter 75 is perhaps Julian's most polished and precise theological reflection on the Trinitarian economy, based on Revelation IX, the intellectual vision which follows the locution 'Are you well satisfied that I suffered for you'? (p. 216). Then, she told us, 'my understanding was lifted up into heaven'. This chapter also takes account of Revelation XIII, the long text's development of the theme of Christ's 'spiritual thirst'. This is monastic theology at its finest, and it has much in common with the principle which, Dumontier writes, 'furnishes the supreme explanation of the spirituality of St. Bernard. . ."The God who is desired and loved becomes a God of desire and love" '[31]. Bernard uses the same Trinitarian and image-theology and he too is writing of those who will be saved: 'Bernard affirms that the Father expects us and desires us. . .there is the same desire in the Son, avid for us, rejoicing in us, eager for the day when he will enjoy the reward of his labours'[32]. This is precisely Julian's anagogy. Bernard writes: 'And the Holy Spirit also awaits us, the love and the benignity in which we were predestined from eternity; nor can anyone doubt that the Spirit wishes to fulfil that predestination'[33]. This is in a sermon for Christmas Eve, and Julian too is recalling what she has been shown of the mother of the Christ child in the time of his conception, the quality of

---

31. *St. Bernard et la Bible*, 39.
32. *Ibid.*, 40.
33. *Ibid.*, 40 and note 4.

Mary's reverent fear in a contemplation which anticipates the awesome joy of the Beatific Vision:

> *It is proper to God's honourable majesty so to be contemplated by his creatures, trembling and quaking in fear, because of their much greater joy endlessly marvelling at the greatness of God, the Creator, and at the smallest part of all that is created. For the contemplation of this makes the creature marvellously meek and mild (p. 327).*

In chapter 76 Julian proceeds to argue that this reverent fear is the antithesis of sin. She recalls that God has shown her only those souls who dread him—our Lady and the procession of penitent-saints, those who have truly received the Holy Spirit's teaching; for it is the Lord's promise that he will teach us all truth (John 16.13). Such souls hate sin more than any pain, for they contemplate 'the gentleness of Jesus' (p. 328). It is thus God's will that we pray to him for this teaching.

What follows, on how we are to behave when confronted with other men's sins, seems to reflect Julian's experience as a spiritual director; and she implies that the counsellor is expected to share the parenthood of God. He must look upon 'the beauty of God', and behold his neighbour's sin

> *with contrition with him, with compassion on him, and with holy desires to God for him.*

These are the very gifts for which she had asked, before the revelations began, the 'three wounds'. Now she sees them as the components of reverent dread; and we see another measure of her spiritual stature. She knows how the graces she had asked for and had been given can be used, not merely for her own profit, but for the pastoral comforting and strengthening of other souls.

In the last section of this chapter she rehearses how the contemplative penitent should exercise his faith, hope and love when he is assailed by doubtful fear. Again, this is written out of her counsellor's experience; she is speaking of and to

> *creatures who have given themselves to serve our Lord by the inward contemplation of his blessed goodness (p. 329).*

At the end of chapter 76, Julian had insisted that doubtful fear is a diabolic temptation; and this leads her to reflect again on what she has seen of 'the fiend's enmity' (p. 329) in chapter 77. She shares the cosmic view of the Book of Wisdom: 'They did not know the secrets of God, nor did they hope for the wages of justice, nor did they esteem the honour of holy souls. For God created man incorruptible, and he made him to the image of his own likeness; but by the envy of the devil death came into the world' (Wisdom 2.22-24). She then proceeds to a review of the relationship of the Trinity with fallen man. Just as in the previous chapter she imagined the tempter speaking, here she has the penitent resisting the temptation, not with the neurotic self-castigation which marks some contemporary writing, but with a gentle, peaceful contemplation in faith of Father, Son and Spirit:

> *I know well that I have deserved pain; but our Lord is almighty, and may punish me greatly, and he is all wisdom, and can punish me wisely, and he is all goodness, and loves me tenderly. And it is profitable for us to remain in this contemplation (p. 330).*

Again she stresses that sorrow for sin, which is the beginning of reverent fear, is not only a compound of the gifts of the fear of the Lord and of hope, but is based on the humility which she perceived so clearly in Mary's soul. These are the virtues which constitute interior penance, the signs of the change of heart which will be the sinner's response to God's desire for him. Julian saw no other:

As to the penance which one takes upon oneself, that was not revealed to me; that is to say, it was not revealed to me specifically. But what was revealed, specially and greatly and in a most loving manner, is that we ought meekly and patiently to bear and suffer the penance which God himself gives us, with recollection of his blessed Passion.

She is here writing in the context of the infinite depths of the Lord's compassion, as he turns his face to the world of men which is in process of being purified and enlightened by the Spirit, 'freed', as Paul writes, 'from the servitude of corruption to the freedom of the glory of God's sons' (Romans 8.21), the bliss of heaven. Julian reminds us here that the first revelations of Christ's sufferings made her 'to choose him with all my strength for my heaven' (p. 331). She has come to know by experience that though he is 'supreme familiarity' (p. 331), he is also mighty and dreadful, for all creation has its being in him.

'For truly it behoves us to see that in ourselves we are nothing at all but sin and wretchedness' (p. 332). As Julian continues in these concluding chapters to set down the practical spiritual counsel which is the authentic fruit of her intellectual visions of the Trinity and the incarnate Word, it has become her special concern to expose the heresy of Pelagianism and its watered-down version, semi-Pelagianism, which has always contaminated the atmosphere of consecrated life in the Church. The difference between those who are 'highest and closest to God' (p. 333) and 'the least and the lowest of those who will be saved', among whom she is happy to count herself in hope, is simply a matter of degree. All sinfulness is unlikeness to God, and in the clarity of contemplative vision the distinctions of the moral theologians cease to have relevance. 'I am needy and poor' (Psalm 69.6). She echoes this sentiment, and applies it to all God's children, even those who appear to be specially favoured with contemplative graces:

And by this I was taught that though we may be lifted up high into contemplation by the special gift of our Lord, still, together with this, we must necessarily have knowledge and sight of our sin and of our feebleness; for without this knowledge we may not have true meekness, and without this we cannot be safe (chapter 78, p. 333).

Julian, who begins this chapter with yet another rendering of the Trinitarian formula 'from the Father, through the Son, in the Holy Spirit', knows that it is only of God's gift that we see the whole truth of our need of him in our nothingness:

Then are we much indebted to God, who is willing himself for love to show it to us, in the time of mercy and of grace.

'For whatever things were written, were written for our teaching, that through patience and the comfort of the Scriptures we might have hope' (Romans 15.4). As Julian in chapter 79 looks back over the long and complex revelation of the divine compassion, she finds that it simply reinforces her knowledge of sacred Scripture, which she summarizes in one sentence which alludes to Paul:

All this familiar revelation of our courteous Lord is a lesson of love, and a sweet, gracious teaching from himself, in comforting of our soul (p. 334).

She had at first agonized, when 'he revealed to me that I should sin' (p. 333), over the prospect of her personal infidelity. But now she has lived with and through her faithlessness, to find that God outreaches her with

the endlessness and the unchangeability of his love, and also his great goodness and his gracious protection of our spirit.

This is a hope and a comfort which she shares with all God's people, his Church for which hope is the persevering response to his quality of mercy. To this hope belongs the patience which we need to have with ourselves in times of darkness, 'when we have fallen through weakness or blindness' (p. 334); and she shows how patient endurance is related to the Lord's own patient longing for us, as was shown in the allegory. She had written that to her the servant's most astonishing pain 'was that he lay alone' (p. 268). But even so she saw the lord 'waiting for the servant whom he had sent out' (p. 274). Now she knows this to be the 'office and working' here on earth of the Spirit of both the Father and the Son.

In chapter 80, as she continues to instruct us on how God sees us and keeps us in our sinful human condition, Julian turns her attention to what she has learned about ministry, the ministry of Christ in his Church, that ministry which for us (and this applies with special force to contemplatives) is primarily the worship of the Father by Christ in us, and their gaining for us, with the Spirit, our salvation. All the powers and gifts which we have received are designed to achieve this purpose, which is the reason for our existence; and they reflect the Trinitarian mystery:

> *Man endures in this life by three things, by which three God is honoured and we are furthered, protected and saved (p. 335).*

Through our higher powers of knowing and loving, through the teaching which Christ imparts in his word to the Church, through the sacramental presence of his Spirit, we are drawn into collaboration with God himself: 'We are God's fellow-workers' (I Corinthians 3.9). But, as always for Julian, it is God revealed in Christ who is the object of this contemplation, without which there is no ministry for his followers:

> *Christ alone performed all the great works which belong to our salvation, and no one but he; and just so, he alone acts now in the last end, that is to say he dwells here in us, and rules us, and cares for us in this life, and brings us to his bliss,*

where that ministry will have its fulfillment. It is a service as personal as the washing of the apostles' feet (John 13.4-8):

. . . so much so that if there were no such soul on earth except one, he would be with it, all alone, until he had brought it up into his bliss.

When Julian writes:

And when I say that he waits for us, moaning and mourning, that means all the true feelings which we have in ourselves, in contrition and in compassion, and all the moaning and mourning because we are not united with our Lord,

she is certainly treating of the mystery of Christ glorified and yet suffering with his members, as Paul encountered him on the Damascus road (Acts 9.5). She had already expressed this with theological competence and precision in Revelation XIII; here, however, she is offering instruction for contemplative prayer, in which the soul must be prepared to move and to be moved from darkness into light and to be exposed to the visitations of consolation and desolation in which it is enabled to experience, in consciousness of its own sinfulness, that compassion for itself which is integral to the gift of loving sorrow and is destined to become a sharing in the mystery of Christ's suffering compassion.

Julian concludes chapter 80 by recalling that the two particular sins which plague Christ's lovers, despair and doubtful dread, and all that is contained in the last capital sin, sloth, bruise the relationship between him and his Church, whether this concerns one soul or all souls. But she ends by stating firmly that on God's part the covenant remains unshaken; he is everlastingly faithful:

. . . constantly he is with us, and tenderly he excuses us, and always protects us from blame in his sight (p. 336).

In chapter 81 she reinforces this teaching by cataloguing the various modes of this presence as they were shown to her in the revelations. The Johannine influence in this summary is strong, as is the emphasis which she gives to the mode of presence which is his government and guidance of man's spirit from within:

> *He revealed himself several times reigning. . .but principally in man's soul; he has taken there his resting place and his honourable city (p. 337).*

It is not merely the vocabulary of mediaeval courtesy which Julian is using here. She is alluding to the Trinitarian glory which Irenaeus long ago had called 'man fully alive'[34], and of which Christ speaks at the end of his Eucharistic discourse: '. . .that they may see my glory which thou hast given me, because thou hast loved me before the creation of the world. . .and I have made known thy name to them and shall make it known, that the love with which thou hast loved me may be in them, and I in them' (John 17.24-26). Plainly and undoubtedly, the love of the Father and the Son is the Holy Spirit, so that when Christ says 'that the love with which thou hast loved me may be in them, and I in them', it is as if he were to say 'that the Holy Spirit, the Paraclete, may come to them and may teach them all truth, and when he shall have entered their hearts, I too shall dwell there through faith and through that Spirit of love'[35].

Again, Julian's counsel is practical: The presence is dynamic, and demands mutuality, and the right contemplative response to it is to rejoice that the Spirit is at work in us in our penance:

> *For he regards us so tenderly that he sees all our life here to be penance; for the loving longing in us for him is a lasting penance in us, and he makes this penance in us, and mercifully he helps us to bear it.*

The process is that which Paul calls being 'transformed from glory into glory, as by the Spirit of the Lord' (II Corinthians

---

34. *Adversus haereses*, IV 7.
35. Rupert of Deutz, *Commentarium in Johannem* XX.

3.18), 'until the time when we are fulfilled, when we shall have him for our reward'.

The attitudes and dispositions which Julian expects from her readers, as they contemplate with her the indwelling as it has been revealed for them to her in the parable, is finely expressed here. The Lord had said to her, at the beginning of Revelation XIII,

> *Sin is necessary, but all will be well, and all will be well, and every kind of thing will be well (p. 225).*

Now, inevitably, she refers this to the contemplative's passive purification, as she makes the Lord say:

> *. . . but since you do not live without sin, you are depressed and sorrowful, and if you could live without sin, you would suffer for my love all the woe which might come to you, and it is true. But do not be too much aggrieved by the sin which comes to you against your will (p. 338).*

She is showing, too, the nature of this unitive prayer, how the purgative quality of this mourning for our sinfulness, when informed by the virtue of discretion, leads to illumination and then to union, and that these three stages of the interior life, though distinguishable, tend to fuse:

> *He loves us endlessly, and we sin customarily, and he reveals it to us most gently.*

In reflecting that she was never shown anyone who 'is continually protected from falling' on earth, she is opposing with her sound theology the Quietism which was so rife in her day. Pierre Adnès has recently written: 'Even with the saints, half-deliberated faults, spontaneous movements coming from instincts not yet sufficiently controlled, and various weaknesses often attest the persistence of an enfeebled will, the consequences of which have not yet been completely eliminated. This is why they never cease to fear, whilst still firmly hoping for their salvation'[36]. This is exactly Julian's position:

> *For we do not fall in the sight of God, and we do not stand in our own sight (p. 339).*

She then constructs a series of oppositions, in order to illustrate how the progressive knowledge of the self in its sensuality, the 'lower contemplation', is constantly purified and enlightened by what God shows us in contemplation of our life in him, which is the 'higher contemplation'. Thus the process of unitive prayer is always constant, in that it moves from the tropological to the anagogical:

> *But our good Lord always wants us to remain much more in the contemplation of the higher, and not to forsake the knowledge of the lower, until the time that we are brought up above, where we shall have our Lord Jesus for our reward.*

Julian had promised to write in these closing chapters of the long text as clearly and fully as she could of the 'most glorified' of her visions. Now she finds herself able in these last four chapters, 83-86, to offer us a summary of the 'three properties of God, in which consist the strength and the effect of all the revelation' (p. 339). She writes, too, by implication at least, of the spiritual senses with which she has been endowed in order to receive these showings. At the very beginning she had written of her desire for greater 'mind' and 'feeling' for Christ's Passion, and, contemplating the first revelations, she had come to realize that she was being enabled to respond to Paul's exhortation to all Christians:

---

36. 'Impeccabilité', *Dictionnaire de Spiritualité* 7 1620.

. . . But each soul should do as St. Paul says, and feel in himself what is in Christ Jesus (p. 142).

Her 'sight and. . .feeling' were her continued response to the Trinitarian communication, the 'touching' of the intellectual visions which she had received. These 'touchings' she now calls 'life, love and light'. They are the attributes appropriated to all the persons of the Trinity. Her reason, the 'higher part' of her soul, 'wanted to be united and cleave' to these attributes 'in one goodness. . .with all my powers'; for this 'higher part' is the apex both of the affections and of the intelligence, so that she

> *contemplated with reverent fear, greatly marvelling at the sight and the feeling of the sweet harmony, that our reason is in God, understanding that this is the highest gift that we have received, and its foundation is in nature (p. 340).*

Her definition of faith here is one which spiritual theologians tend to describe as 'the spirit of faith': '. . .a living synthesis of light and of movement. . .the impregnation of the human soul by faith in the soul's most spiritual faculties. . .progress in the faith, in the sense that man is more completely submissive to God's invitations. . .a perfecting of faith'[37]. Again, Julian's contemplation is strictly anagogical:

> *And at the end of woe, suddenly our eyes will be opened, and in the clearness of our sight our light will be full, which light is God, our Creator, Father, and the Holy Spirit, in Christ Jesus our saviour (p. 340).*

'This light is love': that is, the luminous faith which is contemplative response and awareness is the virtue and the gift of love.
    Chapter 85 seems to indicate that what Julian has written about God's properties and the relationship between faith and

---

37. André de Bovis, 'Esprit de foi', *Dictionnaire de Spiritualité* 5 611-612.

charity is itself the fruit of immediate contemplation of all the revelations, which are now through grace stored in her memory; and she concludes with the vision of Paradise reflected in the *Sanctus* of the Roman Mass, which itself might be called an anagogical gloss on Isaias's vision of the heavenly temple and of the Lord on his throne (Isaias 6.1-3).

Augustine Baker, to whom, along with his followers among the exiled English Benedictines, we owe the preservation of Julian's long text, quotes the *Golden Epistle* of William of St. Thierry (in Baker's day still attributed to Bernard of Clairvaux) in praise of the contemplative life: 'It is for others to serve God, it is for you to cleave to him. It is for others to believe in God, know him, love and revere him; it is for you to taste him, understand him, perceive and delight in him'. Julian, in her humble realization that she is still aspiring to that fulness of the life of prayer which must be 'begun by God's gift and his grace' (chapter 86, p. 342) in this present moment, but which reaches out into God's eternal present, uses all William's verbs to describe it:

> For charity, let us all join with God's working in prayer, thanking, trusting, rejoicing, for so will our good Lord be entreated, by the understanding which I took in all his own intention (p. 342).

It is only as we fulfil God's will in trusting him that he is the ground of the unitive prayer of petition, that he will 'give us grace to love him and to cleave to him', and this whether we be professed contemplatives or not.

This lesson of love can be heard in its simplest form in the call to 'pray without ceasing'; and certainly all creatures, lettered or unlettered, are gifted by God for its performance, in one mode or another. But as this lesson was learned by Julian, it contains and demands far more. Jean Leclercq has written with great perception about the conflict which can arise, in monastic theology and living, between learning and devotion to heavenly things, and how this conflict can be resolved. Readers of Julian's book must decide how closely his description fits her:

> *To combine a patiently acquired culture with a simplicity won through the power of fervent love, to keep simplicity of soul in the midst of the diverse attractions of the intellectual life and, in order to accomplish this, to place oneself and remain firmly on the plane of conscience, to raise knowledge to its level and never let it fall below: this is what the cultivated monk succeeds in doing. He is a scholar, he is versed in letters, but he is not merely a man of science nor a man of letters nor an intellectual; he is a spiritual man*[38].

---

38. *The Love of Learning*, 317.

·JULIAN OF NORWICH·
SHOWINGS

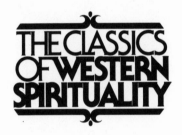

THE CLASSICS OF WESTERN SPIRITUALITY

·JULIAN OF NORWICH·

SHOWINGS

THE SHORT TEXT

Chapter i

Here is a vision shown by the goodness of God to a devout woman, and her name is Julian, who is a recluse at Norwich and still alive, A.D. 1413, in which vision are very many words of comfort, greatly moving for all those who desire to be Christ's lovers.

I desired three graces by the gift of God. The first was to have recollection of Christ's Passion. The second was a bodily sickness, and the third was to have, of God's gift, three wounds. As to the first, it came into my mind with devotion; it seemed to me that I had great feeling for the Passion of Christ, but still I desired to have more by the grace of God. I thought that I wished that I had been at that time with Mary Magdalen and with the others who were Christ's lovers, so that I might have seen with my own eyes our Lord's Passion which he suffered for me, so that I might have suffered with him as others did who loved him, even though I believed firmly in all Christ's pains, as Holy Church shows and teaches, and as paintings of the Crucifixion represent, which are made by God's grace, according to Holy Church's teaching, to resemble Christ's

Passion, so far as human understanding can attain. But despite all my true faith I desired a bodily sight, through which I might have more knowledge of our Lord and saviour's bodily pains, and of the compassion of our Lady and of all his true lovers who were living at that time and saw his pains[1], for I would have been one of them and have suffered with them. I never desired any other sight of God or revelation, until my soul would be separated from the body, for I trusted truly that I would be saved. My intention was, because of that revelation, to have had truer recollection of Christ's Passion. As to the second grace, there came into my mind with contrition—a free gift from God which I did not seek—a desire of my will to have by God's gift a bodily sickness, and I wished it to be so severe that it might seem mortal, so that I should in that sickness receive all the rites which Holy Church had to give me, whilst I myself should believe that I was dying, and everyone who saw me would think the same, for I wanted no comfort from any human, earthly life. In this sickness I wanted to have every kind of pain, bodily and spiritual, which I should have if I were dying, every fear and assault from devils, and every other kind of pain except the departure of the spirit, for I hoped that this would be profitable to me when I should die, because I desired soon to be with my God.

I desired these two, concerning the Passion and the sickness, with a condition, because it seemed to me that neither was an ordinary petition, and therefore I said: Lord, you know what I want. If it be your will that I have it, grant it to me, and if it be not your will, good Lord, do not be displeased, for I want nothing which you do not want. When I was young I desired to have that sickness when I

---

1. The short text reads: 'and of all his true lovers who were believing in his pains, at that time and afterwards', but the long text here clearly is superior. Cf. below, p. 178 and *Showings*, I, 202 and II, 286.

was thirty years old. As to the third, I heard a man of Holy Church tell the story of St. Cecilia, and from his explanation I understood that she received three wounds in the neck from a sword, through which she suffered death. Moved by this, I conceived a great desire, and prayed our Lord God that he would grant me in the course of my life three wounds, that is, the wound of contrition, the wound of compassion and the wound of longing with my will for God. Just as I asked for the other two conditionally, so I asked for this third without any condition. The two desires which I mentioned first passed from my mind, and the third remained there continually.

Chapter ii

And when I was thirty and a half years old, God sent me a bodily sickness in which I lay for three days and three nights; and on the fourth night I received all the rites of Holy Church, and did not expect to live until day. But after this I suffered on for two days and two nights, and on the third night I often thought that I was on the point of death; and those who were around me also thought this. But in this I was very sorrowful and reluctant to die, not that there was anything on earth that it pleased me to live for, or anything of which I was afraid, for I trusted in God. But it was because I wanted to go on living to love God better and longer, and living so, obtain grace to know and love God more as he is in the bliss of heaven. For it seemed to me that all the time that I had lived here was very little and short in comparison with the bliss which is everlasting. So I thought: Good Lord, is it no longer to your glory that I am alive? And my reason and my sufferings told me that I should die;

and with all the will of my heart I assented wholly to be as was God's will.

So I lasted until day, and by then my body was dead from the middle downwards, it felt to me. Then I was moved to ask to be lifted up and supported, with cloths held to my head, so that my heart might be more free to be at God's will, and so that I could think of him whilst my life would last; and those who were with me sent for the parson, my curate, to be present at my end. He came with a little boy, and brought a cross; and by that time my eyes were fixed, and I could not speak. The parson set the cross before my face and said: Daughter, I have brought you the image of your saviour. Look at it and take comfort from it, in reverence of him who died for you and me. It seemed to me that I was well as I was, for my eyes were set upwards towards heaven, where I trusted that I was going; but nevertheless I agreed to fix my eyes on the face of the crucifix if I could, so as to hold out longer until my end came, for it seemed to me that I could hold out longer with my eyes set in front of me rather than upwards. After this my sight began to fail, and it was all dark around me in the room, dark as night, except that there was ordinary light trained upon the image of the cross, I never knew how. Everything around the cross was ugly to me, as if it were occupied by a great crowd of devils.

After that I felt as if the upper part of my body were beginning to die. My hands fell down on either side, and I was so weak that my head lolled to one side. The greatest pain that I felt was my shortness of breath and the ebbing of my life. Then truly I believed that I was at the point of death. And suddenly in that moment all my pain left me, and I was as sound, particularly in the upper part of my body, as ever I was before or have been since. I was astonished by this change, for it seemed to me that it was by God's secret doing and not natural; and even so, in this ease which I felt, I had no more confidence that I should live, nor was the ease complete, for I thought that I would rather have been delivered of this world, because that was what my heart longed for.

Chapter iii

And suddenly it came into my mind that I ought to wish for the second wound, that our Lord, of his gift and of his grace, would fill my body full with recollection and feeling[2] of his blessed Passion, as I had prayed before, for I wished that his pains might be my pains, with compassion which would lead to longing for God. So it seemed to me that I might with his grace have his wounds, as I had wished before; but in this I never wanted any bodily vision or any kind of revelation from God, but only the compassion which I thought a loving soul could have for our Lord Jesus, who for love was willing to become a mortal man. I desired to suffer with him, living in my mortal body, as God would give me grace. And at this, suddenly I saw the red blood trickling down from under the crown, all hot, flowing freely and copiously, a living stream, just as it seemed to me that it was at the time when the crown of thorns was thrust down upon his blessed head. Just so did he, both God and man, suffer for me. I perceived, truly and powerfully, that it was himself who showed this to me, without any intermediary; and then I said: Blessed be the Lord! This I said with a reverent intention and in a loud voice, and I was greatly astonished by this wonder and marvel, that he would so humbly be[3] with a sinful creature living in this wretched

---

2. So the long text (180), which is superior to the short text's 'recollection of feeling'.
3. Or 'would be so familiar'; cf. the long text, p. 181.

flesh. I accepted it that at that time our Lord Jesus wanted, out of his courteous love, to show me comfort before my temptations began; for it seemed to me that I might well be tempted by devils, by God's permission and with his protection, before I died. With this sight of his blessed Passion and with his divinity, of which I speak as I understand[4], I saw that this was strength enough for me, yes, and for all living creatures who will be protected from all the devils of hell and from all their spiritual enemies.

Chapter iv

And at the same time as I saw this corporeal sight, our Lord showed me a spiritual sight of his familiar love. I saw that he is to us everything which is good and comforting for our help. He is our clothing, for he is that love which wraps and enfolds us, embraces us and guides us, surrounds us for his love, which is so tender that he may never desert us. And so in this sight I saw truly that he is everything which is good, as I understand.

And in this he showed me something small, no bigger than a hazelnut, lying in the palm of my hand, and I perceived that it was as round as any ball. I looked at it and thought: What can this be? And I was given this general answer: It is everything which is made. I was amazed that it could last, for I thought that it was so little that it could suddenly fall into nothing. And I was answered in my understanding: It lasts and always will, because God loves it; and thus everything has being through the love of God.

---

4. Or 'which I saw in my understanding'.

In this little thing I saw three properties[5]. The first is that God made it, the second is that he loves it, the third is that God preserves it. But what is that to me? It is that God is the Creator and the lover and the protector. For until I am substantially united to him, I can never have love or rest or true happiness; until, that is, I am so attached to him that there can be no created thing between my God and me. And who will do this deed? Truly, he himself, by his mercy and his grace, for he has made me for this and has blessedly restored me.

In this God brought our Lady to my understanding. I saw her spiritually in her bodily likeness, a simple, humble maiden, young in years, of the stature which she had when she conceived. Also God showed me part of the wisdom and truth of her soul, and in this I understood the reverent contemplation with which she beheld her God, marvelling with great reverence that he was willing to be born of her who was a simple creature created by him[6]. And this wisdom and truth[7], this knowledge of her creator's greatness and of her own created littleness, made her say meekly to the angel Gabriel: Behold me here, God's handmaiden. In this sight I saw truly that she is greater, more worthy and more fulfilled, than everything else which God has created, and which is inferior to her. Above her is no created thing, except the blessed humanity of Christ. This little thing which is created and is inferior to our Lady, St. Mary—God showed it to me as if it had been a hazelnut—seemed to me as if it could have perished because it is so little.

In this blessed revelation God showed me three nothings, of which nothings this is the first that was shown to me. Every man and woman who wishes to live

---

5. 'Properties' (cf. the long text, p. 183) is more probable than the short text's 'parts'.

6. This corrects a scribal error found in both texts. See *Showings*, I, 213.

7. So the long text, which is superior to the short text's 'wisdom of truth'.

contemplatively needs to know of this, so that it may be pleasing to them to despise as nothing everything created, so as to have the love of uncreated God. For this is the reason why those who deliberately occupy themselves with earthly business, constantly seeking worldly well-being, have not God's rest[8] in their hearts and souls; for they love and seek their rest in this thing which is so little and in which there is no rest, and do not know God who is almighty, all wise and all good, for he is true rest. God wishes to be known, and it pleases him that we should rest in him; for all things which are beneath him are not sufficient for us. And this is the reason why no soul has rest until it has despised as nothing all which is created. When the soul has become nothing for love, so as to have him who is all that is good, then is it able to receive spiritual rest.

Chapter v

And during the time that our Lord showed me this spiritual vision which I have now described, I saw the bodily vision of the copious bleeding of the head persist, and as long as I saw it I said, many times: Blessed be the Lord! In this first revelation of our Lord I saw in my understanding six things. The first is the tokens of his blessed Passion, and the plentiful shedding of his precious blood. The second is the virgin who is his beloved mother. The third is the blessed divinity, that always was and is and ever shall be, almighty, all wisdom and all love. The fourth is everything which he has made; it is great and lovely and

---

8. The short text is corrupt, and this is the reading of the long text, p. 184. But Julian may have written 'are not his heirs'; cf. *Showings*, I, 215.

bountiful and good. But the reason why it seemed to my eyes so little was because I saw it in the presence of him who is the Creator. For to a soul who sees the Creator of all things, all that is created seems very little. The fifth is that he has made everything which is made for love, and through the same love is it preserved, and always will be without end, as has been said already. The sixth is that God is everything which is good, and the goodness which everything has is God.

This everything God showed me in the first vision, and he gave me space and time to contemplate it. And then the bodily vision ceased, and the spiritual vision persisted in my understanding, and I waited with reverent fear, rejoicing in what I saw and wishing, as much as I dared, to see more, if that were God's will, or to see for a longer time what I had already seen.

Chapter vi

Everything that I say[9] about myself I mean to apply to all my fellow Christians, for I am taught that this is what our Lord intends in this spiritual revelation. And therefore I pray you all for God's sake, and I counsel you for your own profit, that you disregard the wretched worm, the sinful creature to whom it was shown, and that mightily, wisely, lovingly and meekly you contemplate God, who out of his courteous love and his endless goodness was willing to show this vision generally, to the comfort of us all. And you who hear and see this vision and this teaching, which is from Jesus Christ for the edification of your souls, it is God's will

---

9. 'Say' is here more probable than 'saw'. See *Showings*, I, 219 and II, 319-20.

and my wish that you accept it with as much joy and delight as if Jesus had shown it to you as he did to me. I am not good because of the revelation, but only if I love God better, and so can and so should every man do who sees it and hears it with good will and proper intention. And so it is my desire that it should be to every man the same profit that I asked for myself, and was moved to in the first moment when I saw it; for it is common and general, just as we are all one; and I am sure that I saw it for the profit of many others. For truly it was not revealed to me because God loves me better than the humblest soul who is in a state of grace. For I am sure that there are very many who never had revelations or visions, but only the common teaching of Holy Church, who love God better than I. If I pay special attention to myself, I am nothing at all; but in general I am in the unity of love with all my fellow Christians. For it is in this unity of love that the life consists of all men who will be saved. For God is everything that is good, and God has made everything that is made, and God loves everything that he has made, and if any man or woman withdraws his love from any of his fellow Christians, he does not love at all, because he has not love towards all. And so in such times he is in danger, because he is not at peace; and anyone who has general love for his fellow Christians has love towards everything which is. For in mankind which will be saved is comprehended all, that is, all that is made and the maker of all; for God is in man, and so in man is all. And he who thus generally loves all his fellow Christians loves all, and he who loves thus is safe. And thus will I love, and thus do I love, and thus I am safe—I write as the representative of my fellow Christians—and the more that I love in this way whilst I am here, the more I am like the joy that I shall have in heaven without end, that joy which is the God who out of his endless love willed to become our brother and suffer for us. And I am sure that anyone who sees it so will be taught the truth and be greatly comforted, if he have need of comfort. But God forbid that you should say or assume that I am a teacher, for that is not and never was my intention; for I am a woman, ignorant, weak and frail. But I know very well that what I am saying I have received by the revelation of him who is the sovereign teacher. But it is truly love which moves me to tell it to you, for I want God to be known and my fellow Christians to prosper, as I hope to prosper myself, by hating sin more and loving God more. But because I am a woman, ought I therefore to believe that I should not tell you of the goodness of God, when I saw at that same time that it is his will that it be known? You will see this clearly in what follows, if it be well and truly accepted. Then will you soon forget me who am a wretch, and do this, so that I am no hindrance to you, and you will contemplate Jesus, who is every man's teacher. I speak of those who will be saved, for at this time God showed me no one else; but in everything I believe as Holy Church teaches, for I beheld the whole of this blessed revelation of our Lord as unified in God's sight, and I never understood anything from it which bewilders me or keeps me from the true doctrine of Holy Church.

Chapter vii

All this blessed teaching of our Lord was shown to me in three parts, that is by bodily vision and by words formed in my understanding and by spiritual vision. But I may not and cannot show the spiritual visions to you as plainly and fully as I should wish; but I trust in our Lord God Almighty that he will, out of his goodness and for love of you, make you accept it more spiritually and more sweetly than I can or may tell it to you, and so may it be, for we are all one in love. And in all this I was humbly moved in love towards my fellow Christians, that they might all see and know the same as I saw, for I wished it to be a comfort to them all, as it is to me; for this vision was shown for all men, and not for me alone[10]. Of everything which I saw, this was the greatest comfort to me, that our Lord is so familiar and so courteous, and this most filled my soul with delight and surety. Then I said to the people who were with me: Today is my Doomsday. And I said this because I expected to die; because on the day that a man or a woman dies, he is judged as he will be forever. I said this because I wished them to love God more and to set less store by worldly vanity, and to make them mindful that this life is short, as they could see by my example, for in all this time I was expecting to die.

And after this I saw, in bodily vision, in the face of the crucifix which hung before me, a part of Christ's Passion: contempt, spitting to defoul[11] his body, buffeting of his blessed face, and many woes and pains, more than I can tell; and his colour often changed, and all his blessed face was for a time caked with dry blood. This I saw bodily and sorrowfully and dimly; and I wanted more of the light of day, to have seen it more clearly. And I was answered in my reason that if God wished to show me more he would, but that I needed no light but him.

---

10. Literally, 'shown in general, and not at all specially'.

11. The short text here has *sowlynge*, the long text *solewyng* (Paris, Bibliotheque Nationale Fonds Anglais 40, hereafter cited as P), *sulloing* (Serenus Cressy, *The Revelations of Divine Love*, Paris, 1670, hereafter cited as C), *sollowing* (both Sloan Manuscripts, hereafter cited as SS); but it is conjectured that they all misrepresent 'to soil', 'to defoul'. See *Showings*, II, 324.

Chapter viii

And after this I saw God in an instant of time[12], that is, in my understanding, and by this vision I saw that he is present in all things. I contemplated it carefully, knowing and perceiving through it that he does everything which is done. I marvelled at this vision with a gentle fear, and I thought: What is sin? For I saw truly that God does everything, however small it may be, and that nothing is done by chance, but it is of the endless providence of God's wisdom. Therefore I was compelled to admit that everything which is done is well done, and I was certain that God does no sin. Therefore it seemed to me that sin is nothing, for in all this sin was not shown to me. And I did not wish to go on feeling surprise at this, but I contemplated our Lord and waited for what he would show me. And on another occasion God did show me, nakedly in itself, what sin is, as I shall tell afterwards.

And after this as I watched I saw the body bleeding copiously, the blood hot, flowing freely, a living stream, just as I had before seen the head bleed. And I saw this in the furrows made by the scourging, and I saw this blood run so plentifully that it seemed to me that if it had in fact been happening there, the bed and everything around it would have been soaked in blood.

God has created bountiful waters on the earth for our use and our bodily comfort, out of the tender love he has for us. But it is more pleasing to him that we accept freely his blessed blood to wash us of our sins, for there is no drink that is made which it pleases him so well to give us; for it is so plentiful, and it is of our own nature.

---

12. Literally, 'in a point'. See *Showings*, I, 226 note.

And after this, before God revealed any words to me, he allowed me to contemplate longer all that I had seen and all that was contained in it. And then there was formed in my soul this saying, without voice and without opening of lips: With this the fiend is overcome. Our Lord said this to me with reference to his Passion, as he had shown it to me before; and in this he brought into my mind and showed me a part of the devil's malice and all of his impotence, and this by showing me that his Passion is the overcoming of the fiend. God showed me that he still has the same malice as he had before the Incarnation, and he works as hard, and he sees as constantly as he did before that all chosen souls escape him to God's glory. And in that is all the devil's sorrow; for everything which God permits him to do turns to joy for us and to pain and shame for him, and he has as much sorrow when God permits him to work as when he is not working. And that is because he can never do as much evil as he would wish, for his power is all locked in God's hands. Also I saw our Lord scorning his malice and despising him as nothing, and he wants us to do the same. Because of this sight I laughed greatly, and that made those around me to laugh as well; and their laughter was pleasing to me. I thought that I wished that all my fellow Christians had seen what I saw. Then they would all have laughed with me. But I did not see Christ laugh; nevertheless, it is pleasing to him that we laugh to comfort ourselves, and that we rejoice in God because the devil is overcome. And after that I became serious again, and said: I see. I see three things: sport and scorn and seriousness. I see sport, that the devil is overcome; and I see scorn, that God scorns him and he will be scorned; and I see seriousness, that he is overcome by the Passion of our Lord Jesus Christ and by his death, which was accomplished in great earnest and with heavy labour.

After this our Lord said: I thank you for your service and your labour, and especially in your youth.

Chapter ix

God showed me three degrees of bliss that every soul will have in heaven who has voluntarily served God in any degree here upon earth. The first is the honour of the thanks of our Lord God which he will receive when he is delivered from pain. This thanks is so exalted and so honourable that it will seem to him that this suffices him, if there were no other happiness. For it seemed to me that all the pain and labour which all living men might endure could not earn the thanks that one man will have who has voluntarily served God. As to the second degree, it is that all the blessed in heaven will see the honour of the thanks from our Lord God. This makes a soul's service known to all who are in heaven. And for the third degree, which is that the first joy with which the soul is then received will last forevermore, I saw that this was kindly and sweetly said and revealed to me: Every man's age will be known in heaven, and he will be rewarded for his voluntary service and for the time he has served, and especially the age of those who voluntarily and freely offer their youth to God is fittingly rewarded and wonderfully thanked.

And after this our Lord revealed to me a supreme spiritual delight in my soul. In this delight I was filled full of everlasting surety, and I was powerfully secured without any fear. This sensation was so welcome and so dear to me that I was at peace, at ease and at rest, so that there was nothing upon earth which could have afflicted me.

This lasted only for a time, and then I was changed, and left to myself, oppressed and weary of myself, ruing my life so that I scarcely had the patience to go on living. I felt that there was no ease or comfort for me except hope, faith and love, and truly I felt very little of this. And then presently God gave me again comfort and rest for my soul, delight and security so blessed and so powerful that there was no fear, no sorrow, no pain, physical or spiritual, that one could suffer which might have disturbed me. And then again I felt the pain, and then afterwards the joy and the delight, now the one and now the other, again and again, I suppose about twenty times. And in the time of joy I could have said with Paul: Nothing shall separate me from the love of Christ; and in the pain, I could have said with Peter: Lord, save me, I am perishing.

This vision was shown to me to teach me to understand that every man needs to experience this, to be comforted at one time, and at another to fail and to be left to himself. God wishes us to know that he keeps us safe all the time, in joy and in sorrow, and that he loves us as much in sorrow as in joy. And sometimes a man is left to himself for the profit of his soul, and neither the one nor the other is caused by sin. For in this time I committed no sin for which I ought to have been left to myself, nor did I deserve these sensations of joy; but God gives joy freely as it pleases him, and sometimes he allows us to be in sorrow, and both come from his love. For it is God's will that we do all in our power to preserve our consolation, for bliss lasts forevermore, and pain is passing and will be reduced to nothing. Therefore it is not God's will that when we feel pain we should pursue it, sorrowing and mourning for it, but that suddenly we should pass it over and preserve ourselves in endless delight, because God is almighty, our lover and preserver.

Chapter x

After this Christ showed me part of his Passion, close to his death. I saw his sweet face as it were dry and bloodless, with the pallor of dying, then more dead, pale and languishing, then the pallor turning blue and then more blue, as death took more hold upon his flesh. For all the pains which Christ suffered in his body appeared to me in his blessed face, in all that I could see of it, and especially in the lips. I saw there what had become of the four colours that I had seen before, his freshness, his ruddiness, his vitality and his beauty which I had seen. This was a grievous change to watch, this deep dying, and the nose shrivelled[13] and dried up as I saw. The long torment seemed to me as if he had been dead for a week and had still gone on suffering pain, and it seemed to me as if the greatest and the last pain of his Passion was when his flesh dried up. And in this drying what Christ had said came to my mind: I thirst. For I saw in Christ a double thirst, one physical, the other spiritual. This saying was shown to me to signify the physical thirst, and what was revealed to me of the spiritual thirst I shall say afterwards; and concerning the physical thirst, I understood that the body was wholly dried up, for his blessed flesh and bones were left without blood or moisture. The blessed body was left to dry for a long time, with the wrenching of the nails and the sagging of the head and the weight of the body, with the blowing of the wind around him, which dried up his body and pained him with cold, more than my heart can think of, and with all his other pains I saw such pain that all that I can describe or say is

---

13. *Clonge* (British Museum, Sloan MS, 2499, hereafter cited as S1), *clange* (British Museum, Sloan MS, 3705, hereafter cited as S2), in the long text, are the only variants which give sense. See *Showings*, I, 233.

inadequate, for it cannot be described. But each soul should do as St. Paul says, and feel in himself what is in Christ Jesus. This revelation of Christ's pains filled me full of pains, for I know well that he suffered only once, but it was now his will to show it to me and fill me with its recollection, as I had asked before. My mother, who was standing there with the others, held up her hand in front of my face to close my eyes, for she thought that I was already dead or had that moment died; and this greatly increased my sorrow, for despite all my pains, I did not want to be hindered from seeing, because of my love for him. And with regard to either[14], in all this time that Christ was present to me, I felt no pain except for Christ's pains; and then it came to me that I had little known what pain it was that I had asked for, for it seemed to me that my pains exceeded any mortal death. I thought: Is there any pain in hell like this? And in my reason I was answered that despair is greater, for that is a spiritual pain. But there is no greater physical pain than this; how could I suffer greater pain than to see him who is all my life, all my bliss and all my joy suffer? Here I felt truly that I loved Christ so much more than myself that I thought it would have been a great comfort to me if my body had died.

In this I saw part of the compassion of our Lady, St. Mary, for Christ and she were so united in love that the greatness of her love was the cause of the greatness of her pain. For her pain surpassed that of all others, as much as she loved him more than all others. And so all his disciples and all his true lovers suffered greater pains than they did at the death of their own bodies. For I am sure, by my own experience, that the least of them loved him more than they loved themselves. And here I saw a great unity between Christ and us; for when he was in pain we were in pain, and

14. The cause of her suffering is neither her own sickness nor the sorrow she feels for the Passion, but only the Passion's pains.

142

all creatures able to suffer pain suffered with him. And for those that did not know him, their pain was that all creation, sun and moon, ceased to serve men, and so they were all abandoned in sorrow at that time. So those who loved him suffered pain for their love, and those who did not love him suffered pain because the comfort of all creation failed them.

At this time I wanted to look to the side of the cross, but I did not dare, for I knew well that whilst I looked at the cross I was secure and safe. Therefore I would not agree to put my soul in danger, for apart from the cross there was no safety, but only the horror of devils.

Then there came a suggestion, seemingly friendly, to my reason. It was said to me: Look up to heaven to his Father. Then I saw clearly by the faith which I felt that there was nothing between the cross and heaven which could have grieved me, and that I must either look up or else answer. I answered, and said: No, I cannot, for you are my heaven. I said this because I did not want to look up, for I would rather have remained in that pain until Judgment Day than have come to heaven any other way than by him. For I knew well that he who had bought me so dearly would unbind me when it was his will.

Chapter xi

Thus I chose Jesus for my heaven, whom I saw only in pain at that time. No other heaven was pleasing to me than Jesus, who will be my bliss when I am there; and this has always been a comfort to me, that I chose Jesus as my heaven in all times of suffering and of sorrow. And that has taught me that I should always do so, and choose only him to be my heaven in well-being and in woe. And so I saw my

Lord Jesus languishing for long, because of the union in him of man and God, for love gave strength to his humanity to suffer more than all men could. I mean not only more pain than any other one man could suffer, but also that he suffered more pain than would all men together, from the first beginning to the last day. No tongue may tell, no heart can fully think of the pains which our saviour suffered for us, if we have regard to the honour of him who is the highest, most majestic king, and to his shameful, grievous and painful death. For he who was highest and most honourable was most completely brought low, most utterly despised. But the love which made him suffer all this surpasses all his pains as far as heaven is above earth. For his pains were a deed, performed once through the motion of love; but his love was without beginning and is and ever will be without any end.

Chapter xii

And suddenly, as I looked at the same cross, he changed to an appearance of joy. The change in his appearance changed mine, and I was as glad and joyful as I could possibly be. And then cheerfully our Lord suggested to my mind: Where is there any instant of your pain or of your grief? And I was very joyful.

Then our Lord put a question to me: Are you well satisfied that I suffered for you? Yes, good Lord, I said; all my thanks to you, good Lord, blessed may you be! If you are satisfied, our Lord said, I am satisfied. It is a joy and a bliss and an endless delight to me that ever I suffered my Passion for you, for if I could suffer more, I would. In response to this, my understanding was lifted up into

heaven, and there I saw three heavens; and at this sight I
was greatly astonished, and I thought: I have seen three
heavens, and all are of the blessed humanity of Christ. And
none is greater, none is less, none is higher, none is lower,
but all are equal in their joy.

For the first heaven, Christ showed me his Father, not
in any corporeal likeness, but in his attributes and in his joy.
For the Father's operation is this: He rewards his Son, Jesus
Christ. This gift and this reward is so joyful to Jesus that his
Father could have given him no reward which could have
pleased him better. For the first heaven, which is the
Father's bliss, appeared to me as a heaven, and it was full of
bliss. For Jesus has great joy in all the deeds which he has
done for our salvation, and therefore we are his, not only
through our redemption but also by his Father's courteous
gift. We are his bliss, we are his reward, we are his honour,
we are his crown.

What I am describing now is so great a joy to Jesus that
he counts as nothing his labour and his bitter sufferings and
his cruel and shameful death. And in these words: If I could
suffer more, I would suffer more, I saw truly that if he
could die as often as once for every man who is to be saved,
as he did once for all men, love would never let him rest till
he had done it. And when he had done it, he would count it
all as nothing for love, for everything seems only little to
him in comparison with his love. And that he plainly said to
me, gravely saying this: If I could suffer more. He did not
say: If it were necessary to suffer more, but: If I could suffer
more; for although it might not be necessary, if he could
suffer more he would suffer more. This deed and this work
for our salvation were as well done as he could devise it. It
was done as honourably as Christ could do it, and in this I
saw complete joy in Christ; but his joy would not have been
complete if the deed could have been done any better than it
was. And in these three sayings: It is a joy, a bliss and an

endless delight to me, there were shown to me three heavens, and in this way. By 'joy' I understood that the Father was pleased, by 'bliss' that the Son was honoured, and by 'endless delight' the Holy Spirit. The Father is pleased, the Son is honoured, the Holy Spirit takes delight. Jesus wants us to pay heed to this bliss for our salvation which is in the blessed Trinity, and to take equal delight, through his grace, whilst we are here. And this was shown to me when he said: Are you well satisfied? And by what Christ next said: If you are satisfied, I am satisfied, he made me understand that it was as if he had said: This is joy and delight enough for me, and I ask nothing else for my labour but that I may satisfy you. Generously and completely was this revealed to me.

So think wisely, how great this saying is: That ever I suffered my Passion for you; for in that saying was given exalted understanding of the love and the delight that he had in our salvation.

Chapter xiii

Very merrily and gladly our Lord looked into his side, and he gazed and said this: See how I loved you; as if he had said: My child, if you cannot look on my divinity, see here how I suffered my side to be opened and my heart to be split in two and to send out blood and water, all that was in it; and this is a delight to me, and I wish it to be so for you.

Our Lord showed this to me to make us glad and merry. And with the same joyful appearance he looked down on his right, and brought to my mind where our Lady stood at the time of his Passion, and he said: Do you wish to see her? And I answered and said: Yes, good Lord, great thanks, if it be your will. Often times I had prayed for this, and I expected to see her in a bodily likeness; but I did not see her so. And Jesus, saying this, showed me a spiritual vision of her. Just as before I had seen her small and simple, now he showed her high and noble and glorious and more pleasing to him than all creatures. And so he wishes it to be known that all who take delight in him should take delight in her, and in the delight that he has in her and she in him. And when Jesus said: Do you wish to see her? it seemed to me that I had the greatest delight that he could have given me in this spiritual vision of her which he gave me. For our Lord showed me no particular person except our Lady, St. Mary, and he showed her to me on three occasions. The first was as she conceived, the second was as she had been in her sorrow under the Cross, and the third as she is now, in delight, honour and joy.

And after this our Lord showed himself to me, and he appeared to me more glorified than I had seen him before, and in this I was taught that every contemplative soul to whom it is given to look and to seek will see Mary and pass on to God through contemplation. And after this teaching, simple, courteous, joyful, again and again our Lord said to me: I am he who is highest. I am he whom you love. I am he in whom you delight. I am he whom you serve. I am he for whom you long. I am he whom you desire. I am he whom you intend. I am he who is all. I am he whom Holy Church preaches and teaches to you. I am he who showed himself before to you. I repeat these words only so that every man may accept them as our Lord intended them, according to the grace God gives him in understanding and love.

And after this our Lord brought to my mind the longing that I had for him before; and I saw that nothing hindered me but sin, and I saw that this is true of us all in general, and it seemed to me that if there had been no sin, we should all have been pure and as like our Lord as he created us. And so in my folly before this time I often wondered why, through the great and prescient wisdom of God, sin was not prevented; for it seemed to me that then all would have been well.

The impulse to think this was greatly to be shunned; and I mourned and sorrowed on this account, unreasonably, lacking discretion, filled with pride. Nonetheless in this vision Jesus informed me about everything needful to me. I do not say that I need no more instruction, for after he revealed this our Lord entrusted me to Holy Church, and I am hungry and thirsty and needy and sinful and frail, and willingly submit myself among all my fellow Christians to the teaching of Holy Church to the end of my life.

He answered with these words, and said: Sin is necessary. In the word 'sin', our Lord brought generally to my mind all which is not good: the shameful contempt and the complete denial of himself which he endured for us in this life and in his death, and all the pains and passions, spiritual and bodily, of all his creatures. For we are all in part denied, and we ought to be denied, following our master Jesus until we are fully purged, that is to say until we have completely denied our own mortal flesh and all our inward affections which are not good.

And the beholding of this, with all the pains that ever were or ever will be—and of all this I understood Christ's Passion for the greatest and surpassing pain[15]—was shown to me in an instant, and quickly turned into consolation. For our good Lord God would not have the soul frightened by this ugly sight. But I did not see sin, for I believe that it has no kind of substance, no share in being, nor can it be recognized except by the pains which it causes. And it seems

---

15. 'And of all this. . .surpassing pain': omitted by the short text, supplied from the long. See *Showings*, I, 245.

to me that this pain is something for a time, for it purges us and makes us know ourselves and ask for mercy; for the Passion of our Lord is comfort to us against all this, and that is his blessed will for all who will be saved. He comforts readily and sweetly with his words, and says: But all will be well, and every kind of thing will be well.

These words were revealed very tenderly, showing no kind of blame to me or to anyone who will be saved. So it would be most unkind of me to blame God or marvel at him on account of my sins, since he does not blame me for sin. So I saw how Christ has compassion on us because of sin; and just as I was before filled full of pain and compassion on account of Christ's Passion, so I was now in a measure filled with compassion for all my fellow Christians, and then I saw that every kind of compassion which one has for one's fellow Christians in love is Christ in us.

Chapter xiv

But I[16] shall study upon this, contemplating it generally, heavily and mournfully, saying in intention to our Lord with very great fear: Ah, good Lord, how could all things be well, because of the great harm which has come through sin to your creatures? And I wished, so far as I dared, for some plainer explanation through which my mind might be at ease about this matter. And to this our blessed Lord answered, very meekly and with a most loving manner, and he showed me that Adam's sin was the greatest harm ever done or ever to be done until the end of the world. And he also showed me that this is plainly known to all Holy Church upon earth.

---

16. 'I': ms: 'you'.

Furthermore, he taught me that I should contemplate his glorious atonement, for this atoning is more pleasing to the blessed divinity and more honourable for man's salvation, without comparison, than ever Adam's sin was harmful. So then it is our blessed Lord's intention in this teaching that we should pay heed to this: For since I have set right the greatest of harms, it is my will that you should know through this that I shall set right everything which is less.

He gave me understanding of two portions. One portion is our saviour and our salvation. This blessed portion is open and clear and fair and bright and plentiful, for all men who are or will be of good will are comprehended in this portion. We are bidden to this by God, and drawn and counselled and taught, inwardly by the Holy Spirit and outwardly, through the grace of the same Spirit, by Holy Church. Our Lord wants us to be occupied in this, rejoicing in him, for he rejoices in us. And the more plentifully we accept this with reverence and humility, the more do we deserve thanks from him, and the more profit do we win for ourselves; and so we may rejoice and say: Our portion is our Lord.

The other portion is closed to us and hidden, that is to say all which is additional to our salvation. For this is our Lord's privy counsel, and it is fitting to God's royal dominion to keep his privy counsel in peace, and it is fitting to his subjects out of obedience and respect not to wish to know his counsel.

Our Lord has pity and compassion on us because some creatures occupy themselves so much in this; and I am certain that if we knew how much we should please him and solace ourselves by leaving it alone, we should do so. The saints in heaven wish to know nothing but what our Lord wishes to show them, and furthermore their love and their desire is governed according to our Lord's will; and so we ought to wish to be[17] like him[18]. And then we shall not wish or desire anything but the will of our Lord, for we are all one in God's intention.

And in this I was taught that we shall rejoice only in our blessed saviour Jesus, and trust in him for everything.

Chapter xv

And so our good Lord answered to all the questions and doubts which I could raise, saying most comfortingly in this fashion: I will make all things well, I shall make all things well, I may make all things well and I can make all things well; and you will see that yourself, that all things will be well. When he says that he 'may', I understand this to apply to the Father; and when he says that he 'can', I understand this for the Son; and when he says 'I will', I understand this for the Holy Spirit; and when he says 'I shall', I understand this for the unity of the blessed Trinity, three persons in one truth; and when he says 'You will see yourself', I understand this for the union of all men who will be saved in the blessed Trinity.

And in these five words[19] God wishes to be enclosed in rest and in peace. And so Christ's spiritual thirst has an end. For his spiritual thirst is his longing in love, and that persists and always will until we see him on the day of judgment; for we who shall be saved and shall be Christ's joy and bliss are still here, and shall be until that day. Therefore his thirst is

17. Ms: 'not to be', probably a misunderstanding of 'wilne'.
18. Or 'like them'; see *Showings*, I, 248.
19. 'May', 'can', 'will', 'shall', 'you will see. . .'

this incompleteness of his joy, that he does not now possess us in himself as wholly as he then will.

All this was shown to me as a revelation of his compassion, for on the day of judgment it will cease. So he has pity and compassion on us and he longs to possess us, but his wisdom and his love do not permit the end to come until the best time. And in these same five words[20] said before: 'I may make all things well', I understand powerful consolation from all the deeds of our Lord which are still to be performed; for just as the blessed Trinity created everything from nothing, just so the same blessed Trinity will make well all things which are not well. It is God's will that we pay great heed to all the deeds which he has performed, for he wishes us to know from them all which he will do; and he revealed that to me by those words which he said: And you will see yourself that every kind of thing will be well. I understand this in two ways: One is that I am well content that I do not know it; and the other is that I am glad and joyful because I shall know it. It is God's will that we should know in general that all will be well, but it is not God's will that we should know it now except as it applies to us for the present, and that is the teaching of Holy Church.

Chapter xvi

God showed me the very great delight that he has in all men and women who accept, firmly and humbly and reverently, the preaching and teaching of Holy Church, for he is Holy Church. For he is the foundation, he is the substance, he is the teaching, he is the teacher, he is the

---

20. This seems to refer to 'I may make all things well'. See *Showings*, I, 250.

end, he is the reward[21] for which every faithful soul labours; and he is known and will be known to every soul to whom the Holy Spirit declares this. And I am certain that all who seek in this way will prosper, for they are seeking God.

All this which I have now said and more which I shall presently say is solace against sin; for when I first saw that God does everything which is done, I did not see sin, and then I saw that all is well. But when God did show me sin, it was then that he said: All will be well.

And when almighty God had shown me his goodness so plenteously and fully, I wished to know, concerning a certain person whom I loved, what her future would be; and by wishing this I impeded myself, for I was not then told this. And then I was answered in my reason, as it were by a friendly man[22]: Accept it generally, and contemplate the courtesy of your Lord God as he reveals it to you, for it is more honour to God to contemplate him in all things than in any one special thing. I agreed, and with that I learned that it is more honour to God to know everything in general than it is to take delight in any special thing. And if I were to act wisely, in accordance with this teaching, I should not be glad because of any special thing or be distressed by anything at all, for all will be well.

God brought to my mind that I should sin; and because of the delight that I had in contemplating him, I did not at once pay attention to this revelation. And our Lord very courteously waited until I was ready to attend, and then our Lord brought to my mind, along with my sins, the sins of all my fellow Christians, all in general and none in particular.

---

21. So the long text, p. 230, which is superior to the short text's 'means'.
22. Or, as the long text more probably has, 'a friendly intermediary'. See *Showings*, I, 252.

Chapter xvii

Although our Lord revealed to me that I should sin, I understood everything to apply only to me. In this I conceived a gentle fear, and in answer to this our Lord said: I protect you very safely. This was said to me with more love and assurance of protection for my soul than I can or may tell. For just as it was first revealed to me that I should sin, so was consolation revealed to me—assurance of protection for all my fellow Christians. What can make me love my fellow Christians more than to see in God that he loves all who will be saved, all of them as it were one soul? And in each soul which will be saved there is a good will which never assented to sin and never will. For as there is an animal will in the lower part which cannot will any good, so there is a good will in the higher part which cannot will any evil, but always good, just as the persons of the blessed Trinity. And our Lord revealed this to me in the completeness of his love, that we are standing in his sight, yes, that he loves us now whilst we are here as well as he will when we are there, before his blessed face.

God also showed me that sin is no shame, but honour to man, for in this vision my understanding was lifted up into heaven; and then there came truly to my mind David, Peter and Paul, Thomas of India and Mary Magdalen, how they are known, with their sins, to their honour in the Church on earth. And it is to them no shame that they have sinned—shame is no more in the bliss of heaven—for there the tokens of sin are turned into honours. Just so our Lord showed them to me as examples of all who will come there. Sin is the sharpest scourge with which any chosen soul can be beaten, and this scourge belabours and breaks men and

women, and they become so despicable in their own sight[23]
that it seems to them that they are fit for nothing but as it
were to sink into hell; but when by the inspiration of the
Holy Spirit contrition seizes them, then the Spirit turns
bitterness into hope of God's mercy. And then the wounds
begin to heal and the soul to revive, restored to the life of
Holy Church. The Holy Spirit leads him to confession,
willing to reveal his sins, nakedly and truthfully, with great
sorrow and great shame that he has so befouled God's fair
image. Then he accepts the penance for every sin imposed
by his confessor, for this[24] is established in Holy Church by
the teaching of the Holy Spirit. Every sinful soul must be
healed by this medicine, especially of the sins which are
mortal to him. Though he be healed, his wounds are not
seen by God as wounds but as honours. And as sin is
punished here with sorrow and penance, in contrary fashion
it will be rewarded in heaven by the courteous love of our
Lord God almighty, who does not wish anyone who comes
there to lose his labours.

That reward, which we shall receive there, will not be
small, but it will be high, glorious and honourable. And so
all shame will be turned into honour and into greater joy.
And I am sure by what I feel myself that the more that
every loving soul perceives this in the gentle and courteous
love of God, the more he will hate to sin.

---

23. From this point on the pronouns, singular and plural, are much confused, perhaps
as result of translation from a 'hem' to 'them' dialect of Middle English. But Julian's
intentions are clear.

24. Or 'for he'.

155

Chapter xviii

But if you be moved to say or think: Since this is true, it would be good to sin so as to have more reward, beware of this prompting and despise it, because it comes from the devil. For any soul who deliberately assents to this prompting cannot be saved until he be absolved as though from mortal sin. For if all the pain there is, in hell, in purgatory, on earth, death and other sufferings, were laid before me, together with sin, I should rather choose all that pain than sin. For sin is so vile and so much to be hated that it cannot be compared with any pain which is not sin. For everything is good, except sin, and nothing is wicked, except sin. Sin is neither death nor delight[25], but when a soul deliberately chooses sin, which is pain, to be his god, in the end he has nothing at all. That pain seems to me the cruellest hell, because the soul has not his God. A soul may have God in every pain, but not in sin.

And God's will to save man is as great as his power and his wisdom to save him. For Christ himself is the foundation of all the laws of Christian men, and he has taught us to do good against evil. Here we may see that he himself is this love, and does to us as he teaches us to do; for he wishes us to be like him, in a unity of undying love for ourselves and for our fellow Christians. No more than is his love for us withheld because of our sin does he want us to withhold our love for ourselves and our fellow Christians; we must hate sin utterly, and love souls endlessly as God loves them. For what God said is an endless strengthening, which protects us very safely.

---

25. Or, perhaps, 'deed nor delight'; in either case, the meaning is obscure, and in the long text this passage is omitted. See p. 247 and *Showings*, I, 257.

Chapter xix

After this our Lord revealed to me about prayers. I saw two conditions in those who pray, according to what I have felt myself. One is that they will not pray for anything at all but for the thing which is God's will and to his glory; another is that they apply themselves always and with all their might to entreat the thing which is his will and to his glory. And that is what I have understood from the teaching of Holy Church; for this is what our Lord too taught me now, to accept faith, hope and love as gifts from God, and for us to preserve ourselves in them to the end of life. For this we say the Our Father, Hail Mary, I Believe, with such devotion as God will give us. And so we pray for all our fellow Christians, and for every kind of person as God wishes, for it is our wish that every kind of man and woman might be in the same state of virtue and grace as we ought to wish for ourselves. But still in all this, often our trust is not complete, for we are not certain that almighty God hears us, because of our unworthiness, it seems to us, and because we are feeling nothing at all; for often we are as barren and dry after our prayers as we were before. And thus when we feel so, it is our folly which is the cause of our weakness, for I have experienced this in myself. And our Lord brought all this suddenly to my mind, and gave me great strength and vitality to combat this kind of weakness in praying, and said: I am the foundation of your beseeching. First, it is my will that you should have it, and then I make you to wish it, and then I make you beseech it. And if you beseech, how could it be that you would not have what you beseech? And so in the first reason and in the three that follow it our Lord revealed a great strengthening.

Firstly, where he says: If you beseech, he shows his

great delight, and the everlasting reward that he will give us for our beseeching. And in the fourth[26] reason, where he says: How could it be that you would not have what you beseech? he conveys a serious rebuke, because we have not the firm trust which we need. So our Lord wants us both to pray and to trust, for the reasons I have repeated were given to strengthen us against weakness in our prayers. For it is God's will that we pray, and he moves us to do so in these words I have told, for he wants us to be certain that our prayers are answered, because prayer pleases God. Prayers make a praying man pleased with himself, and make the man serious and humble who before this was contending and striving against himself. Prayer unites the soul to God, for although the soul may always be like God in nature and substance, it is often unlike him in condition, through human sin. Prayer makes the soul like God when the soul wills as God wills; then it is like God in condition, as it is in nature. And so he teaches us to pray and to have firm trust that we shall have what we pray for, because everything which is done would be done, even though we had never prayed for it. But God's love is so great that he regards us as partners in his good work; and so he moves us to pray for what it pleases him to do, for whatever prayer or good desire comes to us by his gift he will repay us for, and give us eternal reward. And this was revealed to me when he said: If you beseech it.

In this saying God showed me his great pleasure and great delight, as though he were much beholden to us for each good deed that we do, even though it is he who does it. Therefore we pray much that he may do what is pleasing to him, as if he were to say: How could you please me more than by entreating me, earnestly, wisely, sincerely, to do the thing that is my will? And so prayer makes harmony

---

26. This has been allowed to stand, although Julian herself probably wrote 'second'. See *Showings*, I, 259 and II, 461.

between God and man's soul, because when man is at ease
with God he does not need to pray, but to contemplate
reverently what God says. For in all the time when this was
revealed to me, I was not moved to pray, but always to keep
this good in my mind[27] for my strength, that when we see
God we have what we desire, and then we do not need to
pray. But when we do not see God, then we need to pray,
because we are failing, and for the strengthening of
ourselves, to Jesus. For when a soul is tempted, troubled and
left to itself in its unrest, that is the time for it to pray and
to make itself simple[28] and obedient to God. Unless the soul
be obedient, no kind of prayer makes God supple to it; for
God's love does not change, but during the time that a man
is in sin he is so weak, so foolish, so unloving that he can
love neither God nor himself.

His greatest harm is his blindness, because he cannot
see all this. Then almighty God's perfect love, which never
changes, gives him sight of himself; and then he believes that
God may be angry with him because of his sin. And then he
is moved to contrition, and through confession and other
good deeds to appease God's anger, till he finds rest of soul
and ease of conscience; and then it seems to him that God
has forgiven his sins, and this is true. And then it seems to
the soul that God has been moved to look upon it, as though
it had been in pain or in prison, saying: I am glad that you
have found rest, for I have always loved you and I love you
now, and you love me. And so with prayers, as I have said,
and with other good works that Holy Church teaches us to
practise, the soul is united to God.

---

27. Or, less probably, 'to keep this well in mind'.

28. 'Simple' has not been emended, but the long text's 'supple' is more suggestive. See
p. 254, and *Showings*, II, 478.

Chapter xx

Before this time I had often great longing, and desired of God's gift to be delivered from this world and this life, for I wanted to be with my God in the bliss in which I surely hope to be without end. For often I beheld the woe that there is here, and the good and the blessed life that is there; and if there had been no other pain on earth except the absence of our Lord God, it seemed to me sometimes that that would be more than I could bear. And this made me mourn and diligently long.

Then God said to me, for my patience and endurance: Suddenly you will be taken out of all your pain, all your unrest and all your woe. And you will come up above, and you will have me for your reward, and you will be filled full of joy and bliss, and you will never have any kind of pain, any kind of sickness, any kind of displeasure, any kind of disappointment, but always endless joy and bliss. Why then should it grieve you to endure for awhile, since it is my will and to my glory?

As God reasoned with me—'Suddenly you will be taken'—I saw how he rewards men for their patience in awaiting the time of his will, and how men have patience to endure throughout the span of their lives, because they do not know when the time for them to die will come. This is very profitable, because if they knew when that would be, they would set a limit to their patience. Then, too, it is God's will that so long as the soul is in the body it should seem to a man that he is always on the point of being taken. For all this life and all the longing we have here is only an instant of time, and when we are suddenly taken into bliss out of pain, it will be nothing.

Therefore our Lord said: Why then should it grieve you

to endure for a while, since that is my will and to my glory? It is God's will that we accept his commands and his consolations as generously and as fully as we are able; and he also wants us to accept our tarrying and our suffering as lightly as we are able, and to count them as nothing. For the more lightly we accept them, the less importance we ascribe to them because of our love, the less pain shall we experience from them and the more thanks shall we have for them.

In this blessed revelation I was truly taught that any man or woman who voluntarily chooses God in his lifetime may be sure that he too is chosen. Pay true heed to this, for it is indeed God's will for us to be as certain in our trust to have the bliss of heaven whilst we are here as we shall be certain of it when we are there.

And always, the more delight and joy that we accept from this certainty, with reverence and humility, the more pleasing is it to God. For I am certain that if there had been no one but I to be saved, God would have done everything which he has done for me. And so ought every soul to think, acknowledging who it is who loves him, forgetting if he can the rest of creation, and thinking that God has done everything he has done for him. And it seems to me that this ought to move a soul to love him and delight in him, and to fear nothing but him; for it is his will that we know that all the power of our enemy is shut in the hand of our friend. And therefore a soul that knows this to be sure will fear nothing but him whom he loves, and count all other fears among the sufferings and bodily sicknesses and illusions which he must endure.

And therefore if a man be in so much pain, so much woe and so much unrest that it seems to him that he can think of nothing at all but the state he is in or what he is feeling, let him, as soon as he may, pass it over lightly and count it as nothing. Why? Because God wants to be known; and because if we knew him and loved him we should have

161

patience and be in great rest, and all that he does would be a delight to us. And our Lord revealed this to me by his words, when he said: Why then should it grieve you to endure for awhile, since that is my will and to my glory? And here came the end of all that our Lord revealed to me on that day.

Chapter xxi

And after this I soon fell back to myself and to my bodily sickness, understanding that I should live, and as the wretched creature that I am, I grieved and mourned for the bodily pains which I felt, and thought how irksome it was that I must go on living. And I was as barren and dry as if the consolation which I had received before were trifling, because my pains had returned and my spiritual perceptions failed.

Then a man of religion came to me and asked me how I did, and I said that during the day I had been raving. And he laughed aloud and heartily. And I said: The cross that stood at the foot of my bed bled profusely; and when I said this, the religious I was speaking to became very serious and surprised. And at once I was very ashamed of my imprudence, and I thought: This man takes seriously every word I could say, and he says nothing in reply. And when I saw that he treated it so seriously and so respectfully, I was greatly ashamed, and wanted to make my confession. But I could not tell it to any priest, for I thought: How could a priest believe me? I did not believe our Lord God. I believed this truly at the time when I saw him, and it was then my will and my intention to do so forever. But like a fool I let it pass from my mind.

See what a wretched creature I am! This was a great sin and a great ingratitude, that I was so foolish, because of a little bodily pain that I felt, as to abandon so imprudently the strength of all this blessed revelation from our Lord God. Here you can see what I am in myself; but our courteous Lord would not leave me so. And I lay still until night, trusting in his mercy, and then I began to sleep.

And as soon as I fell asleep, it seemed to me that the devil set himself at my throat and wanted to strangle me, but he could not. And I awoke, more dead than alive. The people who were with me watched me, and wet my temples, and my heart began to gain strength. And then a little smoke came in at the door, with great heat and a foul stench. I said: Blessed be the Lord! Is everything on fire here? And I thought that it must be actual fire, which would have burned us to death. I asked those who were with me if they were conscious of any stench. They said no, they were not. I said: Blessed be God! for then I knew well that it was the devil who had come to assail me. And at once I assented to all that our Lord had revealed to me on that same day, and to all the faith of Holy Church, for I consider them both to be one, and I fled to them as to my source of strength. And immediately everything vanished, and I was enabled to have rest and peace, without bodily sickness or fear of conscience.

Chapter xxii

But I lay still awake, and then our Lord opened my spiritual eyes, and showed me my soul in the midst of my heart. I saw my soul as wide as if it were a kingdom, and from the state which I saw in it, it seemed to me as if it were a fine city. In the midst of this city sits our Lord Jesus, true God and true man, a handsome person and tall, honourable, the greatest lord. And I saw him splendidly clad in honours. He sits erect there in the soul, in peace and rest, and he rules and he guards heaven and earth and everything that is. The humanity and the divinity sit at rest, and the divinity rules and guards, without instrument or effort. And my soul is blessedly occupied by the divinity, sovereign power, sovereign wisdom, sovereign goodness.

The place which Jesus takes in our soul he will nevermore vacate, for in us is his home of homes, and it is the greatest delight for him to dwell there. This was a delectable and a restful sight, for it is so in truth forevermore; and to contemplate this while we are here is most pleasing to God, and very great profit to us. And the soul who thus contemplates is made like to him who is contemplated, and united to him in rest and peace. And it was a singular joy and bliss to me that I saw him sit, for the contemplation of this sitting revealed to me the certainty that he will dwell in us forever; and I knew truly that it was he who had revealed everything to me before. And when I had contemplated this with great attention, our Lord very humbly revealed words to me, without voice and without opening of lips, as he had done before, and said very seriously: Know it well, it was no hallucination[29] which you saw today, but accept and believe it and hold firmly to it, and you will not be overcome.

These last words were said to me to teach me perfect certainty that it is our Lord Jesus who revealed everything to me; for just as in the first words which our Lord revealed to me, alluding to his blessed Passion: With this the fiend is overcome, just so he said with perfect certainty in these last words: You will not be overcome. And this teaching and this true strengthening apply generally to all my fellow

---

29. Ms: 'raving', an allusion to Julian's remark to the religious.

Christians, as I have said before, and so is the will of God.

And these words: You will not be overcome, were said very insistently and strongly, for certainty and strength against every tribulation which may come. He did not say: You will not be assailed, you will not be belaboured, you will not be disquieted, but he said: You will not be overcome. God wants us to pay attention to his words, and always to be strong in our certainty, in well-being and in woe, for he loves us and delights in us, and so he wishes us to love him and delight in him and trust greatly in him, and all will be well.

And soon afterwards all was hidden, and I saw no more.

Chapter xxiii

After this the devil returned with his heat and his stench, and kept me very busy. The stench was vile and painful, and the physical heat was fearful and oppressive; and I could also hear in my ears chattering and talking, as if between two speakers, and they seemed to be both chattering at once, as if they were conducting a confused debate, and it was all low muttering. And I did not understand what they said, but all this, it seemed, was to move me to despair; and I kept on trusting in God, and spoke words aloud to comfort my soul, as I should have done to another person who was so belaboured. It seemed to me that this commotion could not be compared with anything on earth. I fixed my eyes on the same cross in which I had seen comfort before, and I occupied my tongue in speaking of Christ's Passion and in repeating the faith of Holy Church, and I fixed my heart on God with all the trust and the strength that was in me. And I thought privately to myself: Now you have plenty to do; if from now on you would be so busy in keeping yourself free of sin, that would be a most excellent occupation. For I truly believe that if I were safe from sin I should be very safe from all the devils of hell and the enemies of my soul.

And so they occupied me all that night and into the morning, until it was a little after sunrise; and then all at once they had all gone and disappeared, leaving nothing but their stench, and that persisted for a little while. And I despised them, and so I was delivered from them by the strength of Christ's Passion. For it is so that the fiend is overcome, as Christ said before to me.

O, wretched sin, what are you? You are nothing. For I saw that God is in everything; I did not see you. And when I saw that God has made everything, I did not see you. And when I saw that God is in everything, I did not see you. And when I saw that God does everything that is done, the less and the greater, I did not see you. And when I saw our Lord Jesus Christ seated in our soul so honourably, and love and delight and rule and guard all that he has made, I did not see you. And so I am certain that you are nothing, and all those who love you and delight you and follow you and deliberately end in you, I am sure that they will be brought to nothing with you and eternally confounded. Amen, for love of him.

And I wish to say what wretchedness is, as I am taught by God's revelation. Wretchedness is everything which is not good, the spiritual blindness that we fall into by our first sin, and all that follows from that wretchedness, sufferings and pains, spiritual or physical, and everything on earth or elsewhere which is not good. And then concerning this it may be asked: What are we? and to this I answer: If everything were separated from us which is not good, we should be good. When wretchedness is separated from us, God and the soul are wholly at unity and God and man are

166

wholly one. What is everything on earth which divides us? I answer and say that in the respect in which it serves us it is good, and in the respect in which it will perish it is wretchedness, and in the respect that a man sets his heart upon it otherwise than thus it is sin. And so long as man or woman loves sin, if there be such, he is in pain beyond all pains; and when he does not love sin, but hates it and loves God, all is well. And he who truly does so, though sometimes he sin through weakness or ignorance in his will, he does not fall, because he wishes to exert himself to rise again and look upon God, whom he loves in all his will. God has made things to be loved by men or women who have been sinners; but always he loves and longs to have our love, and when we have a strong and wise love for Jesus, we are at peace.

All the blessed teaching of our Lord God was shown to me in three parts, as I have said before, that is to say by bodily vision, and by words formed in my understanding, and by spiritual vision. About the bodily vision I have said as I saw, as truly as I am able. And about the words formed, I have repeated them just as our Lord revealed them to me. And about the spiritual vision, I have told a part, but I can never tell it in full; and therefore I am moved to say more about this spiritual vision, as God will give me grace.

Chapter xxiv

God showed me two kinds of sickness that we have, of which he wants us to be cured. One is impatience, because we bear our labour and our pain heavily. The other is despair, coming from doubtful fear, as I shall say afterwards. And it is these two which most belabour and assail us, by what our Lord showed me, and it is most pleasing to him that they should be amended. I am speaking of such men and women as for the love of God hate sin and dispose themselves to do God's will. So these are two secret sins, extremely busy in tempting us. Therefore it is God's will that they should be known, and then we shall reject them as we do other sins.

And so very meekly our Lord showed me what patience he had in his cruel Passion, and also the joy and delight that he has in that Passion, because of love. And he showed me this as an example of how we ought gladly and easily to bear our pains, for that is very pleasing to him and an endless profit to us. And the reason why we are oppressed by them is because of our ignorance of love. Though the persons of the blessed Trinity be all alike in their attributes, it was their love which was most shown to me, and that it is closest to us all. And it is about this knowledge that we are most blind, for many men and women believe that God is almighty and may do everything, and that he is all wisdom and can do everything, but that he is all love and wishes to do everything, that is where they fail. And it is this

✳ ignorance which most hinders God's lovers, for when they begin to hate sin and to amend themselves according to the laws of Holy Church, still there persists a fear which moves them to look at themselves and their sins committed in the past. And they take this fear for humility, but it is a reprehensible blindness and weakness; and we do not know how to despise it, as we should at once despise it, like any other sin which we recognize, if we knew it for what it is, because it comes from the enemy, and it is contrary to truth. For of all the attributes of the blessed Trinity, it is God's will that we have most confidence in his delight and his love.

For love makes power and wisdom very humble to us;
✳ for just as by God's courtesy he forgets our sin from the time that we repent, just so does he wish us to forget our sins and all our depression and all our doubtful fears.

Chapter xxv

For I saw four kinds of fear. One is fear of assault, which comes to a man suddenly through timidity. This fear is good, for it helps to purge a man, as does bodily sickness or such other pains which are not sinful; for all such pains help one if they are patiently accepted. The second is fear of pain, through which a man is stirred and wakened from the sleep of sin; for anyone fast asleep in sin is not for that time able to receive the gentle strength of the Holy Spirit, until he has obtained this fear of pain and of the fire of purgatory. And this fear moves him to seek comfort and mercy of God; and so this fear helps him as though by chance, and enables him to have contrition by the blessed teaching of the Holy Spirit. The third is a doubtful fear; if it be recognized for what it is, however little it may be, it is a kind of despair. For I am certain that God hates all doubtful fear, and he wishes us to drive it out, knowing truly how we may live[30]. The fourth is reverent fear, for there is no fear in us which pleases him but reverent fear, and that is very sweet and gentle, because our love is great. And yet this reverent fear is not the same as love; they are different in kind and in effect, and neither of them may be obtained without the other.

Therefore I am sure that he who loves, he fears, though he may feel little of this. Whatever kinds of fear be suggested to us other than reverent fear, though they appear disguised as holiness, they are not so true; and this is how they can be recognized and distinguished, one from the other. The more that one has of this reverent fear, the more it softens and strengthens and pleases and gives rest; and

---

30. The long text, p. 324, has 'love', which is probably superior.

false fear belabours and assails and perturbs. So that the remedy is to recognize them both and to reject false fear, just as we should an evil spirit who presented himself in the likeness of a good angel. For it is so with an evil spirit; though he may come under the disguise and likeness of a good angel, with his dalliance and his operations, however fair he may appear, he first belabours and tempts and perturbs the person he speaks to, and hinders him and leaves him in great unrest; and the more he communicates with him, the more he oppresses him and the further the man is from peace. Therefore it is God's will and to our profit that we recognize them apart; for God wants us always to be strong in our love, and peaceful and restful as he is towards us, and he wants us to be, for ourselves and for our fellow Christians, what he is for us. Amen.

The end of the book of Julian of Norwich.

JULIAN OF NORWICH

SHOWINGS

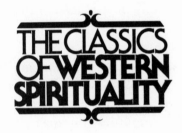

THE CLASSICS
OF WESTERN
SPIRITUALITY

JULIAN OF NORWICH
SHOWINGS

THE LONG TEXT

The First Chapter

Here begins the first chapter.

This is a revelation of love which Jesus Christ, our endless bliss, made in sixteen showings, of which the first is about his precious crowning of thorns; and in this was contained and specified the blessed Trinity, with the Incarnation and the union between God and man's soul, with many fair revelations and teachings of endless wisdom and love, in which all the revelations which follow are founded and connected.

The second revelation is about the discoloration of his fair face, to signify his precious Passion.

The third revelation is that our Lord God almighty, all wisdom and all love, just as truly as he has made everything which is, so truly he does and performs all things which are done.

The fourth revelation is of the scourging of his tender body, with copious shedding of his precious blood.

The fifth revelation is that the fiend is overcome by the precious Passion of Christ.

The sixth revelation is of the honourable thanks with

which our Lord God rewards all his blessed servants in heaven.

The seventh revelation is of the frequent experiences of well-being and of woe. To experience well-being is to be touched and illumined by grace, with true certainty of endless joy; the experience of woe comes as a temptation, through the heaviness and weariness of our mortal life, with spiritual understanding that we are preserved in love by the goodness of God just as truly in woe as in well-being.

The eighth revelation is of Christ's last sufferings and of his cruel death.

The ninth revelation is of the delight which the blessed Trinity has in the cruel Passion of Christ, once his sorrowful death was accomplished, and that he wishes that joy and delight to be our solace and happiness, as it is his, until we come to glory in heaven.

The tenth revelation tells how our Lord Jesus displays his heart split in two for love.

The eleventh revelation is an exalted spiritual showing concerning his dear mother.

The twelfth revelation is that our Lord is all sovereign life.

The thirteenth revelation is that our Lord God wishes us to have great regard for all the deeds which he has performed in the most noble work of creating all things, and it treats of the excellence of man's creation, which is superior to all God's works; and it is about the precious amends which he has made for man's sin, turning all our blame into everlasting honour. Here he says: Behold and see, for by the same power, wisdom and goodness that I have done all this, by the same power, wisdom and goodness I shall make all things well which are not well, and you will see it. And in this it is his wish that we should preserve ourselves in the faith and truth of Holy Church, not wishing to know his mysteries except as that is fitting for us in this life.

The fourteenth revelation is that our Lord God is the foundation of our beseeching. In this two fair qualities were seen. One is proper prayer; the other is true trust, and he wishes them both to be equally generous. And so our prayer is pleasing to him, and he in his goodness fulfils it.

The fifteenth revelation is that suddenly we shall be taken from all our pain and from all our woe, and in his goodness we shall come up above, where we shall have our Lord Jesus for our reward, to be fulfilled with joy and bliss in heaven.

The sixteenth revelation is that the blessed Trinity our Creator dwells eternally in our soul in Christ Jesus our saviour, honourably ruling and commanding all things, powerfully and wisely saving and preserving us out of love; and that we shall not be overcome by our enemy.

The Second Chapter

This revelation was made to a simple, unlettered[1] creature, living in this mortal flesh, the year of our Lord one thousand, three hundred and seventy-three, on the thirteenth day of May; and before this the creature had desired three graces by the gift of God. The first was recollection of the Passion. The second was bodily sickness. The third was to have, of God's gift, three wounds. As to the first, it seemed to me that I had some feeling for the Passion of Christ, but still I desired to have more by the grace of God. I thought that I wished that I had been at that time with Magdalen and with the others who were Christ's lovers, so that I might have seen with my own eyes the Passion which our Lord suffered for me, so that I might have suffered with him as

---

1. Whatever 'unlettered' may mean here, it cannot be 'illiterate'. See *Showings*, I, 43-52, for the editors' reasons for interpreting it as 'lacking in literary skills'.

others did who loved him. Therefore I desired a bodily sight, in which I might have more knowledge of our saviour's bodily pains, and of the compassion of our Lady and of all his true lovers who were living at that time and saw his pains, for I would have been one of them and have suffered with them. I never desired any other sight of God or revelation, until my soul would be separated from the body, for I believed that I should be saved by the mercy of God. This was my intention, because I wished afterwards, because of that revelation, to have truer recollection of Christ's Passion. As to the second grace, there came into my mind with contrition—a free gift which I did not seek—a desire of my will to have by God's gift a bodily sickness. I wished that sickness to be so severe that it might seem mortal, so that I might in it receive all the rites which Holy Church has to give me, whilst I myself should think that I was dying, and everyone who saw me would think the same; for I wanted no comfort from any human, earthly life in that sickness. I wanted to have every kind of pain, bodily and spiritual, which I should have if I had died, every fear and temptation from devils, and every other kind of pain except the departure of the spirit. I intended this because I wanted to be purged by God's mercy, and afterwards live more to his glory because of that sickness; because I hoped that this would be to my reward when I should die, because I desired soon to be with my God and my Creator.

These two desires about the Passion and the sickness which I desired from him were with a condition, for it seemed to me that this was not the ordinary practice of prayer; therefore I said: Lord, you know what I want, if it be your will that I have it, and if it be not your will, good Lord, do not be displeased, for I want nothing which you do not want. When I was young I desired to have this sickness when I would be thirty years old.

As to the third, by the grace of God and the teaching of

Holy Church I conceived a great desire to receive three wounds in my life, that is, the wound of true contrition, the wound of loving compassion and the wound of longing with my will for God. Just as I asked for the other two conditionally, so I asked urgently for this third without any condition. The two desires which I mentioned first passed from my mind, and the third remained there continually.

The Third Chapter

And when I was thirty and a half years old, God sent me a bodily sickness in which I lay for three days and three nights, and on the third night I received all the rites of Holy Church, and did not expect to live until day. And after this I lay for two days and two nights, and on the third night I often thought that I was on the point of death, and those who were with me often thought so. And yet in this I felt a great reluctance to die, not that there was anything on earth which it pleased me to live for, or any pain of which I was afraid, for I trusted in the mercy of God. But it was because I wanted to live to love God better and longer, so that I might through the grace of that living have more knowledge and love of God in the bliss of heaven. Because it seemed to me that all the time that I had lived here was very little and short in comparison with the bliss which is everlasting, I thought: Good Lord, can my living no longer be to your glory? And I understood by my reason and the sensation of my pains that I should die; and with all the will of my heart I assented to be wholly as was God's will.

So I lasted until day, and by then my body was dead from the middle downwards, as it felt to me. Then I was helped to sit upright and supported, so that my heart might be more free to be at God's will, and so that I could think of him whilst my life would last. My curate was sent for to be present at my end; and before he came my eyes were fixed upwards, and I could not speak. He set the cross before my face, and said: I have brought the image of your saviour; look at it and take comfort from it. It seemed to me that I was well, for my eyes were set upwards towards heaven, where I trusted that I by God's mercy was going; but nevertheless I agreed to fix my eyes on the face of the crucifix if I could, and so I did, for it seemed to me that I would hold out longer with my eyes set in front of me rather than upwards. After this my sight began to fail. It grew as dark around me in the room as if it had been night, except that there was ordinary light trained upon the image of the cross, I did not know how. Everything around the cross was ugly and terrifying to me, as if it were occupied by a great crowd of devils.

After this the upper part of my body began to die, until I could scarcely feel anything. My greatest pain was my shortness of breath and the ebbing of my life. Then truly I believed that I was at the point of death. And suddenly at that moment all my pain was taken from me, and I was as sound, particularly in the upper part of my body, as ever I was before. I was astonished by this sudden change, for it seemed to me that it was by God's secret doing and not natural; and even so, in this ease which I felt, I had no more confidence that I should live, nor was the ease I felt complete for me, for I thought that I would rather have been delivered of this world, because that was what my heart longed for.

Then suddenly it came into my mind that I ought to wish for the second wound as a gift and a grace from our Lord, that my body might be filled full of recollection and feeling of his blessed Passion, as I had prayed before, for I wished that his pains might be my pains, with compassion which would lead to longing for God. So it seemed to me that I might with his grace have the wounds which I had before desired; but in this I never wanted any bodily vision or any kind of revelation from God, but the compassion which I thought a loving soul could have for our Lord Jesus, who for love was willing to become a mortal man. I desired to suffer with him, living in my mortal body, as God would give me grace.

The Fourth Chapter

And at this, suddenly I saw the red blood running down from under the crown, hot and flowing freely and copiously, a living stream, just as it was at the time when the crown of thorns was pressed on his blessed head. I perceived, truly and powerfully, that it was he who just so, both God and man, himself suffered for me, who showed it to me without any intermediary.

And in the same revelation[2], suddenly the Trinity filled my heart full of the greatest joy, and I understood that it will be so in heaven without end to all who will come there. For the Trinity is God, God is the Trinity. The Trinity is our maker, the Trinity is our protector, the Trinity is our everlasting lover, the Trinity is our endless joy and our bliss, by our Lord Jesus Christ and in our Lord Jesus Christ. And this was revealed in the first vision and in them all, for where Jesus appears the blessed Trinity is understood, as I see it[3]. And I said: Blessed be the Lord! This I said with a reverent intention and in a loud voice, and I was greatly astonished by this wonder and marvel, that he who is so to be revered and feared would be so familiar[4] with a sinful creature living in this wretched flesh.

---

2. Here the first notable addition in the long text begins. See p. 129.
3. This ends the first addition.
4. Ms: 'homely'; see p. 129.

I accepted it that at that time our Lord Jesus wanted, out of his courteous love, to show me comfort before my temptations began; for it seemed to me that I might well be tempted by devils, by God's permission and with his protection, before I would die. With this sight of his blessed Passion, with the divinity which I saw in my understanding, I knew well that this was strength enough for me, yes, and for all living creatures who were to be saved, against all the devils of hell and against all their spiritual enemies.

In this he brought[5] our Lady St. Mary to my understanding. I saw her spiritually in her bodily likeness, a simple, humble maiden, young in years, grown a little taller than a child, of the stature which she had when she conceived. Also God showed me part of the wisdom and the truth of her soul, and in this I understood the reverent contemplation with which she beheld her God, who is her Creator, marvelling with great reverence that he was willing to be born of her who was a simple creature created by him[6]. And this wisdom and truth, this knowledge of her Creator's greatness and of her own created littleness, made her say very meekly to Gabriel: Behold me here, God's handmaiden. In this sight I understood truly that she is greater, more worthy and more fulfilled, than everything else which God has created, and which is inferior to her. Above her is no created thing, except the blessed humanity of Christ, as I saw.

---

5. The rest of this chapter is a rearrangement of matter from the short text. See p. 131.

6. This corrects a scribal error found in both texts. See *Showings*, II, 297 and p. 131.

The Fifth Chapter

At the same time as I saw this sight of the head bleeding, our good Lord showed a spiritual sight of his familiar love. I saw that he is to us everything which is good and comforting for our help. He is our clothing, who wraps and enfolds us for love, embraces us and shelters us, surrounds us for his love, which is so tender that he may never desert us. And so in this sight I saw that he is everything which is good, as I understand.

And in this he showed me something small, no bigger than a hazelnut, lying in the palm of my hand, as it seemed to me, and it was as round as a ball. I looked at it with the eye of my understanding and thought: What can this be? I was amazed that it could last, for I thought that because of its littleness it would suddenly have fallen into nothing. And I was answered in my understanding: It lasts and always will, because God loves it; and thus everything has being through the love of God.

In this little thing I saw three properties. The first is that God made it, the second is that God loves it, the third is that God preserves it. But what did I see in it?[7] It is that God is the Creator and the protector and the lover. For until I am substantially united to him, I can never have perfect rest or true happiness, until, that is, I am so attached to him that there can be no created thing between my God and me.

This little thing which is created seemed to me as if it could have fallen into nothing because of its littleness. We need to have knowledge of this, so that we may delight in despising as nothing everything created, so as to love and have uncreated God. For this is the reason why our hearts and souls are not in perfect ease, because here we seek rest

---

7. So P, C; but SS, Westminster Cathedral Library, *The Knowledge of Ourselves and of God* (hereafter cited as W) agree with the short text (p. 131): 'But what is that to me?'

in this thing which is so little, in which there is no rest, and we do not know our God who is almighty, all wise and all good, for he is true rest. God wishes to be known, and it pleases him that we should rest in him; for everything which is beneath him is not sufficient for us. And this is the reason why no soul is at rest until it has despised as nothing all things which are created. When it by its will has become nothing for love, to have him who is everything, then is it able to receive spiritual rest.

And also[8] our good Lord revealed that it is very greatly pleasing to him that a simple soul should come naked[9], openly and familiarly. For this is the loving yearning[10] of the soul through the touch of the Holy Spirit, from the understanding which I have in this revelation: God, of your goodness give me yourself, for you are enough for me, and I can ask for nothing which is less which can pay you full worship. And if I ask anything which is less, always I am in want; but only in you do I have everything.

And these words of the goodness of God are very dear to the soul, and very close to touching our Lord's will, for his goodness fills all his creatures and all his blessed works full, and endlessly overflows in them. For he is everlastingness, and he made us only for himself, and restored us by his precious Passion and always preserves us in his blessed love; and all this is of his goodness.

The Sixth Chapter

This revelation was given to my understanding to teach our souls wisely to adhere to the goodness of God; and in that same time our habits of prayer were brought to my

---

8. Here a second, longer addition to the short text begins.
9. SS, W: 'nakedly'.
10. P, C: 'dwelling'; SS: 'yearning'.

mind, how in our ignorance of love we are accustomed to employ many intermediaries. Then I saw truly that it is more honour to God and more true delight if we faithfully pray to him for his goodness, and adhere to this by grace, with true understanding and steadfast belief, than if we employed all the intermediaries of which a heart may think. For if we employ all these intermediaries, this is too little and it is not complete honour to God; but his goodness is full and complete, and in it is nothing lacking.

For what I shall say came to my mind at the same time. We pray to God for his holy flesh and for his precious blood, his holy Passion, his precious death and his glorious wounds, for all the blessings of nature and the endless life that we have of all this, it is of the goodness of God. And we pray to him for the love of the sweet mother who bore him, and all the help that we have of her, it is of his goodness. And we pray for his holy Cross on which he died, and all the help and the strength that we have of that Cross, it is of his goodness. And in the same way, all the help that we have from particular saints and from all the blessed company of heaven, the precious love and the holy, endless friendship that we have from them, it is of his goodness. For the intermediaries which the goodness of God has ordained to help us are very lovely and many. Of them the chief and principal intermediary is the blessed nature which he took of the virgin, with all the intermediaries which preceded and followed, which are a part of our redemption and of our endless salvation.

Therefore it pleases him that we seek him and honour him through intermediaries, understanding and knowing that he is the goodness of everything. For the highest form of prayer is to the goodness of God, which comes down to us to our humblest needs. It gives life to our souls and makes them live and grow in grace and virtue. It is nearest in nature and promptest in grace, for it is the same grace which

the soul seeks and always will, until we truly know our
God, who has enclosed us all in himself.

A man walks upright, and the food in his body is shut
in as if in a well-made purse. When the time of his necessity
comes, the purse is opened and then shut again, in most
seemly fashion. And it is God who does this, as it is shown
when he says that he comes down to us in our humblest
needs. For he does not despise what he has made, nor does
he disdain to serve us in the simplest natural functions of our
body, for love of the soul which he created in his own
likeness. For as the body is clad in the cloth, and the flesh in
the skin, and the bones in the flesh, and the heart in the
trunk, so are we, soul and body, clad and enclosed in the
goodness of God. Yes, and more closely, for all these vanish
and waste away; the goodness of God is always complete,
and closer to us, beyond any comparison. For truly our lover
desires the soul to adhere to him with all its power, and us
always to adhere to his goodness. For of all the things that
the heart can think, this pleases God most and soonest
profits the soul. For it is so preciously loved by him who is
highest that this surpasses the knowledge of all created
beings. That is to say, there is no created being who can
know how much and how sweetly and how tenderly the
Creator loves us. And therefore we can with his grace and
his help persevere in spiritual contemplation, with endless
wonder at this high, surpassing, immeasurable love which
our Lord in his goodness has for us; and therefore we may
with reverence ask from our lover all that we will, for our
natural will is to have God, and God's good will is to have
us, and we can never stop willing or loving until we possess
him in the fulness of joy. And there we can will no more,
for it is his will that we be occupied in knowing and loving
until the time comes that we shall be filled full in heaven.

And therefore this lesson of love was revealed, with all
that follows, as you will see, for the strength and foundation

of everything was revealed in the first vision. For of all things, contemplating and loving the Creator makes the soul to seem less in its own sight, and fills it full with reverent fear and true meekness, and with much love for its fellow Christians.

The Seventh Chapter

And to teach us this[11], as I understand, our good Lord showed our Lady St. Mary at the same time, that is to signify the exalted wisdom and truth which were hers as she contemplated her Creator. This wisdom and truth showed her in contemplation how great, how exalted, how mighty and how good was her God. The greatness and nobility of her contemplation of God filled her full of reverent fear; and with this she saw herself so small and so humble, so simple and so poor in comparison with her God that this reverent fear filled her with humility. And founded on this, she was filled with grace and with every kind of virtue, and she surpasses all creatures.

And during all the time[12] that our Lord showed me this spiritual vision which I have now described, I saw the bodily vision of the copious[13] bleeding of the head persist. The great drops of blood[14] fell from beneath the crown like pellets, looking as if they came from the veins, and as they issued they were a brownish red, for the blood was very thick, and as they spread they turned bright red. And as they reached the brows they vanished; and even so the

---

11. The first paragraph of this chapter is a recapitulation, with deeper insights, of the vision of our Lady already recounted.

12. Correspondence with the short text resumes; see p. 132.

13. Ms: 'pituous', altered, perhaps by another hand, to 'ple(n)tuous', with which the short text (p. 132) and C, SS agree.

14. Another addition to the short text begins.

bleeding continued until I had seen and understood many things. Nevertheless, the beauty and the vivacity persisted, beautiful and vivid without diminution.

The copiousness resembles the drops of water which fall from the eaves of a house after a great shower of rain, falling so thick that no human ingenuity can count them. And in their roundness as they spread over the forehead they were like a herring's scales.

At the time three things occurred to me: The drops were round like pellets as the blood issued, they were round like a herring's scales as they spread, they were like raindrops off a house's eaves, so many that they could not be counted. This vision was living and vivid and hideous and fearful and sweet and lovely; and in all this vision which I saw, what gave me most strength was that our good Lord, who is so to be revered and feared, is so familiar and so courteous, and most of all this filled me full of delight and certainty in my soul.

And so that I might understand this, he showed me this plain example[15]. It is the greatest honour which a majestic king or a great lord can do for a poor servant, to be familiar with him; and especially if he makes this known himself, privately and publicly, with great sincerity and happy mien, this poor creature will think: See, what greater honour and joy could this noble lord give me than to demonstrate to me, who am so little, this wonderful familiarity? Truly, this is a greater joy and delight to me than if he were to give me great gifts, and himself always to remain distant in his manner. This bodily example was shown, so exalted that this man's heart could be ravished and he could almost forget his own existence in the joy of this great familiarity.

So it is with our Lord Jesus and us, for truly it is the greatest possible joy, as I see it, that he who is highest and

---

15. This anticipates the allegory of the lord and the servant in chapter 51, also not found in the short text.

mightiest, noblest and most honourable, is lowest and humblest, most familiar and courteous. And verily and truly he will manifest to us all this marvellous joy when we shall see him. And our good Lord wants us to believe this and trust, rejoice and delight, strengthen and console ourselves, as we can with his grace and with his help, until the time that we see it in reality. For the greatest abundance of joy which we shall have, as I see it, is this wonderful courtesy and familiarity of our Father, who is our Creator, in our Lord Jesus Christ, who is our brother and our saviour. But no man can know this wonderful familiarity in this life, unless by a special revelation from our Lord, or from a great abundance of grace, given within by the Holy Spirit. But faith and belief together with love deserve the reward, and so it is received by grace. For our life is founded on faith with hope and love. This is revealed to whom God wills, and he plainly teaches and expounds and declares it, with many secret details which are a part of our faith and belief, which are to be known to God's glory. And when the revelation, given only for a time, has passed and is hidden, then faith preserves it by the grace of the Holy Spirit to the end of our lives. And so in the revelation there is nothing different from the faith, neither less nor more, as will be seen by our Lord's intention in this same matter[16], when the whole revelation is completed.

The Eighth Chapter

And as long as I saw this vision[17] of the copious bleeding of the head, I could not stop saying these words: Blessed be the Lord! In this revelation I understood six

---

16. Julian's meaning seems to be that these general reflections on authentic private revelation will be seen to be confirmed in her own case when she has concluded her account of her revelations.

17. Correspondence with the short text resumes. See p. 132.

things. The first is the tokens of his blessed Passion and the plentiful shedding of his precious blood. The second is the virgin who is his beloved mother. The third is the blessed divinity, that always was and is and shall be, almighty, all wisdom and all love. The fourth is everything which he has made, for I know well that heaven and earth and all creation are great, generous and beautiful and good. But the reason why it seemed to my eyes so little was because I saw it in the presence of him who is the Creator. To any soul who sees the Creator of all things, all that is created seems very little. The fifth is that he who created it created everything for love, and by the same love is it preserved, and always will be without end, as has been said already. The sixth is that God is everything which is good, as I see, and the goodness which everything has is God.

God showed me this in the first vision, and he gave me space and time to contemplate it. And then the bodily vision ceased, and the spiritual vision persisted in my understanding. And I waited with reverent fear, rejoicing in what I saw and wishing, as much as I dared, to see more, if that were God's will, or to see the same vision for a longer time.

In all this[18] I was greatly moved in love towards my fellow Christians, that they might all see and know the same as I saw, for I wished it to be a comfort to them, for all this vision was shown for all men.

Then I said to those who were with me: Today is my Doomsday. And I said this because I expected to die; because on the day that a man or a woman dies he receives particular judgment as he will be forever, as I understand. I said this because I wished them to love God better, and to make them mindful that this life is short, of which they could see me as an example. For in all this time I was expecting to die, and that was wonderful to me and

---

18. These two paragraphs are from chapter vii of the short text; see p. 136.

somewhat surprising, for it seemed to me that this vision was revealed for those who would go on living.

Everything that I say[19] about me I mean to apply to all my fellow Christians, for I am taught that this is what our Lord intends in this spiritual revelation. And therefore I pray you all for God's sake, and I counsel you for your own profit, that you disregard the wretch to whom it was shown, and that mightily, wisely and meekly you contemplate upon God, who out of his courteous love and his endless goodness was willing to show it generally, to the comfort of us all. For it is God's will that you accept it with great joy and delight, as[20] Jesus has[21] shown it to you.

The Ninth Chapter

I am not good because of the revelations, but only if I love God better; and inasmuch as you love God better, it is more to you than to me. I do not say this to those who are wise, because they know it well. But I say it to you who are simple, to give you comfort and strength; for we are all one in love, for truly it was not revealed to me that[22] God loves me better than the humblest soul who is in a state of grace. For I am sure that there are many who never had revelations or visions, but only the common teaching of Holy Church, who love God better than I. If I pay special attention to myself, I am nothing at all; but in general I am, I hope, in the unity of love with all my fellow Christians. For it is in this unity that the life of all men consists who will be saved. For God is everything that is good, as I see; and God has

---

19. This reverts to chapter vi; see p. 133.
20. S2 agrees with the short text: 'as if'.
21. SS agree with the short text: 'had'.
22. C: 'for that'; S2: 'because that', which agree with the short text, p. 134.

made everything that is made, and God loves everything that he has made. And he who has general love for all his fellow Christians in God has love towards everything that is. For in mankind which will be saved is comprehended all, that is to say all that is made and the maker of all. For God is in man and in God is all[23]. And he who loves thus loves all. And I hope by the grace of God that he who may see it so will be taught the truth and greatly comforted, if he has need of comfort.

I speak of those[24] who will be saved, for at this time God showed me no one else. But in everything I believe as Holy Church preaches and teaches[25]. For the faith of Holy Church, which I had before I had understanding[26], and which, as I hope by the grace of God, I intend to preserve whole and to practise, was always in my sight, and I wished and intended never to accept anything which might be contrary to it. And to this end and with this intention I contemplated the revelation with all diligence, for throughout this blessed revelation I contemplated it as God intended.

All this was shown in three parts[27], that is to say, by bodily vision and by words formed in my understanding and by spiritual vision. But I may not and cannot show the spiritual visions as plainly and fully as I should wish. But I trust in our Lord God almighty that he will, out of his goodness and for love of you, make you accept it more spiritually and more sweetly than I can or may tell it.

---

23. SS: 'and God is in all'. Both readings differ from the short text's 'and so in man is all', p. 134.

24. There is the significant omission, here, of the passage in chapter vi of the short text beginning: 'But God forbid that you should say. . .', p. 135.

25. Most of the rest of this paragraph is original to the long text, and its conclusion varies somewhat from the end of the short text's chapter vi.

26. That is, of the revelations; see *Showings*, II, 333.

27. That is, 'different modes'.

The Second Revelation
The Tenth Chapter

And after this I looked with bodily vision into the face of the crucifix which hung before me, in which I saw a part of Christ's Passion: contempt, foul spitting, buffeting, and many long-drawn pains, more than I can tell; and his colour often changed. At one time I saw how half his face, beginning at the ear, became covered with dried blood, until it was caked to the middle of his face, and then the other side was caked in the same fashion, and meanwhile the blood vanished on the other side, just as it had come.

This I saw bodily, frighteningly and dimly, and I wanted more of the light of day, to have seen it more clearly. And I was answered in my reason: If God wishes to show you more, he will be your light; you need none but him. For I saw him[28] and sought him, for we are now so blind and so foolish that we can never seek God until the time when he in his goodness shows himself to us. And when by grace we see something of him, then we are moved by the same grace to seek with great desire to see him for our greater joy. So I saw him and sought him, and I had him and lacked him; and this is and should be our ordinary undertaking in this life, as I see it.

Once my understanding was let down into the bottom of the sea, and there I saw green hills and valleys, with the appearance of moss strewn with seaweed and gravel. Then I understood in this way: that if a man or woman were there under the wide waters, if he could see God, as God is continually with man, he would be safe in soul and body, and come to no harm. And furthermore, he would have more consolation and strength than all this world can tell.

---

28. The rest of chapter ten is original to the long text.

193

For it is God's will that we believe that we see him
continually, though it seems to us that the sight be only
partial; and through this belief he makes us always to gain
more grace, for God wishes to be seen, and he wishes to be
sought, and he wishes to be expected, and he wishes to be
trusted.

This second revelation was so humble and so small and
so simple that my spirit was greatly distressed as I
contemplated it, mourning, fearing, longing; for sometimes I
was fearful of whether it was a revelation. And then several
times our Lord gave me more insight, by which I
understood truly that it was a revelation. It symbolized and
resembled our foul, black death, which our fair, bright,
blessed Lord bore for our sins. It made me think of the holy
Vernicle at Rome, which he imprinted with his own blessed
face, when he was in his cruel Passion, voluntarily going to
his death, and of his often-changing colour, the brownness
and the blackness[29], his face sorrowful and wasted. Many
marvelled how it could be the case that he imprinted this
image with his blessed face, which is the fairest of heaven,
the flower of earth and the fruit of the virgin's womb. Then
how could this image be so discoloured and so far from
beauty? I wish to say what, by God's grace, I have
understood.

We know in our faith and our belief, by the teaching
and preaching of Holy Church, that the blessed Trinity
made mankind in their image and their likeness. In the same
way we know that when man fell so deeply and so
wretchedly through sin, there was no other help for
restoring him, except through him who created man. And he
who created man for love, by the same love wanted to
restore man to the same blessedness and to even more. And
just as we were made like the Trinity in our first making,

---

29. Of the oozing and caking blood which she had seen.

our Creator wished us to be like Jesus Christ our saviour in
heaven forever, through the power of our making again[30].
Then, between these two, Jesus wished, for his love and for
man's honour, to make himself as much like man in this
mortal life, in our foulness and our wretchedness, as a man
could be without sin; and this is meant where it is said
before that the revelation symbolized and resembled our
foul, black mortality, in which our fair, bright, blessed Lord
concealed his divinity. But truly I dare to say—and we
ought to believe—that there was never so beautiful a man as
he, until the time when his lovely complexion was changed
by labour and grief, suffering and dying. This is mentioned
in Revelation Eight, in the sixteenth chapter[31], where more
is said of the same resemblance. And as concerns the
Vernicle of Rome, it changes its colour and appearance[32]
from time to time, sometimes more consoling and vivid,
sometimes more sorrowful and deathly, as can be seen. And
this vision taught me to understand that the soul's constant
search pleases God greatly. For it cannot do more than seek,
suffer and trust. And this is accomplished in every soul, to
whom it is given by the Holy Spirit. And illumination by
finding is of the Spirit's special grace, when it is his will.
Seeking with faith, hope and love pleases our Lord, and
finding pleases the soul and fills it full of joy. And so I was
taught to understand that seeking is as good as contemplating, during the time that he wishes to permit the soul to
be in labour. It is God's will that we seek on until we see
him, for it is through this that he will show himself to us, of
his special grace, when it is his will.

And he will teach a soul himself how it should bear
itself when it contemplates him, and that is the greatest
honour to him and the greatest profit to the soul, and it

---

30. 'Again': so SS; P, C have 'own'.

31. C, P: 'in Revelation Two, in the eighteenth chapter'; SS: 'in Revelation Eight'. See
p. 207.

32. So SS; P: 'it means its colour, and either. . .'; C: 'it means its colour'.

receives most[33] humility and other virtues, by the grace and guidance of the Holy Spirit. For it seems to me that the greatest honour which a soul can pay to God is simply to surrender itself to him with true confidence, whether it be seeking or contemplating. These are the two activities which can be seen in this vision: one is seeking, the other is contemplating. Seeking is common to all, and every soul can have through grace and ought to have discretion[34] and teaching from Holy Church.

It is God's will that we receive three things from him as gifts as we seek. The first is that we seek willingly and diligently without sloth, as that may be with his grace, joyfully and happily, without unreasonable depression and useless sorrow. The second is that we wait for him steadfastly, out of love for him, without grumbling and contending against him, to the end of our lives, for that will last only for a time. The third is that we have great trust in him, out of complete and true faith, for it is his will that we know that he will appear, suddenly and blessedly, to all his lovers. For he works in secret, and he will be perceived, and his appearing will be very[35] sudden. And he wants to be trusted, for he is very accessible, familiar and courteous[36], blessed may he be.

---

33. So SS, W, which seem preferable to P, C: 'it is most accepted'.

34. For Julian and her contemporaries, 'discretion' in this context means 'grace and knowledge to distinguish good inspirations from bad'.

35. 'Very': so SS, W; P, C: 'sweet' (a misunderstanding of ME 'swithe').

36. So W; P, C have not 'accessible', SS have not 'courteous'.

The Third Revelation
The Eleventh Chapter

And after this[37] I saw God in an instant of time, that is to say in my understanding, by which vision I saw that he is present in all things. I contemplated it carefully, seeing and recognizing through it that he does everything which is done. I marvelled at that vision with a gentle fear, and I thought: What is sin? For I saw truly that God does everything, however small it may be, and that nothing is done by chance, but all by God's prescient[38] wisdom. If it seem[39] chance in man's sight, our blindness and lack of prescience is the reason. For those things which are in God's prescient[40] wisdom since before time, which duly and to his glory he always guides to their best conclusion, as things come about, come[41] suddenly upon us when we are ignorant; and so through our blindness and our lack of prescience we say that these things are by chance.

So I understood in this revelation of love, for I know well that in our Lord's sight there is no chance; and therefore[42] I was compelled to admit that everything which is done is well done, for our Lord God[43] does everything. For at this time the work of creatures was not revealed, but the work of our Lord God in creatures; for he is at the centre of everything, and he does everything. And[44] I was

---

37. Correspondence with the short text (chapter viii) resumes; see p. 137.
38. 'Prescient': so SS, W; P, C: 'aforesaid'.
39. What follows does not correspond with the short text.
40. See note 38.
41. 'Come': so SS; P, C: 'coming'.
42. Correspondence with the short text resumes; see p. 137.
43. What follows is an addition to the short text.
44. Correspondence with the short text resumes.

certain that he does no sin; and here I was certain that sin is no deed[45], for in all this sin was not shown to me. And I did not wish to go on wondering about this, but I contemplated our Lord and waited for what he would show. And thus[46] the rightfulness of God's dealing was shown to the soul, as well as could be in that time. Rightfulness has two fine qualities: It is right and it is full. And so are all the works of our Lord, and they lack no operation of mercy or of grace, for they are all rightful and nothing whatever is lacking in them. And on another occasion[47] he did show sin, undisguised, for my contemplation, as I shall tell afterwards, when he performs works of mercy and of grace.

This vision[48] was revealed to my understanding, for our Lord wants to have the soul truly converted to contemplation of him and of all his works in general. For they are most good, and all his judgments are easy and sweet, bringing to great rest the soul which is converted from contemplating men's blind judgments to the judgments, lovely and sweet, of our Lord God. For a man regards some deeds as well done and some as evil, and our Lord does not regard them so, for everything which exists in nature is of God's creation, so that everything which is done has the property of being of God's doing. For it is easy to understand that the best of deeds is well done; and the smallest of deeds which is done is as well done as the best and the greatest, and they all have the property and the order ordained for them as our Lord had ordained, without beginning[49], for no one does but he.

I saw most truly that he never changed his purpose in any kind of thing, nor ever will eternally. For there was nothing unknown to him in his just ordinance before time

---

45. In the short text, 'is nothing'.
46. What follows is an addition to the short text.
47. This sentence corresponds with the short text, p. 137.
48. The rest of this chapter is not in the short text.
49. SS: 'as our Lord had ordained them to, from without beginning'.

began, and therefore all things were set in order, before anything was made, as it would endure eternally. And no kind of thing will fail in that respect, for he has made everything totally good.

And therefore the blessed Trinity is always wholly pleased with all its works; and God revealed all this most blessedly, as though to say: See, I am God. See, I am in all things. See, I do all things. See, I never remove[50] my hands from my works, nor ever shall without end. See, I guide all things to the end that I ordain them for, before time began, with the same power and wisdom and love with which I made them; how should anything be amiss? So was the soul examined, powerfully, wisely and lovingly, in this vision. Then I saw truly that I must agree, with great reverence and joy in God.

The Fourth Revelation
The Twelfth Chapter

And after this[51] as I watched, I saw the body bleeding copiously in representation of[52] the scourging, and it was thus. The fair skin[53] was deeply broken into the tender flesh through the vicious blows delivered all over the lovely body. The hot blood ran out so plentifully that neither skin nor wounds could be seen, but everything seemed to be blood. And as it flowed down to where it should have fallen, it disappeared. Nonetheless, the bleeding continued for a time, until it could be plainly seen. And I saw it so plentiful that

---

50. Or 'removed'.
51. Correspondence with the short text resumes; see p. 137.
52. Ms: 'in semyng', which could also mean 'in the furrows made by'.
53. The rest of this paragraph differs from the short text.

it seemed to me that if it had in fact and in substance been happening there, the bed and everything all around it would have been soaked in blood.

Then it came into my mind that God has created[54] bountiful waters on the earth for our use and our bodily comfort, out of the tender love he has for us. But it is more pleasing to him that we accept for our total cure his blessed blood to wash us of our sins, for there is no drink that is made which it pleases him so well to give us. For it is most plentiful, as it is most precious, and that through the power of the blessed divinity. And it is of our own nature, and blessedly flows over us by the power of his precious love.

The precious blood[55] of our Lord Jesus Christ, as truly as it is most precious, so truly is it most plentiful. Behold and see the power of this precious plenty of his precious blood. It descended into hell and broke its[56] bonds, and delivered all who were there and who belong to the court of heaven. The precious plenty of his precious blood overflows all the earth, and it is ready to wash from their sins all creatures who are, have been and will be of good will. The precious plenty of his precious blood ascended into heaven in the blessed body of our Lord Jesus Christ, and it is flowing there in him, praying to the Father for us, and this is and will be so long as we have need. And furthermore, it flows in all heaven, rejoicing in the salvation of all mankind which is and will be there, and filling up the number which is lacking.

---

54. Correspondence with the short text resumes.
55. The rest of this chapter is not in the short text.
56. Or 'their' (the Holy Souls).

The Fifth Revelation
The Thirteenth Chapter

And after this[57], before God revealed any words, he allowed me to contemplate him for a fitting length of time, and all that I had seen, and all the significance that was contained in it, as well as my soul's simplicity could accept it. And then he, without voice and without opening of lips, formed in my soul this saying: With this the fiend is overcome. Our Lord said this to me with reference to his blessed Passion, as he had shown it before. In this he showed a part of the fiend's malice, and all of his impotence, because he showed that his Passion is the overcoming of the fiend. God showed me that the fiend has now the same malice as he had before the Incarnation, and he works as hard, and he sees as constantly as he did before that all souls who will be saved escape him to God's glory by the power of our Lord's precious Passion. And that is the devil's sorrow, and he is put to terrible shame, for everything which God permits him to do turns to joy for us and to pain and shame for him. And he has as much sorrow when God permits him to work as when he is not working. And that is because he can never do as much evil as he would wish, for his power is all locked in God's hands. But in God[58] there can be no anger, as I see it, and it is with power and justice, to the profit of all who will be saved, that he opposes the damned, who in malice and malignity work to frustrate and oppose God's will.

Also I saw our Lord scorn his malice and despise him as nothing, and he wants us to do so. Because of this sight I laughed greatly, and that made those around me to laugh as

---

57. Correspondence with the short text resumes; see p. 138.
58. This sentence is not in the short text.

well; and their laughter was pleasing to me. I thought that I wished that all my fellow Christians had seen what I saw. Then they would all have laughed with me; but I did not see Christ laughing, but I know well that it was the vision he showed me which made me laugh, for I understood that we may laugh, to comfort ourselves and rejoice in God, because the devil is overcome. And when I saw[59] our Lord scorn his malice, that was through the fixing of my understanding on him[60], that is, that this was an interior revelation of his truth, in which his demeanour did not change. For as I see it, this is an attribute of God which must be honoured, and which lasts forever.

And after this I became serious again, and said: I see three things: sport and scorn and seriousness. I see sport, that the devil is overcome; and I see scorn, that God scorns him and he will be scorned; and I see seriousness, that he is overcome by the blessed Passion and death of our Lord Jesus Christ, which was accomplished in great earnest and with heavy labour. And when I said[61] that he is scorned, I meant that God scorns him, that is, because he sees him now as he will forever. For in this God revealed that the devil is damned. And I meant this when I said that he ought to be scorned; for I saw that on Judgment Day he will be generally scorned by all who will be saved, of whose salvation he has had great envy. For then he will see that all the woe and tribulation which he has caused them will be changed into the increase of their eternal joy. And all the pain and the sorrow that he wanted to bring them into will go forever with him to hell.

---

59. The rest of this paragraph is not in the short text.
60. Or, as C has: 'this was a vision, to my understanding, of him'.
61. The rest of this chapter is not in the short text.

The Sixth Revelation
The Fourteenth Chapter

After this[62] our Lord said: I thank you for your service and your labour in your youth. And in this my understanding was lifted up into heaven, where I saw our Lord God as a lord in his own house, who has called all his friends to a splendid feast. Then I did not see him seated anywhere in his own house; but I saw him reign in his house as a king and fill it all full of joy and mirth, gladdening and consoling his dear friends with himself, very familiarly and courteously, with wonderful melody in endless love in his own fair blissful countenance, which glorious countenance fills all heaven full of the joy and bliss of the divinity.

God showed[63] three degrees of bliss that every soul will have in heaven who has voluntarily served God in any degree upon earth. The first is the honour and thanks from our Lord God which he will receive when he is delivered from pain. The thanks is so exalted and so honourable that it may seem to him that this suffices him, if there were no more. For it seemed to me that all the pain and labour which all living men might endure could not earn the honourable thanks that one man will have who has voluntarily served God.

As to the second degree, it is that all the blessed in heaven will see the honour of the thanks. God makes the soul's service known to all who are in heaven; and at this time[64] this example was revealed. If a king thank his subjects, it is a great honour for them; and if he make this

---

62. This first sentence, but not the rest of the paragraph, is from the short text.
63. Correspondence with the short text resumes; see p. 139.
64. The rest of this paragraph is not in the short text.

known to all the kingdom, then their honour is much increased.

And for the third degree: It is that the first joy with which the soul is then received will last forevermore. And I saw that this was familiarly and sweetly revealed, that every man's age will be known in heaven, and he will be rewarded for his voluntary service and for the time that he has served, and especially the age of those who voluntarily and freely offer their youth to God is fittingly rewarded and wonderfully thanked. For I saw[65] that whenever or for how long a man or woman is truly turned to God, for the service of one day and for his enduring will he will have all these three degrees of love. And the more that the loving soul sees this courtesy of God, the gladder it is to serve him all its life.

The Seventh Revelation

The Fifteenth Chapter

And after this[66] he revealed a supreme spiritual delight in my soul. In this delight I was filled full of everlasting surety, powerfully secured without any painful fear. This sensation was so welcome and so spiritual that I was wholly at peace, at ease and at rest, so that there was nothing upon earth which could have afflicted me.

This lasted only for a time, and then I was changed, and abandoned to myself, oppressed and weary of my life and ruing myself, so that I hardly had the patience to go on living. I felt that there was no ease or comfort for me except

---

65. The rest of this chapter is not in the short text.
66. Correspondence with the short text resumes; see p. 139.

faith, hope and love, and truly I felt very little of this. And then presently God gave me again comfort and rest for my soul, delight and security so blessedly and so powerfully that there was no fear, no sorrow, no pain, physical or spiritual, that one could suffer which might have disturbed me. And then again I felt the pain, and then afterwards the delight and the joy, now the one and now the other, again and again, I suppose about twenty times. And in the time of joy I could have said with St. Paul: Nothing shall separate me from the love of Christ; and in the pain I could have said with St. Peter: Lord, save me, I am perishing.

This vision was shown to teach me to understand that some souls profit by experiencing this, to be comforted at one time, and at another to fail and to be left to themselves. God wishes us to know that he keeps us safe all the time, in sorrow and in joy; and sometimes a man is left to himself for the profit of his soul, although his sin is not always the cause. For in this time I committed no sin for which I ought to have been left to myself, for it was so sudden. Nor did I deserve these feelings of joy, but our Lord gives it freely when he wills, and sometimes he allows us to be in sorrow, and both are one love. For it is God's will that we do all in our power to preserve our consolation, for bliss lasts forevermore, and pain is passing, and will be reduced to nothing for those who will be saved. Therefore it is not God's will that when we feel pain we should pursue it in sorrow and mourning for it, but that suddenly we should pass it over, and preserve ourselves in the endless delight which is God.

The Eighth Revelation
The Sixteenth Chapter

After this Christ showed me part of his Passion, close to his death. I saw his sweet face as it were dry and bloodless with the pallor of dying, and then deadly pale, languishing, and then the pallor turning blue and then the blue turning brown, as death took more hold upon his flesh. For his Passion appeared to me most vividly in his blessed face, and especially in the lips. I saw there what had become of these four colours, which had appeared to me before as fresh and ruddy, vital and beautiful. This was a painful change to watch, this deep dying, and his nose shrivelled and dried up as I saw; and the sweet body[67] turned brown and black, completely changed and transformed from his naturally beautiful, fresh and vivid complexion into a shrivelled image of death. For at the time when our blessed saviour died upon the Cross, there was a dry, bitter wind, I saw; and when all the precious blood that might had flowed out of his sweet body, still there was some moisture in the sweet flesh as it was revealed. It was dried up from within by bloodlessness and anguish, from without by the blowing of the wind and the cold, all concentrated upon Christ's sweet body; and as the hours passed these four circumstances dried up Christ's flesh. And though this pain was bitter and piercing, still it lasted a very long time. And this pain dried up all the vital fluids in Christ's flesh. Then I saw the sweet flesh drying before my eyes, part after part drying up with astonishing pain. And as long as there was any vital fluid in Christ's flesh, he went on suffering. The long torment[68] impressed me as if he had been dead for a week, dying and on the

---

67. What follows is not in the short text.
68. Correspondence with the short text resumes; see p. 141.

point of death, always suffering this great pain. And when I say[69] that it seemed as if he had been dead for a week, that means, as I have explained, that the sweet body was so discoloured, so dry, so shrivelled, so deathly and so pitiful that he might have been dead for a week, though he went on dying. And it seemed to me as if the greatest and the last pain of his Passion was when his flesh dried up.

The Seventeenth Chapter[70]

And in this drying, what Christ had said came to my mind: I thirst. For I saw in Christ a double thirst, one physical, the other spiritual. This saying was shown for the physical thirst, and what was revealed of the spiritual thirst I shall say afterwards; and concerning the physical thirst, I understood that the body was wholly dried up, for his blessed flesh and bones were left without blood or moisture. The blessed body was left to dry for a long time, with the wrenching of the nails and the weight of the body; for I understood[71] that because of the tenderness of the sweet hands and the sweet feet, through the great and cruel hardness of the nails the wounds grew wide, and the body sagged because of its weight, hanging there for a long time, and the piercing and scraping of the head and the binding of the crown, all clotted with dry blood, with the sweet hair attaching the dry flesh to the thorns, and the thorns attaching to the flesh. And at the beginning, whilst the flesh was fresh and bleeding, the continual pressure of the thorns made the wounds wide. And, too, I saw that the sweet skin and the tender flesh with the hair and the blood was all

---

69. This sentence is not in the short text.
70. The manuscripts make this the beginning of Revelation IX; for the editors' reasons for rejecting this, see *Showings*, I, 95-97.
71. A long passage not in the short text begins here.

scraped and loosened above[72] by the thorns and broken into many fragments, and they were hanging as if they would soon have fallen whilst the body still had natural fluid. How this had happened I did not see, but I understood that it was caused by the sharp thorns and the rough and painful imposition, pitiless, ruthless, of the crown, so that the sweet skin and the flesh broke all in pieces and the hair pulled it from the bones. Through this it was torn in pieces like a cloth, and sagged down, seeming as if it would soon have fallen because it was so heavy and so loose. And that caused me great sorrow and fear, for it seemed to me that I would sooner have died than see it fall.

This continued for a time, and then it began to change; and I watched, and was amazed at how this could be. And then I saw that it was so; what adhered to the crown began to dry and lose weight, and so it was surrounded, as it were crown upon crown. The crown made of thorns was dyed with the blood, and the other crown and the head were all one colour, like congealed dried blood. The skin and the flesh of the face and the body which showed were covered with fine wrinkles, and of a tawny colour, like a dry board which has aged, and the face was more brown than the body.

I saw four ways in which the body dried. The first was through bloodlessness, the second was the consequent pain, the third was that he was hanging up in the air as people hang up a cloth to dry, the fourth was that his physical nature needed liquid, and there was no kind of comfort ministered to him. Ah, hard and grievous was the pain, but it was far harder and more grievous when the fluid failed and everything began to dry, shrivelling so. These were the two pains which showed in the blessed head. The first contributed to the drying, whilst the body was moist, and

---

72. That is, on the forehead. C has 'about'.

the other was slow, with shrivelling and drying as the wind blew on the body from outside, which dried him and tormented him with cold, more than my heart can ponder; and with all his other pains, I saw that all that I can say[73] is inadequate, for it cannot be described.

This revelation of Christ's pains filled me full of pains, for I know well that he suffered only once, but it was his will now to show it to me and fill me with mind of it, as I had asked before[74]. And in all this time that Christ was present to me, I felt no pain except for Christ's pains; and then it came to me that I had little known what pain it was that I had asked, and like a wretch[75] I regretted it, thinking that if I had known what it had been, I should have been reluctant to ask for it. For it seemed to me that my pains exceeded any mortal death. I thought: Is there any pain in hell like this pain? And in my reason I was answered[76]: Hell is a different pain, for in it there is despair. But of all the pains that lead to salvation, this is the greatest, to see the lover[77] suffer. How could any pain be greater than to see him who is all my life, all my bliss and all my joy suffer? Here I felt unshakably that I loved Christ so much more than myself that there was no pain[78] which could be suffered like the sorrow which I felt to see him in pain.

---

73. Correspondence with the short text resumes; see p. 142.
74. The detail which follows in the short text, Julian's mother making to close her eyes, thinking her dead, is omitted here.
75. The rest of this sentence is not in the short text.
76. This answer varies slightly from that in the short text; see p. 142.
77. SS: 'to see your beloved'.
78. The rest of this sentence differs from the short text.

The Eighteenth Chapter

Here I saw part of the compassion of our Lady, St. Mary; for Christ and she were so united in love that the greatness of her love was the cause of the greatness of her pain. For in this[79] I saw a substance of natural love, which is developed by grace, which his creatures have for him, and this natural love was most perfectly and surpassingly revealed in his sweet mother; for as much as she loved him more than all others, her pain surpassed that of all others. For always, the higher, the stronger, the sweeter that love is, the more sorrow it is to the lover to see the body which he loved in pain. And so all his disciples and all his true lovers suffered more pain than they did at the death of their own bodies. For I am sure, by my own experience, that the least of them loved him so much more than they did themselves that it surpasses all that I can say.

Here I saw a great unity between Christ and us, as I understand it; for when he was in pain we were in pain, and all creatures able to suffer pain suffered with him. That is to say[80], all creatures which God has created for our service, the firmament and the earth, failed in their natural functions because of sorrow at the time of Christ's death, for it is their natural characteristic to recognize him as their Lord, in whom all their powers exist. And when he failed, their nature constrained them to fail with him, insofar as they could, because of the sorrow of his sufferings. And so those who were his friends suffered pain because of love, and all creation suffered in general; that is to say, those who did not recognize him suffered because the comfort of all creation failed them, except for God's powerful, secret preservation

---

79. The next two sentences elaborate 'For her pain. . .than all other' in the short text; see p. 142.

80. What follows, leading to the examples of Pilate and Denis, is an elaboration of the short text; see p. 143.

of them. I write of two kinds of people who did not recognize him, who can be understood by two persons.

One was Pilate; the other was St. Denis of France[81], who at that time was a pagan. For when he saw wonders and marvels, sorrows and fears which came at that time, he said: Either the world is coming to an end, or else he who is the Creator of nature is suffering. Therefore he caused to be written on an altar: This is an altar of the unknown god. God in his goodness, who makes the planets and the elements to function according to their natures for the man who is blessed and the man who is accursed, in that time withdrew this from both. So it was that they who did not recognize him were in sorrow at that time.

So was our Lord Jesus afflicted for us; and we all stand in this way of suffering with him, and shall till we come to his bliss, as I shall afterwards say.

The Nineteenth Chapter

At this time[82] I wanted to look away from the cross, but I did not dare, for I knew well that whilst I contemplated the cross I was secure and safe. Therefore I would not agree to put my soul in danger, for apart from the cross there was no safety from the fear of devils.

Then there came a suggestion, seemingly said in friendly manner, to my reason: Look up to heaven to his Father. And then I saw clearly by the faith which I felt that there was nothing between the cross and heaven which could have grieved me. Here I must look up or else answer. I answered inwardly with all the power of my soul, and said: No, I cannot, for you are my heaven. I said this because I

---

81. On the mediaeval conflation of (1) Dionysius the Areopagite, Paul's convert, (2) 'pseudo-Denis', the mystical theologian, and (3) St. Denis, patron of France, see *Showings*, II, 368.

82. Correspondence with the short text resumes; see p. 143.

did not want to look up, for I would rather have remained in that pain until Judgment Day than have come to heaven any other way than by him. For I knew well that he who had bound[83] me so fast would unbind me when it was his will.

So was I taught to choose Jesus for my heaven, whom I saw only in pain at that time. No other heaven was pleasing to me than Jesus, who will be my bliss when I am there. And this has always been a comfort to me, that I chose Jesus by his grace to be my heaven in all this time of suffering and of sorrow. And that has taught me that I should always do so, to choose only Jesus to be my heaven, in well-being and in woe.

And though like a wretch[84] I had regretted what I had asked, as I have said—if I had known the pain for what it was I should have been loath to pray for it—now I saw truly that this was the reluctance and domination of the flesh, to which my soul did not assent, and to which God imputes no blame. Reluctance and deliberate choice are in opposition to one another, and I experienced them both at the same time; and these are two parts, one exterior, the other interior. The exterior part is our mortal flesh, which is sometimes in pain, sometimes in sorrow, and will be so during this life, and I felt it very much at this time; and it was in that part of me that I felt regret. The interior part is an exalted and blessed life which is all peace and love; and this is more secretly experienced; and it was in this part of me that I powerfully, wisely and deliberately chose Jesus for my heaven.

And in this I truly saw that the interior part is the master and ruler of the exterior, attaching no importance, paying no heed to what the exterior part may will, but forever fixing its intention and will upon being united with our Lord Jesus. But it was not revealed to me that the

83. For the editors' reasons for thinking 'bound' more probable than the short text's 'bought' (p. 143), see *Showings*, II, 371.
84. The rest of this chapter is not in the short text.

exterior part would induce agreement in the interior part; but it was revealed that the interior part draws the exterior by grace, and both will be eternally united in bliss through the power of Christ.

The Twentieth Chapter

And so I saw[85] our Lord Jesus languishing for long, because the union in him of the divinity gave strength to his humanity to suffer more than all men could. I mean not only more pain than any other one man could suffer, but also that he suffered more pain than all men who are to be saved, from the first beginning to the last day, may tell or fully think, if we have regard to the honour of the highest, most majestic king and to his shameful, grievous and painful death. For he who is highest and most honourable was most foully brought low, most utterly despised; for the most important[86] point to apprehend in his Passion is to meditate and come to see that he who suffered is God, and then to consider two lesser particulars. One is what he suffered; the other is for whom he suffered.

And in this he partly brought to my mind the exaltedness and nobility of the glorious divinity, and at the same time the preciousness and tenderness of his blessed body united with it, and also the reluctance that there is in human nature to suffer pain. For just as he was most tender and most pure, so he was most strong and powerful to suffer. And he suffered for the sins of every man who will be saved; and he saw and he sorrowed for every man's sorrow, desolation and anguish, in his compassion and love. For as much as our Lady sorrowed for his pains, so much did he suffer sorrow for her sorrows. And furthermore, since

---

85. Correspondence with the short text resumes; see p. 143.
86. The rest of this chapter is not in the short text.

his sweet humanity was more honourable by nature, so long as he was capable of suffering he suffered for us and sorrowed for us. And now he has risen again and is no longer capable of suffering; and yet he suffers with us, as I shall afterwards say. And contemplating all this through his grace, I saw that the love in him which he has for our souls was so strong that he willingly chose suffering with a great desire, and suffered it meekly with a great joy. For when a soul touched by grace contemplates this so, he will truly see that those pains of Christ's Passion surpass all pains, all pains, that is, which will be turned into everlasting joy by the power of Christ's Passion.

It is God's will, as I understand it, that we contemplate his blessed Passion in three ways. Firstly, that we contemplate with contrition and compassion the cruel pain he suffered; and our Lord revealed that at this time, and gave me strength and grace to see it[87].

The Ninth Revelation
The Twenty-First Chapter[88]

And I watched with all my might for the moment when Christ would expire, and I expected to see his body quite dead; but I did not see him so, and just at the moment when by appearances it seemed to me that life could last no longer, and that the revelation of his end must be near, suddenly[89],

---

87. At first sight it appears that the end of chapter 20 has suffered truncation; but the second way of contemplating the Passion will be described in chapter 22, the third in chapter 23.

88. For the editors' reasons for making Revelation IX begin here, and not, as do the manuscripts, with chapter 22, and for making chapter 21 begin here, and not with 'Suddenly, as I looked on the same cross. . .', see *Showings*, I, 95-97.

89. Correspondence with the short text resumes; see p. 144.

as I looked at the same cross, he changed to an appearance of
joy. The change in his blessed appearance changed mine,
and I was as glad and joyful as I could possibly be. And
then cheerfully our Lord suggested to my mind: Where is
there now any instant of your pain or of your grief? And I
was very joyful; I understood[90] that in our Lord's intention
we are now on his cross with him in our pains, and in our
sufferings we are dying, and with his help and his grace we
willingly endure on that same cross until the last moment of
life. Suddenly he will change his appearance for us, and we
shall be with him in heaven. Between the one and the other
all will be a single era[91]; and then all will be brought into
joy. And this was what he meant in this revelation: Where is
there now any instant of your pain or of your grief? And we
shall be full of joy. And here I saw truly that if he revealed
to us now his countenance of joy, there is no pain on earth
or anywhere else which could trouble us, but everything
would be joy and bliss for us. But because he shows us his
suffering countenance, as he was in this life as he carried his
cross, we are therefore in suffering and labour with him as
our nature requires. And the reason why he suffers is
because in his goodness he wishes to make us heirs with him
of his joy. And for this little pain which we suffer here we
shall have an exalted and eternal knowledge in God which
we could never have without it. And the harder our pains
have been with him on his cross, the greater will our glory
be with him in his kingdom.

---

90. The rest of this chapter is not in the short text.
91. Literally, 'all will be one time', but SS have 'no time'. P, C seem to mean that
this side of eternity we shall not find the world changing, SS that we shall be in eternity in
no time at all, 'In a moment, in a twinkling of an eye' (I Corinthians 15.22).

The Twenty-Second Chapter

Then our good Lord[92] put a question to me: Are you well satisfied that I suffered for you? I said: Yes, good Lord, all my thanks to you; yes, good Lord, blessed may you be. Then Jesus our good Lord said: If you are satisfied, I am satisfied. It is a joy, a bliss, an endless delight to me that ever I suffered my Passion for you; and if I could suffer more, I should suffer more. In response to this my understanding was lifted up into heaven, and there I saw three heavens; and at this sight I was greatly astonished, and I thought: I see three heavens, and all are of the blessed humanity of Christ. And none is greater, none is less, none is higher, none is lower, but all are equal in their joy.

For the first heaven, Christ showed me his Father, not in any bodily likeness but in his attributes and in his operations[93]. That is to say[94], I saw in Christ that the Father is. For the Father's operation is this: He rewards his Son, Jesus Christ. This gift and this reward is so joyful to Jesus that his Father could have given him no reward which could have pleased him better. For the first heaven, which is the pleasure of the Father, appeared to me as a heaven, and it was full of bliss. For he[95] is well pleased with all the deeds that Jesus has done for our salvation; and therefore we are his, not only through our redemption but also by his Father's courteous gift. We are his bliss, we are his reward, we are his honour, we are his crown. And this[96] was a singular wonder and a most delectable contemplation, that we are his crown.

---

92. Correspondence with the short text resumes; see p. 144.
93. Compare the short text, p. 145, 'and in his joy', and *Showings*, II, 383.
94. This sentence is not in the short text.
95. In the short text this is ambiguous, and has been given as 'Jesus'; here, plainly, it refers to the Father.
96. This phrase is not in the short text.

What I am describing now is so a great joy to Jesus that he counts as nothing his labour and his sufferings and his cruel and shameful death. And in these words: If I could suffer more, I should suffer more, I saw truly that as often as he could die, so often should he die, and love would never let him rest till he had done it. And I contemplated[97] with great diligence to know how often he should die if he would. And truly the number so far exceeded my understanding and intelligence that my reason had not leave or power to comprehend or accept it.

And when[98] he had died or would die so often, he would count it all as nothing for love, for everything seems only little to him in comparison with his love. For although[99] the sweet humanity of Christ could suffer only once, his goodness can never cease offering it. Every day he is ready to do the same, if that might be. For if he said that he would for love of me make new heavens and new earths, that would by comparison be only little, for this he could do if he wished every day without any labour. But to die for my love so often that the number exceeds human reckoning, that is the greatest offer that our Lord God could make to man's soul, as I see it.

Then his meaning is this: How could it be that I should not do for love of you all that I was able? To do this does not grieve me, since I would for love of you die so often, paying no heed to my cruel pains. And this I saw as the second way of contemplating his blessed Passion. The love which made him suffer it surpasses all his sufferings, as much as heaven is above earth; for the suffering was a noble, precious and honourable deed, performed once in time by the operation of love. And love was without beginning, it is and shall be without end. And for this love he said very

---

97. The rest of this paragraph is not in the short text.
98. This sentence is in the short text; see p. 145.
99. What follows is not in the short text.

sweetly this: If I could suffer more[100], I should suffer more. He did not say: If it were necessary to suffer more, but: If I could suffer more; for although it might not have been necessary, if he could suffer more he would. This deed and this work for our salvation were as well devised as God could devise it. It was done as honourably as Christ could do it, and here I saw complete joy in Christ, for his joy would not have been complete if the deed could have been done any better than it was.

The Twenty-Third Chapter

And in these three sayings: It is a joy, a bliss and an endless delight to me, there were shown to me three heavens, and in this way. By 'joy' I understood that the Father was pleased, and by 'bliss' that the Son was honoured, and by 'endless delight' the Holy Spirit. The Father is pleased, the Son is honoured, the Holy Spirit takes delight. And here[101] I saw the third way of contemplating his blessed Passion, that is to say the joy and the bliss which make him take delight in it. For our courteous Lord showed his Passion to me in five ways, of which the first is the bleeding of the head, the second the discolouration of his blessed face, the third is the copious bleeding of the body in the furrows made by the scourging[102], the fourth is the deep drying—these four ways, as is said before, were for the sufferings of the Passion—and the fifth is this which was revealed for the joy and the bliss of the Passion.

For it is God's will that we have true delight with him in our salvation, and in it he wants us to be greatly comforted and strengthened, and so joyfully he wishes our

---

100. Correspondence with the short text resumes; see p. 145.
101. What follows is not in the short text.
102. Or 'a representation of the scourging'; see p. 199, note 52.

souls to be occupied with his grace. For we are his bliss, because he endlessly delights in us; and so with his grace shall we delight in him. All that he does for us and has done and will do was never expense or labour to him, nor could it be, except only that he died[103] in our humanity, beginning at the sweet Incarnation and lasting until his blessed Resurrection on Easter morning. So long did the labour and expense of our redemption last, in which deed he always and endlessly rejoices, as it is said before.

Ah, Jesus[104], let us pay heed to this bliss over our salvation which is in the blessed Trinity, and let us desire to have as much spiritual delight by his grace, as it is said before. That is to say[105], let our delight in our salvation be like the joy which Christ has in our salvation, as much as that may be whilst we are here.

All the Trinity worked in Christ's Passion, administering abundant virtues and plentiful grace to us by him; but only the virgin's Son suffered, in which all the blessed Trinity rejoice. And this was shown[106] to me when he said: Are you well satisfied? And by what Christ next said: If you are well satisfied, I am well satisfied; it was as if he had said: This is joy and delight enough for me, and I ask nothing else from you for my labour but that I may satisfy you.

And in this[107] he brought to my mind the qualities of a cheerful giver. Always a cheerful giver pays only little attention to the thing which he is giving, but all his desire and all his intention is to please and comfort the one to whom he is giving it. And if the receiver accept the gift gladly and gratefully, then the courteous giver counts as

---

103. S2: 'what he did'.
104. Correspondence with the short text resumes (see p. 146); but what is there statement of fact here becomes apostrophe.
105. What follows is not in the short text.
106. Correspondence with the short text resumes.
107. The next three sentences are not in the short text.

nothing all his expense and his labour, because of the joy and the delight that he has because he has pleased and comforted the one whom he loves. Generously[108] and completely was this revealed to me.

So think wisely how great is this word 'ever', for in that was revealed exalted understanding of the love that he has in our salvation, with the manifold joys[109] which follow from the Passion of Christ. One is that he rejoices that he has accomplished the deed and will suffer no more. Another is that he has by it redeemed us from endless torment in hell. Another is that he brought us up into heaven and made us his crown and his everlasting bliss.

The Tenth Revelation
The Twenty-Fourth Chapter

With a kindly countenance our good Lord looked into his side[110], and he gazed with joy, and with his sweet regard he drew his creature's understanding into his side by the same wound; and there he revealed a fair and delectable place, large enough for all mankind that will be saved and will rest in peace and in love. And with that he brought to mind the dear and precious blood and water which he suffered to be shed for love. And in this sweet sight he showed his blessed heart split in two, and as he rejoiced he showed to my understanding a part of his blessed divinity, as much as was his will at that time, strengthening my poor soul to understand what can be said, that is the endless love

---

108. Correspondence with the short text resumes; see p. 146.
109. The rest of this chapter is not in the short text.
110. Correspondence with the short text resumes (see p. 146); but after this first sentence the rest of the chapter is original to the long text.

which was without beginning and is and always shall be.

And with this our good Lord said most joyfully: See how I love you, as if he had said, my darling, behold and see your Lord, your God, who is your Creator and your endless joy; see your own brother, your saviour; my child, behold and see what delight and bliss I have in your salvation, and for my love rejoice with me.

And for my greater understanding, these blessed words were said: See how I love you, as if he had said, behold and see that I loved you so much, before I died for you, that I wanted to die for you. And now I have died for you, and willingly suffered what I could. And now all my bitter pain and my hard labour is turned into everlasting joy and bliss for me and for you. How could it now be that you would pray to me for anything pleasing to me which I would not very gladly grant to you? For my delight is in your holiness and in your endless joy and bliss in me.

This is the understanding, as simply as I can say it, of these blessed words: See how I loved you. Our Lord revealed this to make us glad and joyful.

The Eleventh Revelation
The Twenty-Fifth Chapter

And with this same appearance[111] of mirth and joy our good Lord looked down on his right, and brought to my mind where our Lady stood at the time of his Passion, and he said: Do you wish to see her? And these sweet words[112] were as if he had said, I know well that you wish to see my

---

111. Correspondence with the short text resumes; see p. 146.
112. What follows is not in the short text.

blessed mother, for after myself she is the greatest joy that I
could show you, and the greatest delight and honour to me,
and she is what all my blessed creatures most desire to see.
And because of the wonderful, exalted and singular love that
he has for this sweet maiden, his blessed mother, our Lady
St. Mary, he reveals her bliss and joy through the sense of
these sweet words, as if he said, do you wish to see how I
love her, so that you could rejoice with me in the love which
I have in her and she has in me?

And for greater understanding of these sweet words our
good Lord speaks in love to all mankind who will be saved,
addressing them all as one person[113], as if he said, do you
wish to see in her how you are loved? It is for love of you
that I have made her so exalted, so noble, so honourable;
and this delights me. And I wish it to delight you. For next
to him, she is the most blissful to be seen. But in this matter
I was not taught to long to see her bodily presence whilst I
am here, but the virtues of her blessed soul, her truth, her
wisdom, her love, through which I am taught to know
myself and reverently to fear my God.

And when our good Lord had revealed this, and said
these words: Do you wish to see her? I answered[114] and
said: Yes, good Lord, great thanks, yes, good Lord, if it be
your will. Often times I had prayed for this, and I had
expected to see her in a bodily likeness[115]; but I did not see
her so. And Jesus, saying this, showed me a spiritual vision
of her. Just as before I had seen her small and simple, now
he showed her high and noble and glorious and more
pleasing to him than all creatures. And so he wishes it to be
known that all who take delight in him should take delight in

---

113. In the original all Julian's locutions are in the second person singular: 'Wilt
thou. . .?'

114. Correspondence with the short text resumes; see p. 146.

115. P, C have 'lykyng', 'delight', which is defensible; but SS have 'presence', and see
the short text, 'likeness', which seems superior.

her, and in the delight that he has in her and she in him[116].

And for greater understanding[117] he showed this example, as if, when a man loves some creature particularly, more than all other creatures, he will make all other creatures to love and delight in that creature whom he loves so much. And in these words which Jesus said: Do you wish to see her? it seemed to me that these were the most delectable words which he could give me in this spiritual vision of her which he gave me. For our Lord showed me no particular person except our Lady St. Mary, and he showed her on three occasions. The first was as she conceived, the second was as she had been under the Cross, and the third was as she is now, in delight, honour and joy.

The Twelfth Revelation
The Twenty-Sixth Chapter

And after this our Lord showed himself to me, and he appeared to me more glorified than I had seen him before, in which I was taught[118] that our soul will never have rest till it comes into him, acknowledging that he is full of joy, familiar and courteous and blissful and true life. Again and again our Lord said: I am he, I am he, I am he who is highest. I am he whom you love. I am he in whom you delight. I am he whom you serve. I am he for whom you long. I am he whom you desire. I am he whom you intend. I am he who is all. I am he whom Holy Church preaches and teaches to you. I am he who showed himself before to you. The

---

116. 'And in the delight. . .she in him': supplied from SS, which agree with the short text; P, C omit.

117. This sentence is not in the short text.

118. In what follows, this sentence is significantly different from the short text; see p. 147.

number[119] of the words surpasses my intelligence and my understanding and all my powers, for they were the most exalted, as I see it, for in them is comprehended I cannot tell what; but the joy which I saw when they were revealed surpasses all that the heart can think or the soul may desire. And therefore these words are not explained here[120], but let every man accept them as our Lord intended them, according to the grace God gives him in understanding and love.

The Thirteenth Revelation
The Twenty-Seventh Chapter

And after this[121] our Lord brought to my mind the longing that I had for him before, and I saw that nothing hindered me but sin, and I saw that this is true of us all in general, and it seemed to me that if there had been no sin, we should all have been pure and as like our Lord as he created us. And so in my folly before this time I often wondered why, through the great prescient[122] wisdom of God, the beginning of sin was not prevented. For then it seemed to me that all would have been well.

The impulse to think this was greatly to be shunned; and nevertheless I mourned and sorrowed on this account, unreasonably, lacking discretion[123]. But Jesus, who in this vision informed me about everything needful to me,

---

119. The rest of this chapter differs from the short text.
120. On the significance of this for the first and second versions of the long text, see Introduction.
121. Correspondence with the short text resumes; see p. 147.
122. P, C have 'aforesaid'; but SS agree with the short text.
123. The long text omits the short text's 'filled with pride'.

answered with these words[124] and said: Sin is necessary[125], but all will be well, and all will be well, and every kind of thing will be well. In this naked word 'sin', our Lord brought generally to my mind all which is not good, and the shameful contempt and the direst tribulation which he endured for us in this life, and his death and all his pains, and the passions, spiritual and bodily, of all his creatures. For we are all in part troubled[126], and we shall be troubled[127], following our master Jesus until we are fully purged of our mortal flesh and all our inward affections which are not very good.

And with the beholding of this, with all the pains that ever were or ever will be, I understood Christ's Passion for the greatest and surpassing pain. And yet this was shown to me in an instant, and it quickly turned into consolation. For our good Lord would not have the soul frightened by this ugly sight. But I did not see sin, for I believe that it has no kind of substance, no share in being, nor can it be recognized except by the pain caused by it. And it seems to me that this pain is something for a time, for it purges and makes us know ourselves and ask for mercy; for the Passion of our Lord is comfort to us against all this, and that is his blessed will. And because of the tender love which our good Lord has for all who will be saved, he comforts readily and sweetly, meaning this: It is true that sin is the cause of all this pain[128], but all will be well, and every kind of thing will be well.

These words were revealed most tenderly, showing no kind of blame to me or to anyone who will be saved. So it would be most unkind of me to blame God or marvel at him

---

124. This omits 'I do not say that I need. . .' and the rest of that paragraph in the short text.
125. The rest of this sentence is not found at this point in the short text.
126. SS agree with the short text: 'denied'.
127. *Ibid*.
128. 'It is true. . .pain': not in the short text.

on account of my sins, since he does not blame me for sin.

And in these same words[129] I saw hidden in God an exalted and wonderful mystery, which he will make plain and we shall know in heaven. In this knowledge we shall truly see the cause why he allowed sin to come, and in this sight we shall rejoice forever.

The Twenty-Eighth Chapter

So I saw[130] how Christ has compassion on us because of sin; and just as I was before filled full of pain and compassion on account of Christ's Passion, so I was now in part filled with compassion for all my fellow Christians, because[131] he loves very dearly the people who will be saved, that is to say God's servants. Holy Church will be shaken in sorrow and anguish and tribulation in this world as men shake a cloth in the wind; and in this matter our Lord answered, revealing in this way: Ah, I shall turn this into a great thing, of endless honour and everlasting joy, in heaven. Yes, I even saw that our Lord rejoices with pity and compassion over the tribulations of his servants; and he imposes on every person whom he loves, to bring him to his bliss, something that is no defect in his sight, through which souls are humiliated and despised in this world, scorned and mocked and rejected. And he does this to prevent the harm which they might have from the pomps and the pride and the vainglory of this wretched life, and to prepare their way to come to heaven, into endless, everlasting bliss. For he says: I shall completely break down in you your empty affections and your vicious pride, and then I shall gather you

---

129. This last paragraph of chapter 27 is not in the short text.
130. Correspondence with the short text resumes; see p. 149.
131. The rest of this paragraph is not in the short text.

and make you meek and mild, pure and holy through union with me.

And then I saw that every natural compassion which one has for one's fellow Christians in love is Christ in us, and that[132] every kind of self-humiliation which he manifested in his Passion was manifested again in this compassion, in which there were two different understandings of our Lord's intention. One was the bliss that we are brought to, in which he wants us to rejoice. The other is for consolation in our pain, for he wants us to know that it will all be turned to our honour and profit by the power of his Passion, and to know that we suffered in no way alone, but together with him, and to see in him our foundation. And he wants us to see that his pains and his tribulation exceed all that we may suffer so far that it cannot be comprehended in full. And if we well contemplate his will in this, it keeps us from lamenting and despairing as we experience our pains; and if we see truly that our sins deserve them, still his love excuses us. And of his great courtesy he puts away all our blame, and regards us with pity and compassion as innocent and guiltless children.

The Twenty-Ninth Chapter

But in this I stood[133], contemplating it generally, darkly and mournfully, saying in intention to our Lord with very great fear: Ah, good Lord, how could all things be well, because of the great harm which has come through sin to your creatures? And here I wished, so far as I dared, for some plainer explanation through which I might be at ease about this matter. And to this our blessed Lord answered,

132. The rest of this chapter is not in the short text
133. Correspondence with the short text resumes; but see p. 149, 'But I shall study. . .'

very meekly and with a most loving manner, and he showed that Adam's sin was the greatest harm ever done or ever to be done until the end of the world. And he also showed me that this is plainly known to all Holy Church upon earth.

Furthermore, he taught that I should contemplate the glorious atonement, for this atoning is more pleasing to the blessed divinity and more honourable for man's salvation, without comparison, than ever Adam's sin was harmful. So then this is our blessed Lord's intention, and in this teaching we should pay heed to this: For since I have set right the greatest of harms, then it is my will that you should know through this that I shall set right everything which is less.

The Thirtieth Chapter

He gave understanding of two portions. One portion is our saviour and our salvation. This blessed portion is open, clear, fair and bright and plentiful, for all men who are of good will are comprehended in this portion. We are bound[134] to this by God, and drawn and counselled and taught, inwardly by the Holy Spirit, and outwardly through the same grace by Holy Church. Our Lord wants us to be occupied in this, rejoicing in him, for he rejoices in us. And the more plentifully we accept from this with reverence and humility, the more do we deserve thanks from him, and the more profit do we win for ourselves. And so we may see and rejoice that our portion is our Lord.

The other portion is hidden from us and closed, that is to say all which is additional to our salvation; for this is our Lord's privy counsel, and it is fitting to God's royal dominion to keep his privy counsel in peace, and it is fitting to his servants out of obedience and respect not to wish to know his counsel.

---

134. The short text has 'bidden'.

Our Lord has pity and compassion on us because some creatures occupy themselves so much in this; and I am sure that if we knew how greatly we should please him and solace ourselves by leaving it alone, we should do so. The saints in heaven, they wish to know nothing but what our Lord wishes them to know, and furthermore their love and their desire are governed according to our Lord's will; and we should do this, so that our will resembles theirs. Then we shall not wish or desire anything but the will of our Lord, as they do, for we are all one in God's intention.

And in this I was taught that we shall rejoice only in our blessed saviour Jesus, and trust in him for everything.

The Thirty-First Chapter

And so our good Lord answered to all the questions and doubts which I could raise, saying most comfortingly: I may make all things well, and I can make all things well, and I shall make all things well, and I will make all things well; and you will see yourself that every kind of thing will be well. When he says 'I may', I understand this to apply to the Father; and when he says 'I can', I understand it for the Son; and when he says 'I will', I understand it for the Holy Spirit; and when he says 'I shall', I understand it for the unity of the blessed Trinity, three persons and one truth[135]; and when he says 'You will see yourself', I understand it for the union of all men who will be saved in the blessed Trinity.

And in these five words God wishes us to be enclosed[136] in rest and in peace. And so Christ's spiritual

---

135. It will be observed that in the locution the order of the auxiliary verbs differs, but in both texts the expositions follow the same order, 'I may', 'I can', 'I will', 'I shall', suggesting that the long text reports Julian more accurately.

136. This is more plausible than the short text's 'God wishes to be enclosed'.

thirst will have an end. For this is Christ's spiritual thirst, his longing in love, which persists and always will until we see him on the day of judgment, for we who shall be saved and shall be Christ's joy and bliss are still here, and some are yet to come, and so will some be until that day. Therefore this is his thirst and his longing in love for us, to gather us all here into him, to our endless joy, as I see it. For we are not now so wholly in him as we then shall be.

For we know[137] in our faith, and it was also revealed in all this, that Christ Jesus is both God and man; and in his divinity he is himself supreme bliss, and was from without beginning, and he will be without end, which true everlasting bliss cannot of its nature be increased or diminished. And this was plentifully seen in every revelation, and especially in the twelfth, where he says: I am he who is highest[138]. And with respect to Christ's humanity, it is known in our faith and it was also revealed that with all the power of his divinity, for love, to bring us to his bliss, he suffered pains and Passion and he died. And these are the deeds of Christ's humanity, in which he rejoices; and that he revealed in the ninth revelation, where he says: It is a joy, a bliss, an endless delight to me that ever I suffered my Passion for you[139]. And this is the bliss of Christ's deeds, and this is what he means when he says in the same revelation: We are his bliss, we are his reward, we are his honour, we are his crown[140]. For insofar as Christ is our head, he is glorious and impassible; but with respect to his body, to which all his members are joined, he is not yet fully glorified or wholly impassible. For he still has that same thirst and longing which he had upon the Cross, which

---

137. The rest of this chapter and the first paragraph of chapter 32 are not in the short text.

138. See p. 223.

139. See p. 216.

140. See p. 216. In fact, the words are Julian's, and by 'he says' she can only mean that she believes her entire book to be divinely inspired.

desire, longing and thirst, as I see it, were in him from without beginning; and he will have this until the time that the last soul which will be saved has come up into his bliss.

For as truly as there is in God a quality of pity and compassion, so truly is there in God a quality of thirst and longing; and the power of this longing in Christ enables us to respond to his longing, and without this no soul comes to heaven. And this quality of longing and thirst comes from God's everlasting goodness, just as the quality of pity comes from his everlasting goodness. And though he may have both longing and pity, they are different qualities, as I see them; and this is the characteristic of spiritual thirst, which will persist in him so long as we are in need, and will draw us up into his bliss.

And all this was seen to reveal his compassion, for on Judgment Day that will cease. So he has pity and compassion for us, and he has longing to possess us, but his wisdom and his love do not allow the end to come until the best time.

The Thirty-Second Chapter

On one occasion our good Lord said: Every kind of thing will be well[141]; and on another occasion he said: You will see yourself that every kind of thing will be well[142]. And from these two the soul gained different kinds of understanding. One was this: that he wants us to know that he takes heed not only of things which are noble and great, but also of those which are little and small, of humble men and simple, of this man and that man. And this is what he means when he says: Every kind of thing will be well. For he wants us to know that the smallest thing will not be

---

141. See p. 225.
142. See p. 229.

forgotten. Another understanding is this: that there are many deeds which in our eyes are so evilly done and lead to such great harms that it seems to us impossible that any good result could ever come of them. And we contemplate this and sorrow and mourn for it so that we cannot rest in the blessed contemplation of God as we ought to do. And the cause is this: that the reason which we use is now so blind, so abject and so stupid that we cannot recognize God's exalted, wonderful wisdom, or the power and the goodness of the blessed Trinity. And this is his intention when he says: You will see yourself that every kind of thing will be well, as if he said: Accept it now in faith and trust, and in the very end you will see truly, in fulness of joy.

And so[143] in the same five words said before: I may make all things well[144], I understand a powerful comfort from all the works of our Lord God which are still to come.

There is a deed[145] which the blessed Trinity will perform on the last day, as I see it, and what the deed will be and how it will be performed is unknown to every creature who is inferior to Christ, and it will be until the deed is done. The goodness and the love of our Lord God want us to know that this will be, and his power and his wisdom, through the same love, want to conceal it and hide it from us, what it will be and how it will be done. And the cause why he wants us to know it like this is because he wants us to be at ease in our souls and at peace in love, disregarding every disturbance which could hinder our true rejoicing in him.

This is the great deed ordained by our Lord God from without beginning, treasured and hidden in his blessed breast, known only to himself, through which deed he will

---

143. This paragraph corresponds with the short text; see p. 152.
144. See p. 229
145. The rest of this chapter, and the first two paragraphs of chapter 33, are not in the short text.

make all things well. For just as the blessed Trinity created
all things from nothing, just so will the same blessed Trinity
make everything well which is not well. And I marvelled
greatly at this sight, and contemplated our faith, with this in
my mind: Our faith is founded on God's word, and it
belongs to our faith that we believe that God's word will be
preserved in all things. And one article of our faith is that   ✶
many creatures will be damned, such as the angels who fell
out of heaven because of pride, who now are devils, and
many men upon earth who die out of the faith of Holy
Church, that is to say those who are pagans and many who
have received baptism and who live unchristian lives and so
die out of God's love. All these will be eternally condemned
to hell, as Holy Church teaches me to believe.

And all this being so, it seemed to me that it was
impossible that every kind of thing should be well, as our
Lord revealed at this time. And to this I had no other
answer as a revelation from our Lord except this: What is
impossible to you is not impossible to me. I shall preserve
my word in everything, and I shall make everything well.
And in this I was taught by the grace of God that I ought to
keep myself steadfastly in the faith, as I had understood   ✶ ✶
before, and that at the same time I should stand firm and
believe firmly that every kind of thing will be well, as our
Lord revealed at that same time. For this is the great deed
which our Lord will do, and in this deed he will preserve his
word in everything. And he will make well all which is not
well. But what the deed will be and how it will be done,
there is no creature who is inferior to Christ who knows it,
or will know it until it has been done, according to the
understanding which I received of our Lord's meaning at this
time.

The Thirty-Third Chapter

And yet in this I desired, so far as I dared, that I might have had some sight of hell and of purgatory; but it was not my intention to make trial of anything which belongs to our faith, for I believed steadfastly that hell and purgatory exist for the same ends as Holy Church teaches. But my intention was to have seen for instruction in everything which belongs to my faith, whereby I could live more to God's glory and to my profit. But for all that I could wish, I could see nothing at all of this except what has already been said in the fifth revelation, where I saw that the devil is reproved by God and endlessly condemned[146]. By this sight I understand that every creature who is of the devil's condition in this life and so dies is no more mentioned before God and all his saints than is the devil, notwithstanding that they belong to the human race, whether they have been baptized or not; for although the revelation was shown to reveal goodness, and little mention was made in it of evil, still I was not drawn by it away from any article of the faith which Holy Church teaches me to believe. For I had sight of Christ's Passion in various revelations, in the first, in the second, in the fourth, in the eighth, as is already related, in which I had partial feeling of our Lady's sorrow, and of his faithful friends who saw his pains. But I saw nothing so exactly specified concerning the Jews who put him to death; and nonetheless I knew in my faith that they were eternally accursed and condemned, except those who were converted by grace.

And I was strengthened and generally taught to preserve myself in every article of the faith, and in everything which I had before understood, hoping that I was, by God's mercy and grace, in faith, and intending with desire and prayers to continue in it until my life's end.

---

146. See p. 202.

It is God's will[147] that we pay great heed to all the deeds which he has performed, for he wishes us to know from them and to trust and believe all which he will do. But always[148] we must avoid pondering what the deed will be, and wish to be like our brothers, who are the saints in heaven, who want nothing else than God's will. Then shall we rejoice only in God, and be well satisfied both with what he conceals and what he reveals. For I saw truly in our Lord's intention that the more we busy ourselves in that or in anything else, the further we shall be from knowing.

The Thirty-Fourth Chapter

Our Lord showed[149] two kinds of mystery. One is this great mystery, with all the individual mysteries pertaining to it, and these he wishes us to know as hidden until the time that he wishes to reveal them to us plainly. The other is the mysteries which he himself plainly showed in this revelation, for these are mysteries which he wishes to make open and known to us, for he wishes us to know that it is his will that we know them. They are mysteries to us, but not only because he wants them to be mysteries to us, but also because of our blindness and our ignorance. And therefore he has great pity, and therefore he wants to make them plain to us himself, so that we may know him and love him and cling to him. For everything which is profitable for us to understand and know our good Lord will most courteously show to us by all the preaching and teaching of Holy Church.

God showed the very great delight that he has in all men and women who accept, firmly and wisely, the

---

147. Correspondence with the short text resumes; see p. 152.
148. The rest of the paragraph is not in the short text.
149. This first paragraph is not in the short text.

preaching and teaching of Holy Church, for he is that Holy Church. He is the foundation, he is the substance, he is the teacher, he is the end, he is the reward[150] for which every loving soul labours; and this[151] is known and will be known to every soul to whom the Holy Spirit declares this. And I truly hope[152] that all those who seek in this way will prosper, for they are seeking God.

All this which I have now said, and more which I shall presently say, is a solace against sin; for in the third revelation, when I saw that God does everything which is done[153], I did not see sin, and then I saw that all is well. But when God did show me about sin, then he said: All will be well.

The Thirty-Fifth Chapter

And when almighty God had shown me his goodness so plenteously and so fully, I wished to know, concerning a certain creature whom I loved, if it would continue in the good living which I hoped had been begun by the grace of God[154]; and in this particular wish it seemed that I impeded myself, for I was not then told this. And then I was answered in my reason, as it were by a friendly intermediary: Accept it generally, and contemplate the courtesy of your Lord God as he revealed it to you, for it is more honour to God to contemplate him in all things than in any one special thing. I agreed, and with that I learned that it is more honour to God to know everything in general than it is to take delight in any special thing. And if I were to act

---

150. This is more plausible than the short text's 'means', p. 153.
151. The short text has 'he'.
152. The short text has 'And I am certain'.
153. See p. 197.
154. See the short text, p. 153: 'concerning a certain person whom I loved, what her future would be'.

wisely, in accordance with this teaching, I should not be
glad because of any special thing or be greatly distressed by
anything at all, for all will be well; for the fulness[155] of joy
is to contemplate God in everything.

For by the same blessed power, wisdom and love by
which he made all things, our good Lord always leads them
to the same end, and he himself will bring them there, and
at the right time we shall see it. And the foundation of this
was shown in the first revelation, and more plainly in the
third, where it says: I saw God in an instant of time[156].
Everything which our Lord God does is righteous, and all
which he tolerates is honourable; and in these two are good
and evil comprehended. For our Lord does everything which
is good, and our Lord tolerates what is evil. I do not say that
evil is honourable, but I say that our Lord God's toleration
is honourable, through which his goodness will be known
eternally, and his wonderful meekness and mildness by this
working of mercy and grace.

Righteousness is that which is so good that it cannot be
better than it is, for God himself is true righteousness, and
all his works are righteously performed, as they are ordained
from eternity by his exalted power, his exalted wisdom, his
exalted goodness. And what he has ordained for the best he
constantly brings to pass in the same way, and directs to the
same end. And he is always fully pleased with himself and
with all his works. And the contemplation of this blessed
harmony is most sweet to the soul which sees it by grace.
All the souls which will be saved in heaven without end are
made righteous in the sight of God and by his own
goodness, in which righteousness we are endlessly and
marvellously protected, above all creatures.

And mercy is an operation which comes from the
goodness of God, and it will go on operating so long as sin is

---

155. The rest of this chapter is not in the short text.
156. See p. 197.

permitted to harass righteous souls. And when sin is no longer permitted to harass, then the operation of mercy will cease. And then all will be brought into righteousness and stand fast there forever. By his toleration we fall, and in his blessed love, with his power and his wisdom, we are protected, and by mercy and grace we are raised to much more joy. And so in righteousness and in mercy he wishes to be known and loved, now and forever. And the soul that wisely contemplates[157] in grace is well satisfied with both, and endlessly delights.

The Thirty-Sixth Chapter[158]

Our Lord God revealed that a deed will be done[159], and he himself will do it, and it will be honourable and wonderful and plentiful, and it will be done with respect to me[160], and he himself will do it. And this is the highest joy that the soul understood, that God himself will do it, and I shall do nothing at all but sin; and my sin will not impede the operation of his goodness. And I saw that the contemplation of this is a heavenly joy in a soul which fears God and always lovingly through grace desires the will of God. This deed will be begun here, and it will be honour to God and to the plentiful profit of all his lovers on earth; and as we come to heaven each one of us will see it with wonderful joy; and it will go on operating until the last day. And the honour and the bliss of it will last in heaven before God and all his holy saints eternally.

Thus was this deed seen and understood in our Lord's

---

157. SS: 'contemplates it'.
158. This chapter is not in the short text.
159. See chapter 32, p. 232.
160. P, C (SS do not report): 'by him'; but this is plainly the emendation of some scribe-editor. What Julian means is clear later in this chapter, p. 239: 'And this is the meaning. . .'

intention, and the reason why he revealed it is to make us rejoice in him and in all his works.

When I saw how the revelation continued, I understood that it was revealed as a great thing which was to come, which God revealed that he himself would do; and this deed has the properties[161] already described. And this he showed most blessedly, intending me to accept it wisely, faithfully and trustfully. But what the deed would be was kept secret from me. And in this I saw that he does not wish us to be afraid to know those things which he reveals. He reveals them because he wants us to know them, and by that knowledge he wants us to love him and delight in him and endlessly rejoice in him. And for the great love which he has for us he reveals to us everything which is at the time to his glory and our profit. And those things which he now wants to keep secret he still in his great goodness reveals, but not openly[162]. In this revelation he wants us to believe and understand that we shall truly see it in his endless bliss. Then we ought to rejoice in him for everything which he reveals and for everything which he conceals; and if we do so, willingly and meekly, we shall find great comfort in it, and we shall have endless thanks from him for it.

And this is the meaning of this saying, that it will be done with respect to me, that is, men in general, that is to say all who will be saved; it will be honourable, wonderful and plentiful, and it will be done with respect to me; and God himself will do it; and this will be the highest joy which can be contemplated in the deed, that God himself will do it, and that man will do nothing at all but sin.

So our good Lord means as if he said, behold and see; here you have the matter[163] of meekness, here you have the

---

161. That is, it is 'honourable and wonderful and plentiful'.

162. Ms: 'close'. Julian probably has in mind chancery practice, when letters were issued 'close' (sealed) or 'open'. See *Showings*, II, 433.

163. Julian uses the term in its philosophical sense—the existence, first result of creation, to which form is to be given.

matter of love, here you have the matter of self-knowledge, here you have the matter of rejoicing in me. And for my love rejoice in me, for in this of all things you could most please me. And so long as we are in this life, whenever we in our folly revert to the contemplation of those who are damned, our Lord tenderly teaches us and blessedly calls us, saying in our souls: Leave me alone, my beloved child, attend to me. I am enough for you, and rejoice in your saviour and in your salvation. And I am sure that this is our Lord working in us. The soul which is pierced with this[164] by grace will see it and feel it. And even though this deed may truly be accepted as done for men in general, still this does not exclude particular men; for what our good Lord wishes to do with respect to his poor creatures is not known to me.

But this deed and the other described before[165] are not both the same, but two and separate. But this deed will be sooner known, and the other will be when we come to heaven; and by them to whom our Lord gives it, this may partly be known here, but the great deed described before will be known neither in heaven nor on earth until it is done.

And furthermore, he gave special understanding and teaching about the working and revelation of miracles, thus: It is known that I have performed miracles in time past, many, most great and wonderful, glorious and splendid, and what I have done I always go on doing, and I shall in times to come. It is known that before miracles come sorrows and anguish and trouble, and that because we ought to know our own weakness and the harm that we have fallen into through sin, to humble us and make us cry to God for help and grace. And afterwards great miracles come, and that is from

---

164. SS: 'the soul which is perceived in this', which is less probable.
165. See chapter 32, p. 232: 'There is a deed which the blessed Trinity will perform. . .'

God's great power and wisdom and goodness, showing his might and the joys of heaven, so much as this may be in this passing life, and that is for the strengthening of our faith, and as this may increase our hope in love. Therefore it pleases him to be known and worshipped in miracles. Then this is his intention: He wishes us not to be oppressed because of the sorrows and travails which come to us, for it has always been so before the coming of miracles.

The Thirty-Seventh Chapter

God brought to mind[166] that I should sin; and because of the delight that I had in contemplating him, I did not at once pay attention to that revelation. And our Lord very mercifully waited, and gave me grace[167] to attend; and I applied this revelation particularly to myself[168]. But by all the consolations of grace which follow, as you will see, I was taught to apply it to all my fellow Christians, to all in general and not to any in particular.

Though our Lord revealed to me that I should sin, by me is understood everyone. And in this I conceived a gentle fear, and in answer to this our Lord said: I protect you very safely. This word was said with more love and assurance of protection for my soul than I can or may tell. For just as it was first revealed to me that I should sin, so was consolation revealed—assurance of protection for all my fellow Christians. What can make me love my fellow Christians more than to see in God that he loves all who will be saved, all of them as it were one soul? For in every soul which will be saved there is a godly will which never assents[169] to sin

---

166. Correspondence with the short text resumes; see p. 153.
167. In the short text, 'until I was ready'.
168. The short text mentions no such particular application.
169. C: 'finally assents', Cressy's theological caution, which does not accord with what Julian here is teaching.

and never will. Just as there is an animal will in the lower part which cannot will any good, so there is a godly will in the higher part, which will is so good that it cannot ever will any evil, but always good. And therefore[170] we are they whom he loves, and eternally we do what he delights in. And our Lord revealed this to me in the completeness of his love, that we are standing in his sight, yes, that he loves us now whilst we are here as well as he will when we are there, before his blessed face; but[171] all our travail is because love is lacking on our side.

The Thirty-Eighth Chapter

And God showed that sin will be no shame, but honour to man, for just[172] as there is indeed a corresponding pain for every sin, just so love gives to the same soul a bliss for every sin. Just as various sins are punished with various pains, the more grievous are the sins, so will they be rewarded with various joys in heaven to reward the victories over them, to the degree in which the sin may have been painful and sorrowful to the soul on earth. For the soul which will come to heaven is so precious to God, and its place there so honourable, that God's goodness never suffers the soul to sin finally which will come there. But who are the sinners who will be so rewarded is known to Holy Church, on earth and also in heaven, by their surpassing honours. For in this sight[173] my understanding was lifted up into heaven; and then God brought joyfully[174] to my mind David and innumerable others with him in the Old Law; and in the New Law he brought to my mind first Magdalen,

---

170. This sentence replaces the short text's 'just as the persons of the blessed Trinity'.
171. The rest of the sentence is not in the short text.
172. What follows differs from the short text, p. 154.
173. Correspondence with the short text resumes.
174. Short text: 'and then there came truly'.

Peter and Paul, Thomas of India[175], St. John of Beverly[176] and others too without number; how they and their sins are known to the Church on earth, and this is no shame to them, but everything is turned to their honour. And therefore our courteous Lord gives a partial revelation about them here of what is there in fulness; for there the mark of sin is turned to honour.

And St. John of Beverly[177]—our Lord revealed him as exalted and yet a familiar, for our comfort, and he brought to my mind how he is a kind neighbour and of our acquaintance; and God called him 'St. John of Beverly', openly, as we do, and that in a very happy and sweet manner, revealing that he is in God's sight a most exalted and blissful saint. And with this God mentioned that in his youth and in his tender years he was a beloved servant of God, greatly loving and fearing him. And nevertheless God allowed him to fall[178], mercifully protecting him so that he did not perish or lose any time[179]; and afterwards God raised him to many times more grace, and for the contrition and the meekness that he had as he lived, God has given him in heaven manifold joys, exceeding what he would have had if he had not sinned or fallen. And God shows on earth that this is true by constantly working many miracles about his body. And all this was to make us glad and happy in love.

---

175. This is wrongly copied in P, C, S1; but has been intelligently corrected in S2.
176. He does not appear in the short text.
177. The rest of this chapter is not in the short text.
178. For possible traces elsewhere of this otherwise lost legend of the saint's fall, see *Showings*, II, 447 note.
179. In chapter 62 Julian will allude again to 'loss of time'.

The Thirty-Ninth Chapter

Sin is the sharpest scourge[180] with which any chosen soul can be struck, which scourge belabours man or woman, and breaks a man, and purges[181] him in his own sight so much that at times he thinks himself that he is not fit for anything but as it were to sink into hell, until contrition seizes him by the inspiration of the Holy Spirit and turns bitterness into hope of God's mercy. And then the wounds begin to heal and the soul to revive, restored to the life of Holy Church. The Holy Spirit leads him to confession, willing to reveal his sins, nakedly and truthfully, with great sorrow and great shame that he has so befouled God's fair image. Then he accepts the penance for every sin imposed by his confessor, for this[182] is established in Holy Church by the teaching of the Holy Spirit, and this[183] is one meekness which greatly pleases God; and he also meekly accepts bodily sickness sent by God, and sorrows and outward shames, with the reproofs and contempt of the world and with all kinds of affliction and temptations into which we are cast, spiritually and bodily.

Our good Lord protects us with the greatest of loving care when it seems to us that we are almost forsaken and abandoned because of our sins and because we see that we have deserved it. And because of the meekness that we obtain from this, we are raised very high in God's sight by his grace. And also God in his special grace visits whom he will with such great contrition, and also with compassion and true longing for him, that they are suddenly delivered from sin and from pain, and taken up into bliss and made

---

180. Correspondence with the short text resumes; see p. 154.
181. This seems to be a replacement for an incomprehensible word, rendered as 'noyeth' in SS, somehow related to the short text's 'noughts', 'makes despicable'.
182. Or 'for he'.
183. The rest of this paragraph and the next are not in the short text.

equal with the saints. By contrition we are made clean, by compassion we are made ready, and by true longing for God we are made worthy. These are three means, as I understand, through which all souls come to heaven, those, that is to say, who have been sinners on earth and will be saved.

For every sinful soul[184] must be healed by these medicines[185]. Though he be healed, his wounds are not seen by God as wounds but as honours. And as we are punished here with sorrow and penance, in contrary fashion we shall be rewarded in heaven by the courteous love of our almighty God, who does not wish anyone who comes there to lose his labours[186] in any degree. For he regards sin as sorrow and pains for his lovers, to whom for love he assigns no blame.

The reward which we shall receive will not be small, but it will be great, glorious and honourable. And so all shame will be turned into honour and joy[187]. For our courteous Lord does not want his servants to despair because they fall often and grievously; for our falling does not hinder him in loving us. Peace and love are always in us, living and working, but we are not always in peace and in love; but he wants us so to take heed that he is the foundation of our whole life in love, and furthermore that he is our everlasting protector, and mightily defends us against all our enemies, who are very cruel and very fierce towards us, and so our need is great, the more so because by our falling we give them occasion.

---

184. Correspondence with the short text resumes; see p. 155.
185. Here is omitted the short text's 'especially of the sins which are mortal to him'.
186. The rest of this paragraph is not in the short text.
187. The rest of this chapter and most of chapter 40 are not in the short text.

The Fortieth Chapter

And this is a supreme friendship of our courteous Lord, that he protects us so tenderly whilst we are in our sins; and furthermore he touches us most secretly, and shows us our sins by the sweet light of mercy and grace. But when we see ourselves so foul[188], then we believe that God may be angry with us because of our sins. Then we are moved by the Holy Spirit through contrition to prayer, and we desire with all our might an amendment of ourselves to appease God's anger, until the time that we find rest of soul and ease of conscience. And then we hope that God has forgiven us our sin; and this is true. And then our courteous Lord shows himself to the soul, happily and with the gladdest countenance, welcoming it as a friend, as if it had been in pain and in prison, saying: My dear darling, I am glad that you have come to me in all your woe. I have always been with you, and now you see me loving, and we are made one in bliss.

So[189] sins are forgiven by grace and mercy, and our soul is honourably received in joy, as it will be when it comes into heaven, as often as it comes by the operation of grace of the Holy Spirit and the power of Christ's Passion.

Here I truly understood that every kind of thing is made available to us by God's great goodness, so much so that when we ourselves are at peace and in charity we are truly safe. But because we cannot have this completely whilst we are here, therefore it is fitting for us to live always in sweet prayer and in loving longing with our Lord Jesus. For he always longs to bring us to the fulness of joy, as has been said before[190], where he reveals his spiritual thirst. But

---

188. What follows, to the end of the paragraph, corresponds in outline, though not in detail, with chapter xix of the short text, p. 157.

189. From here to the end of Revelation XV, p. 310, is generally independent of the short text.

190. See chapter 31, p. 230.

now, because of all this spiritual consolation which has been described, if any man or woman be moved by folly to say or to think 'If this be true, then it would be well to sin so as to have the greater reward, or else to think sin less important', beware of this impulse, for truly, should it come, it is untrue and from the fiend.

For the same true love which touches us all by its blessed strength, that same blessed love teaches us that we must hate sin only because of love. And I am sure by what I feel that the more that each loving soul sees this in the courteous love of our Lord God, the greater is his hatred of sinning and the more he is ashamed. For if it were laid in front of us, all the pain there is in hell and in purgatory and on earth, death and all the rest, we should choose all that pain rather than sin. For sin is so vile and so much to be hated that it can be compared with no pain which is not itself sin. And no more cruel hell than sin was revealed to me, for a loving soul hates no pain but sin; for everything is good except sin, and nothing is evil except sin. And when by the operation of mercy and grace we set our intention on mercy and grace, we are made all fair and spotless.

And God is as willing as he is powerful and wise to save man. And Christ himself is the foundation of all the laws of Christian men, and he taught us to do good in return for evil. Here we may see that he is himself this love, and does to us as he teaches us to do; for he wishes us to be like him in undiminished, everlasting love towards ourselves and our fellow Christians. No more than his love towards us is withdrawn because of our sin does he wish our love to be withdrawn from ourselves or from our fellow Christians; but we must unreservedly hate sin and endlessly love the soul as God loves it. Then we should hate sin just as God hates it, and love the soul as God loves it. For these words which God said[191] are an endless strength: I protect you most truly.

---

191. See p. 241.

The Fourteenth Revelation
The Forty-First Chapter

After this our Lord revealed about prayer, in which revelation I saw two conditions[192] in our Lord's intention. One is rightful[193] prayer; the other is confident trust. But[194] still our trust is often not complete, because we are not sure that God hears us, as we think, because of our unworthiness and because we are feeling nothing at all; for often we are as barren and dry after our prayers as we were before. And thus when we feel so, it is our folly which is the cause of our weakness, for I have experienced this in myself. And our Lord brought all this suddenly to my mind, and revealed these words and said: I am the ground of your beseeching. First, it is my will that you should have it, and then I make you to wish it, and then I make you to beseech it. If you beseech it, how could it be that you would not have what you beseech? And so in the first reason and in the three that follow, our Lord reveals a great strengthening, as can be seen in the same words.

And in the first reason[195], where he says: if you beseech, he shows his great delight, and the everlasting reward that he will give us for our beseeching. And in the second[196] reason, where he says: How could it be?[197] this was said as an impossibility; for it is the most impossible that that may be that we should seek mercy and grace and not have it. For everything which our good Lord makes us

---

192. This corresponds with that of the short text's chapter xix, p. 157.
193. The short text indicates what is meant by 'rightful': 'One is that they will not pray for anything at all but for the thing which is God's will and to his glory'.
194. From here to '. . .a great strengthening' follows the short text.
195. From here to 'How could it be. . .' follows the short text.
196. For the editors' reasons for emending 'sixth' to 'second', see *Showings*, II, 461 and note.
197. Correspondence with the short text ceases.

to beseech he himself has ordained for us from all eternity. So here we may see that our beseeching is not the cause of the goodness and grace which he gives us, but his own goodness. And that he truly revealed in all these sweet words, where he says[198]: I am the foundation. And our good Lord wants this to be known by his lovers on earth. And the more that we know this, the more shall we beseech, if it be wisely accepted, and this is our Lord's intention.

Beseeching is a true and gracious, enduring will of the soul, united and joined to our Lord's will by the sweet, secret operation of the Holy Spirit. Our Lord himself is the first receiver of our prayer, as I see it, and he accepts it most thankfully, and greatly rejoicing he sends it up above, and puts it in a treasure-house where it will never perish. It is there before God with all his holy saints, continually received, always furthering our needs. And when we shall receive our bliss, it will be given to us as a measure of joy, with endless, honourable thanks from him.

Our Lord is most glad and joyful because of our prayer; and he expects it, and he wants to have it, for with his grace it makes us like to himself in condition as we are in nature, and such is his blessed will. For he says: Pray wholeheartedly[199], though it seems to you that this has no savour for you; still it is profitable enough, though you may not feel that. Pray wholeheartedly, though you may feel nothing, though you may see nothing, yes, though you think that you could not, for in dryness and in barrenness[200], in sickness and in weakness, then is your prayer most pleasing to me, though you think it almost tasteless to you. And so is all your living prayer in my sight.

Because of the reward and the endless thanks that he

---

198. See chapter 34, p. 236 (where direct speech is not used).
199. P: 'interly, inwardly', of which the other witnesses have made nonsense. See *Showings*, II, 464 and note.
200. P: 'barness' ('bareness, deprivation'), which fits the context well; but the other witnesses have 'barrenness', and see p. 157, 'we are as barren and dry'.

will give us there, because he covets to have us praying continually in his sight, God accepts the good will and the labour of his servants, however we may feel, and therefore it pleases him that we work in prayer and in good living by his help and his grace, reasonably and with discretion, preserving our powers for him until we have in the fulness of joy him whom we seek, who is Jesus. And that he revealed in the fifteenth revelation[201], where he says: You will have me for your reward.

Thanksgiving also belongs to prayer. Thanksgiving is a true inward acknowledgment, we applying ourselves with great reverence and loving fear and with all our powers to the work that our Lord moved us to, rejoicing and giving thanks inwardly. And sometimes the soul is so full of this that it breaks out in words and says: Good Lord, great thanks, blessed may you be. And sometimes the heart is dry and feels nothing, or else, by the temptation of our enemy, reason and grace drive the soul to implore our Lord with words, recounting his blessed Passion and his great goodness. And so the power of our Lord's word enters the soul and enlivens the heart and it begins by his grace faithful exercise, and makes the soul to pray most blessedly, and truly to rejoice in our Lord. This is a most loving thanksgiving in his sight.

The Forty-Second Chapter

Our Lord wants us to have true understanding, and especially in three things which belong to our prayer.

The first is with whom and how our prayer originates. He reveals with whom when he says[202]: I am the ground;

---

201. See p. 306.
202. See p. 248.

and he reveals how by his goodness, because he says[203]:
First it is my will.

As to the second, in what manner and how we should
perform our prayers, that is that our will should be turned,
rejoicing, into the will of our Lord. And he means this when
he says[204]: I make you to wish it.

As to the third, it is that we know the fruit and the end
of our prayer, which is to be united and like to our Lord in
all things. And with this intention and for this end was all
this loving lesson revealed, and he wishes to help us, and he
will make it so, as he says himself, blessed may he be.

For this is our Lord's will, that our prayer and our trust
be both equally generous. For if we do not trust as much as
we pray, we do not pay full honour to our Lord in our
prayer, and also we impede and hurt ourselves; and the
reason is, as I believe, because we do not truly know that
our Lord is the ground from which our prayer springs, and
also because we do not know that it is given to us by grace
from his love. For if we knew this, ·it would make us trust to
have all we desire from our Lord's gift.

For I am sure that no man asks for mercy and grace
with a right intention unless mercy and grace be first given
to him. But sometimes it comes to our mind that we have
prayed a long time, and still it seems to us that we do not
have what we ask for. But we should not be too depressed
on this account, for I am sure, according to our Lord's
meaning, that either we are waiting for a better occasion, or
more grace, or a better gift. He wants us to have true
knowledge in himself that he is being; and in this knowledge
he wants our understanding to be founded, with all our
powers and all our purpose and all our intention. And he
wants us to take our place and our dwelling in this
foundation. And he wants us to have understanding, by his

---

203. See p. 248.
204. See p. 248.

own light of grace, of three things which follow.

The first is our noble and excellent making, the second our precious and lovable redemption, the third everything which he has made inferior to us to serve us and which he protects for love of us. So he means as if he said: Behold and see that I have done all this before your prayer, and now you are, and you pray to me. And so he means that it is for us to know that the greatest deeds are done as Holy Church teaches.

And contemplating this with thanksgiving, we ought to pray for the deed which is now being done, that is that he may rule us and guide us to his glory in this life, and bring us to his bliss; and therefore he has done everything. So he means us to see that he does it and to pray for it. For the one is not enough, for if we pray and do not see that he does it, it makes us depressed and doubting; and that is not to his glory. And if we see that he does it and do not pray, we do not do our duty. And it cannot be so, that is to say, it is not so in his sight. But to see that he does it, and at the same time to pray, in this way is he worshipped and we are helped. It is our Lord's will that we pray for everything which he has ordained to do, either in particular or in general. And the joy and the bliss that this is to him, and the thanks and the honour that we shall have for it, this is beyond the understanding of all creatures in this life, as I see it.

For prayer is a right understanding of that fulness of joy which is to come, with true longing and trust. The savouring or seeing of our bliss, to which we are ordained, by nature makes us to long; true understanding and love, with a sweet recollection in our savour[205], by grace makes us to trust[206]. And in these two operations our Lord constantly

---

205. All the witnesses have 'saviour', which is plainly wrong; see *Showings*, II, 473 note.

206. P, C: 'thirst', which again is plainly wrong; SS omit, but seem to derive from an ancestor with 'trust'; see *Showings*, II, 473 note.

regards us, for this is our duty, and his goodness cannot assign any less to us than[207] it is our obligation diligently to perform. And when we do it, still it will seem to us that it is nothing. And this is true. But let us do what we can, and meekly ask mercy and grace, and everything which is lacking in us we shall find in him. And this is what he means when he says[208]: I am the foundation of your beseeching.

And so in these blessed words with the revelation I saw a complete overcoming of all our weakness[209] and all our doubting fears.

The Forty-Third Chapter

Prayer[210] unites the soul to God, for though the soul may be always like God in nature and in substance restored by grace[211], it is often unlike him in condition, through sin on man's part. Then prayer is a witness that the soul wills as God wills, and it eases the conscience and fits man for grace. And so he teaches us to pray and to have firm trust that we shall have it; for he beholds us in love, and wants to make us partners in his good will and work. And so he moves us to pray for what it pleases him to do, and for this prayer and good desire which come to us by his gift he will repay us, and give us eternal reward. And this was revealed to me when he said[212]: If you beseech it.

In this saying God showed such great pleasure and such great delight, as though he were much beholden to us for each good deed that we do; and yet it is he who does it.

---

207. So SS; P, C: 'that'.
208. See p. 248.
209. So SS; P, C: 'wickedness', which in this context is nonsensical.
210. What follows derives, though not in detail, from the short text's chapter xix; see p. 158.
211. 'Restored by grace' is not in the short text; for the editors' reasons for suspecting this as a scribe's interpolation, see *Showings*, II, 475 note.
212. See p. 248.

Therefore we pray to him urgently that he may do what is pleasing to him, as if he were to say: How could you please me more than by entreating me, urgently, wisely and sincerely, to do the thing that I want to have done? And so the soul by prayer is made of one accord with God.

But when[213] our courteous Lord of his special grace shows himself to our soul, we have what we desire, and then for that time we do not see what more we should pray for, but all our intention and all our powers are wholly directed to contemplating him. And as I see it, this is an exalted and imperceptible prayer; for the whole reason why we pray is to be united into the vision and contemplation of him to whom we pray, wonderfully rejoicing with reverent fear, and with so much sweetness and delight in him that we cannot pray at all except as he moves us at the time.

And well I know that the more the soul sees of God, the more she desires him by grace; but when we do not see him so[214], then we feel need and reason to pray, because we are failing and unfit for Jesus. For when a soul is tempted, troubled and left to herself in her unrest, that is the time for her to pray and to make herself supple and obedient to God. But he[215] by no kind of prayer makes God supple to him; for God's love does not change. And so[216] I saw that when we see the need for us to pray, then our Lord God is following us, helping our desire. And when we by his special grace behold him plainly, seeing no other, we then necessarily follow him, and he draws us to him by love. For I saw and felt that his wonderful and total goodness fulfils all our powers; and with that I saw that his continual working in every kind of thing is done so divinely[217], so wisely and

---

213. The rest of this paragraph is not in the short text.
214. Correspondence with the short text resumes; see p. 159.
215. That is, the soul. All the witnesses have the same change of gender.
216. What follows differs from the short text.
217. P: 'godly'; S2: 'goodly'; but in this markedly Johannine and Trinitarian passage, the word can only mean 'divinely'.

so powerfully that it surpasses all our imagining and everything that we can understand or think. And then we can do no more than contemplate him and rejoice, with a great and compelling desire to be wholly united into him, and attend to his motion and rejoice in his love and delight in his goodness.

And so we shall by his sweet grace in our own meek continual prayer come into him now in this life by many secret touchings of sweet spiritual sights and feelings, measured out to us as our simplicity may bear it. And this is done and will be done by the grace of the Holy Spirit, until the day that we die, still longing for love. And then we shall all come into our Lord, knowing ourselves clearly and wholly possessing God, and we shall all be endlessly hidden in God, truly seeing and wholly feeling, and hearing him spiritually and delectably smelling him and sweetly tasting him. And there we shall see God face to face, familiarly and wholly. The creature which is made will see and endlessly contemplate God who is the maker; for so can no man see God and live afterwards, that is to say in this mortal life. But when he of his special grace wishes to show himself here, he gives the creature more than its own strength, and he measures the revelation according to his own will, and it is profitable for that time.

The Forty-Fourth Chapter

God often showed in all the revelations that man[218] always works his will and to his glory, continually, without ceasing. And what this working is was shown in the first revelation[219], and that in a marvellous setting, for it was

---

218. That is, the perfect man who will be seen in the parable of the lord and the servant.
219. See p. 182.

shown in the working of the blessed soul of our Lady St. Mary, by truth and wisdom; and I hope that by the grace of the Holy Spirit I shall say as I saw how this was.

Truth sees God, and wisdom contemplates God, and of these two comes the third, and that is a marvellous delight in God, which is love. Where truth and wisdom are, truly there is love, truly coming from them both, and all are of God's making. For God is endless supreme truth, endless supreme wisdom, endless supreme love uncreated; and a man's soul is a creature in God which has the same properties created. And always it does what it was created for; it sees God and it contemplates God and it loves God. Therefore God rejoices in the creature and the creature in God, endlessly marvelling, in which marvelling he sees his God, his Lord, his maker, so exalted, so great and so good in comparison with him who is made that the creature scarcely seems anything to itself. But the brightness and clearness of truth and wisdom make him see and know that he is made for love, in which love God endlessly protects him.

The Forty-Fifth Chapter

God judges us in our natural substance, which is always kept one in him, whole and safe, without end; and this judgment is out of his justice. And man judges us in our changeable sensuality, which now seems one thing and now another, as it derives from parts and presents an external appearance. And this judgment is mixed, for sometimes it is good and lenient, and sometimes it is hard and painful. And inasmuch as it is good and lenient it pertains to God's justice, and inasmuch as it is hard and painful, our good Lord Jesus reforms it by mercy and grace through the power of the blessed Passion, and so brings it into justice. And though these two are so reconciled and joined, still both will be known in heaven forever.

The first judgment, which is from God's justice, is from his own great endless love, and that is that fair, sweet judgment which was shown in all the fair revelation[220] in which I saw him assign to us no kind of blame. And though this was sweet and delectable, I could not be fully comforted only by contemplating it, and that was because of the judgment of Holy Church, which I had understood before, and which was continually in my sight. And therefore it seemed to me that by this judgment I must necessarily know myself a sinner. And by the same judgment I understood that sinners sometimes deserve blame and wrath, and I could not see these two in God, and therefore my desire[221] was more than I can or may tell, because of the higher judgment which God himself revealed at the same time, and therefore I had of necessity to accept it. And the lower judgment had previously been taught me in Holy Church, and therefore I could not in any way ignore the lower judgment.

This then was my desire, that I might see in God in what way the judgment of Holy Church here on earth is true in his sight, and how it pertains to me to know it truly, whereby they might both be reconciled as might be glory to God and the right way for me. And to all this I never had any other answer than a wonderful example[222] of a lord and a servant, as I shall tell later[223], and that was very mysteriously revealed. And still it was my desire and my will until the end of my life by grace to know these two judgments, as it pertains to me. For all heavenly things and all earthly things which belong to heaven are comprehended in these two judgments. And the more knowledge and understanding that we have by the gracious leading of the Holy Spirit of these two judgments, the more shall we see

---

220. See p. 214.
221. So SS; P, C: 'my advice and desire', probably a marginal (and mistaken) gloss from an earlier manuscript incorporated in the text.
222. That is, an illustrative story or parable such as a preacher might use.
223. See p. 267 and following.

and know our feelings. And always, the more that we see
them, the more, according to our nature by the working of
grace, shall we long to be filled with endless joy and bliss,
for we are made for this. And our natural substance is now
full of blessedness in God, and has been since it was made,
and will be without end.

The Forty-Sixth Chapter

But our passing life which we have here does not know
in our senses what our self is, but we know in our faith.
And when we know and see, truly and clearly, what our self
is, then we shall truly and clearly see and know our Lord
God in the fulness of joy. And therefore it must necessarily
be that the nearer that we are to our bliss, the more we shall
long, both by nature and by grace. We may have knowledge
of ourselves in this life by the continuing help and power of
our exalted nature, in which knowledge we may increase and
grow by the furthering and help of mercy and grace. But we
may never fully know ourselves until the last moment, at
which moment this passing life and every kind of woe and
pain will have an end. And therefore this belongs to our
properties, both by nature and by grace to long and desire
with all our powers to know ourselves, in which full
knowledge we shall truly and clearly know our God in the
fulness of endless joy. And yet in all this time, from the
beginning to the end, I had two kinds of contemplation. The
one was endless continuing love, with certainty of protection
and blessed salvation, for all the revelation was about this.
The other was the common teaching of Holy Church, in
which before I had been instructed and grounded, and had
by my will practised and understood. And the contemplation
of this did not leave me, for by the revelation I was not
moved or led away from it in any way at all; but I was
taught in the revelation to love it and rejoice in it, so that I

might with the help of our Lord and his grace increase and rise to more heavenly knowledge and a higher loving.

And so in all this contemplation it seemed to me that it was necessary to see and to know that we are sinners and commit many evil deeds which we ought to forsake, and leave many good deeds undone which we ought to do, so that we deserve pain, blame and wrath. And despite all this, I saw truly that our Lord was never angry, and never will be. Because he is God, he is good, he is truth, he is love, he is peace; and his power, his wisdom, his charity and his unity do not allow him to be angry. For I saw truly that it is against the property of his power to be angry, and against the property of his wisdom and against the property of his goodness. God is that goodness which cannot be angry, for God is nothing but goodness. Our soul is united to him who is unchangeable goodness. And between God and our soul there is neither wrath nor forgiveness in his sight. For our soul is so wholly united to God, through his own goodness, that between God and our soul nothing can interpose.

And the soul was led to this understanding by love, and drawn by power in every revelation; that it is so, our good Lord revealed, and how it is so, truly of his great goodness he wishes that we desire to know, that is to say, inasmuch as it is appropriate for a creature of his to know it. For everything which the simple soul understood, God wants that to be revealed and known; for he himself, powerfully and wisely, out of love, hides the things which he wishes to be secret. For I saw in the same revelation that there are many hidden mysteries which can never be known until the time when God in his goodness has made us worthy to see them. And with this I am well satisfied, waiting upon our Lord's will in this great marvel. And now I submit myself to my mother, Holy Church, as a simple child should.

The Forty-Seventh Chapter

There are two particular debts which our soul has to pay. One is that we reverently marvel; the other is that we meekly suffer, always rejoicing in God. For he wants us to know that in a short time we shall see clearly in him all that we desire. And notwithstanding all this, I contemplated and wondered greatly what is the mercy and forgiveness of God; for by the teaching which I had before, I understood that the mercy of God will be remission of his wrath after we have sinned. For it seemed to me that to a soul whose intention and desire is to love, God's wrath would be harder than any other pain. And therefore I accepted that the remission of his wrath would be one of the chief characteristics of his mercy. But for anything which I could see or desire, I could not see this characteristic in all the revelation. But I shall describe something of how I saw and understood the operation of mercy, as God will give me grace.

I understood in this way. Man is changeable in this life, and falls into sin through naivete and ignorance. He is weak[224] and foolish in himself, and also his will is overpowered in the time when he is assailed and in sorrow and woe. And the cause is blindness, because he does not see God[225]; for if he saw God continually, he would have no harmful feelings nor any kind of prompting, no sorrowing which is conducive to sin.

So I saw and felt at the same time, and it seemed to me that the sight and the feeling were great and plentiful and gracious in comparison with what is our common feeling in this life. But still it seemed to me humble and petty in

---

224. Correspondence with the short text resumes; see p. 159.
225. From here until the end of chapter 63 (p. 305) is wholly independent of the short text.

comparison with the great desire which the soul has to see
God. For I felt in myself five kinds of activity, and they are
these: rejoicing, mourning, desire, fear and true[226] hope.
Rejoicing, because God gave me knowledge and
understanding that it was himself whom I saw. Mourning,
and that was because of weakness[227]. Desire, which was that
I might see him always more and more; understanding and
knowing that we shall never have perfect rest until we see
him clearly and truly in heaven. The fear was because it
seemed to me in all that time that that sight would fail and I
should be left to myself. The true hope was in the endless
love, for I saw that I should be protected by his mercy and
brought to bliss.

And the rejoicing in his sight with this true[228] hope of
his merciful protection made me have feeling and comfort, so
that the mourning and fear were not very painful. And still
in all this I contemplated in this revelation by God that this
kind of vision of him cannot persist in this life, and that is
for his own glory and for the increase of our endless joy.
And therefore often we fail to perceive him, and presently
we fall back upon ourselves, and then we find that we feel
nothing at all but the opposition that is in ourselves, and that
comes from the old root of our first sin, with all that follows
from our own persistence; and in this we are belaboured and
tempted with the feeling of sin and of pain in many different
ways, spiritually and bodily, as is known to us in this life.

The Forty-Eighth Chapter

But our good Lord the Holy Spirit, who is endless life
dwelling in our soul, protects us most faithfully and
produces in the soul a peace, and brings it to ease through

---

226. SS: 'sure'.
227. P, C, S2: 'feeling'; but S1 has emended intelligently, or had a better copy.
228. SS: 'sure'.

grace, and makes it obedient and reconciles it to God. And this is the mercy and the way on which our good Lord constantly leads us, so long as we are in this changeable life. For I saw no wrath except on man's side, and he forgives that in us, for wrath is nothing else but a perversity and an opposition to peace and to love. And it comes from a lack of power or a lack of wisdom or a lack of goodness, and this lack is not in God, but it is on our side. For we through sin and wretchedness have in us a wrath and a constant opposition to peace and to love; and he revealed that very often in his lovely look of compassion and pity. For the foundation of mercy is in love, and the operation of mercy is our protection in love; and this was revealed in such a way that I could not perceive, about mercy's properties, in any other way than as if it were all love in love.

That is to say, as I see it, mercy is a sweet, gracious operation in love, mingled with plentiful pity, for mercy works, protecting us, and mercy works, turning everything to good for us. Mercy for love allows us to fail to a certain extent; and inasmuch as we fail, in so much we fall, and inasmuch as we fall, in so much we die. For we must necessarily die inasmuch as we fail to see and feel God, who is our life. Our failing is dreadful, our falling is shameful, and our dying is sorrowful. But yet in all this the sweet eye of pity is never turned away from us, and the operation of mercy does not cease.

For I contemplated the property of mercy, and I contemplated the property of grace, which have two ways of operating in one love. Mercy is a compassionate property, which belongs to motherhood in tender love; and grace is an honourable property, which belongs to royal dominion in the same love. Mercy works, protecting, enduring, vivifying and healing, and it is all of the tenderness of love; and grace works with mercy, raising, rewarding, endlessly exceeding what our love and labour deserve, distributing[229] and displaying the vast plenty and generosity of God's royal dominion in his wonderful courtesy. And this is from the abundance of love, for grace transforms our dreadful failing into plentiful and endless solace; and grace transforms our shameful falling into high and honourable rising; and grace transforms our sorrowful dying into holy, blessed life.

For I saw most truly[230] that always, as our contrariness makes for us here on earth pain, shame and sorrow, just so in contrary manner grace makes for us in heaven solace, honour and bliss, so superabundant that when we come up and receive that sweet reward which grace has made for us, there we shall thank and bless our Lord, endlessly rejoicing that we ever suffered woe; and that will be because of a property of the blessed love which we shall know in God, which we might never have known without woe preceding it. And when I saw all this, I was forced to agree that the mercy of God and his forgiveness abate and dispel our wrath.

The Forty-Ninth Chapter

For it was a great marvel, constantly shown to the soul in all the revelations, and the soul was contemplating with great diligence that our Lord God cannot in his own judgment forgive, because he cannot be angry—that would be impossible. For this was revealed, that our life is all founded and rooted in love, and without love we cannot live. And therefore to the soul which by God's special grace sees

---

229. Literally, 'spreading abroad'; on the associations for Julian of the term with the doctrine of *circumincessio*, the interpenetration in the Trinity of the attributes and operations of the persons, see *Showings*, 1, 126–127.
230. SS: 'surely'.

so much of his great and wonderful goodness as that we are endlessly united to him in love, it is the most impossible thing which could be that God might be angry, for anger and friendship are two contraries; for he dispels and destroys our wrath and makes us meek and mild—we must necessarily believe that he is always one in[231] love, meek and mild, which is contrary to wrath. For I saw most truly that where our Lord appears, peace is received and wrath has no place; for I saw no kind of wrath in God, neither briefly nor for long. For truly, as I see it, if God could be angry for any time, we should neither have life nor place nor being; for as truly as we have our being from the endless power of God and from his endless wisdom and from his endless goodness, just as truly we have our preservation in the endless power of God and in his endless wisdom and in his endless goodness. For though we may feel in ourselves anger, contention and strife, still we are all mercifully enclosed in God's mildness and in his meekness, in his benignity and in his accessibility.

For I saw very truly that all our endless friendship, our place, our life and our being are in God. For that same endless goodness which protects us when we sin so that we do not perish, that same endless goodness constantly draws into us a peace, opposing our wrath and our perverse falling, and makes us see our need with true fear, and urgently to beseech God that we may have forgiveness, with a grace-given desire for our salvation. For we cannot be blessedly saved until we are truly in peace and in love, for that is our salvation.

And though we may be angry, and the contrariness which is in us be now in tribulation, distress and woe, as we fall victims to our blindness and our evil propensities, still we are sure and safe by God's merciful protection, so that we do not perish. But we are not blessedly safe, possessing

---

231. So SS, which seem superior to P's 'in one'.

our endless joy, until we are all in peace and in love, that is to say wholly contented with God and with all his works and with all his judgments, and loving and content with ourselves and with our fellow Christians and with everything which God loves, as is pleasing to love. And God's goodness does this in us.

So I saw that God is our true peace; and he is our safe protector when we ourselves are in disquiet, and he constantly works to bring us into endless peace. And so when by the operation of mercy and grace we are made meek and mild, then we are wholly safe. Suddenly the soul is united to God, when she is truly pacified in herself, for in him is found no wrath. And so I saw that when we are wholly in peace and in love, we find no contrariness in any kind of hindrance, and our Lord God in his goodness makes the contrariness which is in us now very profitable for us. For contrariness is the cause of all our tribulation and all our woe; and our Lord Jesus takes them and sends them up to heaven, and then they are made more sweet and delectable than heart can think or tongue can tell. And when we come there, we shall find them ready, all turned into true beauty and endless honour.

So is God our steadfast foundation, and he will be our whole joy, and he will make us as unchangeable as he is when we are there.

The Fiftieth Chapter

And in this mortal life mercy and forgiveness are the path which always leads us to grace; and through the temptations and the sorrow into which on our side we fall, we often are dead by the judgment of men on earth. But in the sight of God the soul which will be saved was never dead, and never will be. But still here I wondered and marvelled with all the diligence of my soul, after this fashion: Good Lord, I see in you that you are very truth, and I know truly that we sin grievously all day and are very blameworthy; and I can neither reject my knowledge of this truth, nor see that any kind of blame is shown to us. How can this be? For I know by the ordinary teaching of Holy Church and by my own feeling that the blame of our sins continually hangs upon us, from the first man until the time that we come up into heaven. This, then, was my astonishment, that I saw our Lord God showing no more blame to us than if we were as pure and as holy as the angels are in heaven. And between these two oppositions my reason was greatly afflicted by my blindness, and I could have no rest for fear that his blessed presence would pass from my sight, and I should be left in ignorance of how he may look on us in our sin. For either I ought to see in God that sin was all done away with, or else I ought to see in God how he sees it, by which I might truly know how it is fitting for me to see sin and the way in which we have blame.

My longing endured as I constantly beheld him; and yet I could have no patience because of great fear and perplexity, thinking that if I were to take it that we are not sinners and not blameworthy, it seems as if I should err and fail to recognize the truth. And if it be true that we are sinners and blameworthy, good Lord, how can it then be that I cannot see this truth in you, who are my God, my maker in whom I desire to see all truth?

Three circumstances gave me courage to ask this. The first is because it is so humble a thing, for if it were a great one I should be afraid. The second is that it is so general; for if it were special or secret, I should also be afraid. The third is that it is something which I need to know, it seems to me, if I shall live here, so as to tell good from evil, whereby I may through reason and grace separate them more distinctly, and love goodness and hate evil as Holy Church teaches. I cried within me with all my might, beseeching God for help, in this fashion: Ah, Lord Jesus, king of bliss, how shall I be comforted, who will tell me and teach me what I need to know, if I cannot at this time see it in you?

The Fifty-First Chapter

And then our courteous Lord answered very mysteriously, by revealing a wonderful example[232] of a lord who has a servant, and gave me sight for the understanding of them both. The vision was shown doubly with respect to the lord, and the vision was shown doubly with respect to the servant. One part was shown spiritually, in a bodily likeness. The other part was shown more spiritually, without bodily likeness. So, for the first, I saw two persons in bodily likeness, that is to say a lord and a servant; and with that God gave me spiritual understanding. The lord sits in state, in rest and in peace. The servant stands before his lord, respectfully, ready to do his lord's will. The lord looks on his servant very lovingly and sweetly and mildly. He sends him to a certain place to do his will. Not only does the servant go, but he dashes off and runs at great speed, loving to do his lord's will. And soon he falls into a dell and is greatly injured; and then he groans and moans and tosses about and writhes, but he cannot rise or help himself in any way. And of all this, the greatest hurt which I saw him in was lack of consolation, for he could not turn his face to look on his loving lord, who was very close to him, in whom is all consolation; but like a man who was for the time extremely feeble and foolish, he paid heed to his feelings and his continuing distress, in which distress he suffered seven great pains. The first was the severe bruising which he took in his fall, which gave him great pain. The second was the clumsiness of his body. The third was the weakness which

232. See p. 257, note 222.

followed these two. The fourth was that he was blinded in his reason and perplexed in his mind, so much so that he had almost forgotten his own love. The fifth was that he could not rise. The sixth was the pain most astonishing to me, and that was that he lay alone. I looked all around and searched, and far and near, high and low, I saw no help for him. The seventh was that the place in which he lay was narrow and comfortless and distressful.

I was amazed that this servant could so meekly suffer all this woe; and I looked carefully to know if I could detect any fault in him, or if the lord would impute to him any kind of blame; and truly none was seen, for the only cause of his falling was his good will and his great desire. And in spirit he was as prompt and as good as he was when he stood before his lord, ready to do his will.

And all this time his loving lord looks on him most tenderly, and now with a double aspect, one outward, very meekly and mildly, with great compassion and pity, and this belonged to the first part; the other was inward, more spiritual, and this was shown with a direction of my understanding towards the lord, and I was brought again[233] to see how greatly he rejoiced over the honourable rest and nobility which by his plentiful grace he wishes for his servant and will bring him to. And this belonged to the second vision[234]. And now my understanding was led back to the first, keeping both in mind.

Then this courteous lord said this: See my beloved servant, what harm and injuries he has had and accepted in my service for my love, yes, and for his good will. Is it not reasonable that I should reward him for his fright and his fear, his hurt and his injuries and all his woe? And furthermore, is it not proper for me to give him a gift, better

---

233. This perhaps refers to Revelation IX, chapter 22, where Julian describes how her understanding was lifted up into heaven. On this difficult passage (which defeated the SS scribes) see *Showings*, II, 517 note 42.

234. That is, the second 'part' of it.

for him and more honourable than his own health could have
been? Otherwise, it seems to me that I should be
ungracious.

And in this an inward spiritual revelation of the lord's
meaning descended into my soul, in which I saw that this
must necessarily be the case, that his great goodness and his
own honour require that his beloved servant, whom he loved
so much, should be highly and blessedly rewarded forever,
above what he would have been if he had not fallen, yes,
and so much that his falling and all the woe that he received
from it will be turned into high, surpassing honour and
endless bliss.

And at this point the example which had been shown
vanished, and our good Lord led my understanding on to the
end of what was to be seen and shown in the revelation. But
despite this leading on, the wonder of the example never left
me, for it seemed to me that it had been given as an answer
to my petition. And yet at that time I could not understand
it fully or be comforted. For in the servant, who was shown
for Adam, as I shall say, I saw many different characteristics
which could in no way be attributed to Adam, that one man;
and so at that time I relied greatly on three insights, for the
complete understanding of that wonderful example was not
at that time given to me. The secrets of the revelation were
deeply hidden in this mysterious example; and despite this I
saw and understood that every showing is full of secrets.
And therefore I must now tell of three attributes through
which I have been somewhat consoled.

The first is the beginning of the teaching which I
understood from it at the time. The second is the inward
instruction which I have understood from it since. The third
is all the whole revelation from the beginning to the end,
which our Lord God of his goodness freely and often brings
before the eyes of my understanding. And these three are so
unified, as I understand it, that I cannot and may not
separate them. And by these three as one I have instruction

269

by which I ought to believe and trust that our Lord God, that out of the same goodness and for the same purpose as he revealed it, by the same goodness and for the same purpose will make it clear to us when it is his will.

For twenty years after the time of the revelation except for three months, I received an inward instruction, and it was this: You ought to take heed to all the attributes, divine and human[235], which were revealed in the example, though this may seem to you mysterious and ambiguous. I willingly agreed with a great desire, seeing inwardly with great care all the details and the characteristics which were at that time revealed, so far as my intelligence and understanding will serve, beginning with when I looked at the lord and the servant, at how the lord was sitting and the place where he sat, and the colour of his clothing and how it was made, and his outward appearance and his inward nobility and goodness; and the demeanour of the servant as he stood, and the place where and how, and his fashion of clothing, the colour and the shape, his outward behaviour and his inward goodness and willingness. I understood that the lord who sat in state in rest and peace is God. I understood that the servant who stood before him was shown for Adam, that is to say, one man was shown at that time and his fall, so as to make it understood how God regards all men and their falling. For in the sight of God all men are one man, and one man is all men. This man was injured in his powers and made most feeble, and in his understanding he was amazed, because he was diverted from looking on his lord, but his will was preserved in God's sight. I saw the lord[236] commend and approve him for his will, but he himself was blinded and hindered from knowing this will. And this is a great sorrow and a cruel suffering to him, for he neither sees clearly his loving lord, who is so meek and mild to him, nor

---

235. Literally, 'to all the properties and the conditions'; see *Showings*, II, 520 and note 88.

236. 'Our Lord', that is, God the Father.

does he truly see what he himself is in the sight of his loving lord. And I know well that when these two things are wisely and truly seen, we shall gain rest and peace, here in part and the fulness in the bliss of heaven, by God's plentiful grace.

And this was a beginning of the teaching which I saw at the same time, whereby I might come to know in what manner he looks on us in our sin. And then I saw that only pain blames and punishes, and our courteous Lord comforts and succours, and always he is kindly disposed to the soul, loving and longing to bring us to his bliss.

The place which the lord sat on was unadorned, on the ground, barren and waste, alone in the wilderness. His clothing was wide and ample and very handsome, as befits a lord. The colour of the clothing was azure blue, most dignified and beautiful. His demeanour was merciful, his face was a lovely pale brown with a very seemly countenance, his eyes were black, most beautiful and seemly, revealing all his loving pity, and within him there was a secure[237] place of refuge, long and broad, all full of endless heavenliness. And the loving regard which he kept constantly on his servant, and especially when he fell, it seemed to me that it could melt our hearts for love and break them in two for joy. This lovely regard had in it a beautiful mingling which was wonderful to see. Part was compassion and pity, part was joy and bliss. The joy and bliss surpass the compassion and pity, as far as heaven is above earth. The pity was earthly and the bliss was heavenly.

The compassion and the pity of the Father were for Adam, who is his most beloved creature. The joy and the bliss were for the falling of his dearly beloved Son, who is equal with the Father. The merciful regard of his lovely countenance filled all the earth, and went down with Adam into hell, and by this continuing pity Adam was kept from endless death. And this mercy and pity abides with mankind

---

237. Literally, 'high'.

.

until the time that we come up to heaven. But man is blinded in this life, and therefore we cannot see our Father, God, as he is. And when he of his goodness wishes to show himself to man, he shows himself familiar, like a man, even though I saw truly that we ought to know and believe that the Father is not man. But his sitting on the ground, barren and waste, signifies this: He made man's soul to be his own city and his dwelling place, which is the most pleasing to him of all his works. And when man had fallen into sorrow and pain, he was not wholly proper to serve in that noble office, and therefore our kind Father did not wish to prepare any other place, but sat upon the ground, awaiting human nature, which is mixed with earth, until the time when by his grace his beloved Son had brought back his city into its noble place of beauty by his hard labour.

The blueness of the clothing signifies his steadfastness; the brownness of his fair face with the lovely blackness of the eyes was most suitable to indicate his holy solemnity; the amplitude, billowing[238] splendidly all about him, signifies that he has enclosed within himself all heavens and all endless joy and bliss; and this was shown in a brief moment, when I perceived that my understanding was directed to the lord. In this I saw him greatly rejoice over the honourable restoration to which he wants to bring and will bring his servant by his great and plentiful grace. And still I was amazed, contemplating the lord and the servant as I have said.

I saw the lord sitting in state, and the servant standing respectfully before his lord, and in this servant there is a double significance, one outward, the other inward. Outwardly he was simply dressed like a labourer prepared to work, and he stood very close to the lord, not immediately in front of him but a little to one side, and that on the left;

---

238. 'Flammyng' (P), 'flaming' (C), 'flamand' (SS); the word might also mean 'shining', or all the readings may be corrupt.

his clothing was a white tunic, scanty, old and all worn, dyed with the sweat of his body, tight fitting and short, as it were a hand's breadth below his knee, looking threadbare as if it would soon be worn out, ready to go to rags and to tear. And in this I was much amazed, thinking: This is not fitting clothing for a servant so greatly loved to stand in before so honourable a lord. And, inwardly, there was shown in him a foundation of love, the love which he had for the lord, which was equal to the love which the lord had for him. The wisdom of the servant saw inwardly that there was one thing to do which would pay honour to the lord; and the servant, for love, having no regard for himself or for anything which might happen to him, went off in great haste and ran when his lord sent him, to do the thing which was his will and to his honour; for it seemed by his outer garment as if he had been a constant labourer and a hard traveller[239] for a long time. And by the inward perception which I had of both the lord and the servant, it seemed that he was newly appointed, that is to say just beginning to labour, and that this servant had never been sent out before.

There was a treasure in the earth which the lord loved. I was astonished, and considered what it could be; and I was answered in my understanding: It is a food which is delicious and pleasing to the lord. For I saw the lord sitting like a man, and I saw neither food nor drink with which to serve him. This was one astonishment; another astonishment was that this stately lord had only one servant, and him he sent out. I watched, wondering what kind of labour it could be that the servant was to do. And then I understood that he was to do the greatest labour and the hardest work there is. He was to be a gardener, digging and ditching and sweating and turning the soil over and over, and to dig deep down, and to water the plants at the proper time. And he was to persevere in his work, and make sweet streams to run, and

---

239. On the *double entendre* here, see *Showings*, II, 529 note 182.

fine and plenteous[240] fruit to grow, which he was to bring
before the lord and serve him with to his liking. And he was
never to come back again until he had made all this food
ready as he knew was pleasing to the lord; and then he was
to take this food, and drink, and carry it most reverently
before the lord. And all this time the lord was to sit in
exactly the same place, waiting for the servant whom he had
sent out.

And still I wondered where the servant came from, for I
saw in the lord that he has in himself endless life and every
kind of goodness, except for the treasure which was in the
earth, and that was founded in the lord in a marvellous
depth of endless love. But it was not wholly to his honour
until his servant had prepared it so finely and carried it
before him into the lord's own presence. And except for the
lord, there was nothing at all but wilderness; and I did not
understand everything which this example meant. And
therefore I wondered where the servant came from.

In the servant is comprehended[241] the second person of
the Trinity, and in the servant is comprehended Adam, that
is to say all men. And therefore when I say 'the Son', that
means the divinity which is equal to the Father, and when I
say 'the servant', that means Christ's humanity, which is the
true Adam. By the closeness of the servant is understood the
Son, and by his standing to the left is understood Adam.
The lord is God the Father, the servant is the Son, Jesus
Christ, the Holy Spirit is the equal love which is in them
both. When Adam fell, God's Son fell; because of the true
union which was made in heaven, God's Son could not be
separated from Adam, for by Adam I understand all
mankind. Adam fell from life to death, into the valley of this
wretched world, and after that into hell. God's Son fell with

---

240. So SS; P, C: 'fine plentiousness'.
241. Julian appears to use 'comprehend' in the same ambiguous sense which is found
in John 1.5, to suggest both 'include, surround' and 'understand'.

Adam, into the valley of the womb of the maiden who was the fairest daughter of Adam, and that was to excuse Adam from blame in heaven and on earth; and powerfully he brought him out of hell. By the wisdom and the goodness which were in the servant is understood God's Son, by the poor labourer's clothing and the standing close by on the left is understood Adam's humanity with all the harm and weakness which follow. For in all this our good Lord showed his own Son and Adam as only one man. The strength and the goodness that we have is from Jesus Christ, the weakness and blindness that we have is from Adam, which two were shown in the servant.

And so has our good Lord Jesus taken upon him all our blame; and therefore our Father may not, does not wish to assign more blame to us than to his own beloved Son Jesus Christ. So he was the servant before he came on earth, standing ready in purpose before the Father until the time when he would send him to do the glorious deed by which mankind was brought back to heaven. That is to say, even though he is God, equal with the Father as regards his divinity, but with his prescient purpose that he would become man to save mankind in fulfillment of the will of his Father, so he stood before his Father as a servant, willingly taking upon him all our charge[242]. And then he rushed off very readily at the Father's bidding, and soon he fell very low into the maiden's womb, having no regard for himself or for his cruel pains.

The white tunic is his flesh, the scantiness signifies that there was nothing at all separating the divinity from the humanity. The tight fit is poverty, the age is Adam's wearing, the wornness is the sweat of Adam's labour, the shortness shows the servant-labourer.

And so I saw the Son stand, saying in intention: See,

---

242. Again, the word is calculatedly ambiguous, and seems to suggest 'burden', 'cost', 'responsibility'.

my dear Father, I stand before you in Adam's tunic, all ready to hasten and run. I wish to be on earth to your glory, when it is your will to send me. How long shall I desire it? Very truly the Son knew when was the Father's will, and how long he would desire it, that is to say as regards his divinity, for he is the wisdom of the Father. Therefore this meaning was shown for understanding of Christ's humanity. For all mankind which will be saved by the sweet Incarnation and the Passion of Christ, all is Christ's humanity, for he is the head, and we are his members, to which members the day and the time are unknown when every passing woe and sorrow will have an end, and everlasting joy and bliss will be fulfilled, which day and time all the company of heaven longs and[243] desires to see. And all who are under heaven and will come there, their way is by longing and desiring, which desiring and longing was shown in the servant standing before the lord, or, otherwise, in the Son standing before the Father in Adam's tunic. For the longing and desire of all mankind which will be saved appeared in Jesus, for Jesus is in all who will be saved, and all who will be saved[244] are in Jesus, and all is of the love of God, with obedience, meekness and patience, and the virtues which befit us.

Also in this marvellous example I have teaching within me, as it were the beginning of an ABC, whereby I may have some understanding of our Lord's meaning, for the mysteries of the revelation are hidden in it, even though all the showings are full of mysteries.

The sitting of the Father symbolizes the divinity, that is to say to reveal rest and peace, for in the divinity there can be no labour; and that he shows himself as a lord symbolizes our humanity. The standing of the servant symbolizes labour, and that he stands to the left symbolizes that he was

---

243. So C; P: 'or'; om. SS: 'and desires'.
244. So SS, which seem superior to P, C: 'are saved'.

not fully worthy to stand immediately in front of the lord. His rushing away was the divinity, and his running was the humanity; for the divinity rushed from the Father into the maiden's womb, falling to accept our nature, and in this falling he took great hurt. The hurt that he took was our flesh, in which at once he experienced mortal pains. That he stood fearfully before the lord and not immediately in front symbolizes that his clothing was not seemly for him to stand in immediately in front of the lord, nor could nor should that be his office whilst he was a labourer; nor, further, might he sit with the lord in rest and peace until he had duly won his peace with his hard labour; and that he stood to the left symbolizes that the Father by his will permitted his own Son in human nature to suffer all man's pain without sparing him. By his tunic being ready to go to rags and to tear is understood the rods and the scourges, the thorns and the nails, the pulling and the dragging and the tearing of his tender flesh, of which I had seen a part. The flesh was torn from the skull, falling in pieces until when the bleeding stopped; and then it began to dry again, adhering to the bone. And by the tossing about and writhing, the groaning and moaning, is understood that he could never with almighty power rise from the time that he fell into the maiden's womb until his body was slain and dead, and he had yielded his soul into the Father's hand, with all mankind for whom he had been sent.

And at this moment he first began to show his power, for then he went down into hell; and when he was there, he raised up the great root out of the deep depth[245], which rightly was joined to him in heaven. The body lay in the grave until Easter[246] morning; and from that time it never lay again. For then the tossing about and writhing, the

---

245. For the Scriptural allusions and the rhetorical devices here, see *Showings*, II, 542 notes 301 and 302.

246. So C, SS; P: 'after'.

groaning and the moaning[247] ended, rightly; and our foul
mortal flesh, which God's Son took upon him, which was
Adam's old tunic, tight-fitting, threadbare and short, was
then made lovely by our saviour, new, white and bright and
forever clean, wide and ample, fairer[248] and richer than the
clothing which I saw on the Father. For that clothing was
blue, and Christ's clothing is now of a fair and seemly
mixture, which is so marvellous that I cannot describe it, for
it is all of true glory.

Now the lord does not sit on the ground in the
wilderness, but in his rich and noblest[249] seat, which he
made in heaven most to his liking. Now the Son does not
stand before the Father as a servant before the lord, pitifully
clothed, partly naked, but he stands immediately before the
Father, richly clothed in joyful amplitude, with a rich and
precious crown upon his head. For it was revealed that we
are his crown[250], which crown is the Father's joy, the Son's
honour, the Holy Spirit's delight, and endless marvellous
bliss to all who are in heaven.

Now the Son does not stand before the Father on the
left like a labourer, but he sits at the Father's right hand in
endless rest and peace. But this does not mean that the Son
sits on the right hand side as one man sits beside another in
this life, for there is no such sitting, as I see it, in the
Trinity; but he sits at his Father's right hand, that is to say
right in the highest nobility of the Father's joy. Now the
spouse, God's son, is at peace with his beloved wife, who is
the fair maiden of endless joy. Now the Son, true God and
true man, sits in his city in rest and in peace, which his
Father has prepared for him by his endless purpose, and the
Father in the Son, and the Holy Spirit in the Father and in
the Son.

---

247. So SS; P, C: 'morning' (or 'mourning').
248. So C, SS; P: 'fair'.
249. So SS; P, C: 'noble'.
250. See 216, 230.

The Fifty-Second Chapter

And so I saw that God rejoices that he is our Father, and God rejoices that he is our Mother, and God rejoices that he is our true spouse, and that our soul is his beloved wife. And Christ rejoices that he is our brother, and Jesus rejoices that he is our saviour. These are five great joys, as I understand, in which he wants us to rejoice, praising him, thanking him, loving him, endlessly blessing him, all who will be saved.

During our lifetime here we have in us a marvellous mixture of both well-being and woe. We have in us our risen Lord Jesus Christ, and we have in us the wretchedness and the harm of Adam's falling. Dying, we are constantly protected by Christ, and by the touching of his grace we are raised to true trust in salvation. And we are so afflicted in our feelings by Adam's falling in various ways, by sin and by different pains, and in this we are made dark and so blind that we can scarcely accept any comfort. But in our intention we wait for God, and trust faithfully to have mercy and grace; and this is his own working in us, and in his goodness he opens the eye of our understanding, by which we have sight, sometimes more and sometimes less, according to the ability God gives us to receive. And now we are raised to the one, and now we are permitted to fall to the other. And so that mixture is so marvellous in us that we scarcely know, about ourselves or about our fellow Christians, what condition we are in, these conflicting feelings are so extraordinary, except for each holy act of assent to God which we make when we feel him, truly willing with all our heart to be with him, and with all our soul and with all our might. And then we hate and despise our evil inclinations, and everything which could be an occasion of spiritual and bodily sin. And even so, when this sweetness is hidden, we fall again into blindness, and so in various ways into woe and tribulation. But then this is our comfort, that we know in our faith that by the power of Christ who is our protector we never assent to that, but we complain about it, and endure in pain and in woe, praying until the time that he shows[251] himself again to us. And so we remain in this mixture all the days of our life; but he wants us to trust that he is constantly with us, and that in three ways.

He is with us in heaven, true man in his own person, drawing us up; and that was revealed in the spiritual thirst[252]. And he is with us on earth, leading us; and that was revealed in the third revelation, where I saw God in a moment of time[253]. And he is with us in our soul, endlessly dwelling, ruling and guarding[254]; and that was revealed in the sixteenth revelation, as I shall say[255].

And so in the servant there was shown the blindness and the hurt of Adam's falling; and in the servant there was shown the wisdom and the goodness of God's Son. And in the lord there was shown the compassion and the pity for Adam's woe; and in the lord there was shown the great nobility and the endless honour that man has come to, by the power of the Passion and the death of God's beloved Son. And therefore he greatly rejoices in his falling, for the raising on high and the fulness of bliss which mankind has come to, exceeding what we should have if he had not fallen. And so, to see the surpassing nobility, my understanding was led into God at the same time as I saw the servant fall.

And so we have matter for mourning, because our sin is the cause of Christ's pains, and we have constantly matter for joy, because endless love made him suffer. And therefore the creature which sees and feels the operation of love by

---

251. So SS; P, C: 'showed'.
252. See p. 230.
253. See p. 197.
254. So SS; P, C: 'guiding'.
255. See p. 314.

grace hates nothing but sin, for of all things, as I see it, love and hate are the hardest and most immeasurable contraries. And all this notwithstanding, in our Lord's intention I saw and understood that we cannot in this life keep ourselves completely[256] from sin, in the perfect purity that we shall have in heaven. But we can well by grace keep ourselves from the sins which would lead us to endless torment, as Holy Church teaches us, and eschew venial sin, reasonably, to the extent of our power. And if we through our blindness and our wretchedness at any time fall, then let us quickly rise, knowing the sweet touching of grace, and willingly amend ourselves according to the teaching of Holy Church, as may fit the grievousness of the sin, and go on our way with God in love, and neither on the one side fall too low, inclining to despair, nor on the other side be too reckless, as though we did not care; but let us meekly recognize our weakness, knowing that we cannot stand for the twinkling of an eye·except with the protection of grace, and let us reverently cling to God, trusting only in him.

For God sees one way and man sees another way. For it is for man meekly to accuse himself, and it is for our Lord God's own goodness courteously to excuse man. And these are two parts which were shown in the double demeanour with which the lord saw his beloved servant falling.

The one was shown outwardly, very meekly and mildly, with great compassion and pity; and the other was of inward endless love and justice. So[257] does our good Lord want us willingly to accuse ourselves, and to see truly and know our falling, and all the harms which come from it, seeing and knowing that we can never repair it; and also we willingly and truly see and know[258] the everlasting love which he has for us, and his plentiful mercy. And so by

---

256. Or, less probably, 'all holy'.
257. Or, less probably, 'endless love. And just so. . .'
258. 'Our falling, and all. . .see and know' from SS; P, C omit.

grace to see and know both together is the meek self-accusation which our good Lord asks from us. And he himself works where it is, and this is the lower part of man's life; and it was shown in the outward demeanour, and in this showing I saw two parts. One is man's pitiful falling; the other is the glorious atonement which our Lord has made for man. The other demeanour was inwardly shown, and that was more exaltedly shown, and it was all one; for the life and the power that we have in the lower part is from the higher, and it comes down to us from the substantial love of the self, by grace. In between the one and the other is nothing at all, for it is all one love, which one blessed love now has a double operation in us; for in the lower part there are pains and sufferings, compassions and pities, mercies and forgiveness and other such, which are profitable. But in the higher part there are none of these, but all is one great love and marvellous joy, in which marvellous joy all pains are wholly destroyed. And in this our good Lord showed not only that we are excused, but also the honourable nobility to which he will bring us, turning all our blame into endless honour.

The Fifty-Third Chapter

And thus I saw that he wants us to know that he takes the falling of any creature who will be saved no harder than he took the falling of Adam, who, we know, was endlessly loved and safely protected in the time of all his need, and now is blissfully restored in great and surpassing joys. For our Lord God is so good, so gentle and so courteous that he can never assign final failure to those in whom he will always be blessed and praised.

And in what I have now said my desire was partly answered, and my great fear was somewhat eased by the lovely, gracious revelation of our Lord God. In this revelation I saw and understood very surely that in each soul which will be saved there is a godly will which never assented to sin nor ever will, which will is so good that it can never will evil, but always constantly it wills good and it does good in the sight of God.

Therefore our Lord wants us to know it in our faith and our belief, and particularly and truly that we have all this blessed will whole and safe in our Lord Jesus Christ, because every nature with which heaven will be filled had of necessity and of God's rightfulness to be so joined and united in him that in it a substance was kept which could never and should never be parted from him, and that through his own good will in his endless prescient[259] purpose.

And despite this rightful joining and this endless uniting, still the redemption and the buying-back of mankind is needful and profitable in everything, as it is done with the same intention and for the same end as Holy Church teaches us in our faith. For I saw that God never began to love mankind; for just as mankind will be in endless bliss, fulfilling God's joy with regard to his works, just so has that same mankind been known and loved in God's prescience from without beginning in his righteous intent. And by the endless intent and assent and the full accord of all the Trinity, the mediator[260] wanted to be the foundation and the head of this fair nature, out of whom we have all come, in whom we are all enclosed, into whom we shall all go, finding in him our full heaven in everlasting joy by the prescient purpose of all the blessed Trinity from without beginning. For before he made us he loved us, and when we were made we loved him; and this is made only of the natural substantial goodness of the Holy Spirit, mighty by reason of the might of the Father, wise in mind of the

---

259. SS: 'prescient'; P, C: 'fore said'.
260. Literally, 'the mid person'.

wisdom of the Son. And so is man's soul made by God, and in the same moment joined to God.

And so I understood that man's soul is made of nothing, that is to say that it is made of nothing that is made, in this way: When God was to make man's body, he took the slime of the earth, which is matter mixed and gathered from all bodily things, and of that he made man's body. But to the making of man's soul he would accept nothing at all, but made it. And so is created nature rightfully united to the maker, who is substantial uncreated nature, that is God. And so it is that there may and will be nothing at all between God and man's soul. And in this endless love man's soul is kept whole, as all the matter of the revelation means and shows.

In this endless love we are led and protected by God, and we never shall be lost; for he wants us to know that the soul is a life, which life of his goodness and his grace will last in heaven without end, loving him, thanking him, praising him. And just as we were to be without end, so we were treasured and hidden in God, known and loved from without beginning. Therefore he wants us to know that the noblest thing which he ever made is mankind, and the fullest substance and the highest power is the blessed soul of Christ. And furthermore, he wants us to know that this beloved soul was preciously knitted to him in its making, by a knot so subtle and so mighty that it is united in God. In this uniting it is made endlessly holy. Furthermore, he wants us to know that all the souls which will be saved in heaven without end are knit in this knot, and united in this union, and made holy in this holiness.

The Fifty-Fourth Chapter

And for the great endless love that God has for all
mankind, he makes no distinction in love between the
blessed soul of Christ and the least soul that will be saved.
For it is very easy to believe and trust that the dwelling of
the blessed soul of Christ is very high in the glorious
divinity; and truly, as I understand our Lord to mean, where
the blessed soul of Christ is, there is the substance of all the
souls which will be saved by Christ.

Greatly ought we to rejoice that God dwells in our soul;
and more greatly ought we to rejoice that our soul dwells in
God. Our soul is created to be God's dwelling place, and the
dwelling of our soul is God, who is uncreated. It is a great
understanding to see and know inwardly that God, who is
our Creator, dwells in our soul, and it is a far greater
understanding to see and know inwardly that our soul,
which is created, dwells in God in substance, of which
substance, through God, we are what we are.

And I saw no difference between God and our
substance, but, as it were, all God; and still my
understanding accepted that our substance is in God, that is
to say that God is God, and our substance is a creature in
God. For the almighty truth of the Trinity is our Father, for
he made us and keeps us in him. And the deep wisdom of
the Trinity is our Mother, in whom we are enclosed. And
the high goodness of the Trinity is our Lord, and in him we
are enclosed and he in us. We are enclosed in the Father,
and we are enclosed in the Son, and we are enclosed in the
Holy Spirit. And the Father is enclosed in us, the Son is
enclosed in us, and the Holy Spirit is enclosed in us,
almighty, all wisdom and all goodness, one God, one Lord.
And our faith is a power which comes from our natural
substance into our sensual soul by the Holy Spirit, in which
power all our powers come to us, for without that no man

can receive power, for it is nothing else than right understanding with true belief and certain trust in our being, that we are in God and he in us, which we do not see.

And this power with all the others which God has ordained for us, entering there, works great things in us; for Christ is mercifully working in us, and we are by grace according with him, through the gift and the power of the Holy Spirit. This working makes it so that we are Christ's children and live Christian lives.

The Fifty-Fifth Chapter

And so Christ is our way, safely leading us in his laws, and Christ in his body mightily bears us up into heaven; for I saw that Christ, having us all in him who shall be saved by him, honourably presents his Father in heaven with us, which present his Father most thankfully receives, and courteously gives to his Son Jesus Christ. This gift and operation is joy to the Father and bliss to the Son and delight to the Holy Spirit, and of everything which is our duty, it is the greatest delight to our Lord that we rejoice in this joy which the blessed Trinity has over our salvation.

And this was seen in the ninth revelation[261], where it says more about this matter; and despite all our feelings of woe or of well-being, God wants us to understand and to believe that we are more truly in heaven than on earth. Our faith comes from the natural love of our soul, and from the clear light of our reason, and from the steadfast memory which we have from God in our first creation. And when our soul is breathed into our body, at which time we are made sensual, at once mercy and grace begin to work, having care of us and protecting us with pity and love, in which operation the Holy Spirit forms in our faith the hope

---

261. See p. 218.

that we shall return up above to our substance, into the power of Christ, increased and fulfilled through the Holy Spirit. So I understood that our sensuality is founded in nature, in mercy and in grace, and this foundation enables us to receive gifts which lead us to endless life. For I saw very surely that our substance is in God, and I also saw that God is in our sensuality, for in the same instant and place in which our soul is made sensual, in that same instant and place exists the city of God, ordained for him from without beginning. He comes into this city and will never depart from it, for God is never out of the soul, in which he will dwell blessedly without end.

And this was said in the sixteenth revelation[262], where it says: The place that Jesus takes in our soul he will never depart from. And all the gifts which God can give to the creature he has given to his Son Jesus for us, which gifts he, dwelling in us, has enclosed in him until the time that we are fully grown, our soul together with our body and our body together with our soul. Let either of them take help from the other, until we have grown to full stature as creative nature brings about; and then in the foundation of creative nature with the operation of mercy, the Holy Spirit by grace breathes into us gifts leading to endless life.

And so my understanding was led by God to see in him and to know, to understand and to recognize that our soul is a created trinity, like the uncreated blessed Trinity, known and loved from without beginning, and in the creation united to the Creator, as is said before. This sight was sweet and wonderful to contemplate, peaceful and restful, secure and delectable. And because of the glorious union which was thus made by God between the soul and the body, mankind had necessarily to be restored from a double death, which restoration could never be until the time when the second person in the Trinity had taken the lower part of

---

262. See p. 313.

287

human nature, whose highest part was united to him in its first creation. And these two parts were in Christ, the higher and the lower, which are only one soul. The higher part was always at peace with God in full joy and bliss. The lower part, which is sensuality, suffered for the salvation of mankind. And these two parts were seen and felt in the eighth revelation[263], in which my body was filled full of feeling and memory of Christ's Passion and his dying. And furthermore, together with this there was a perception and a secret inward vision of the higher part[264], and that was shown at the same time, when I could not, in response to the intermediary's suggestion, look up to heaven. And that was because of that same mighty contemplative vision of the inward life, which inward life is that high substance, that precious soul which is endlessly rejoicing in the divinity.

The Fifty-Sixth Chapter

And so I saw most surely that it is quicker for us and easier to come to the knowledge of God than it is to know our own soul. For our soul is so deeply grounded in God and so endlessly treasured that we cannot come to knowledge of it until we first have knowledge of God, who is the Creator to whom it is united. But nevertheless I saw that we have, naturally from our fulness, to desire wisely and truly to know our own soul, through which we are taught to seek it where it is, and that is in God. And so by the leading through grace of the Holy Spirit we shall know them[265] both in one; whether we are moved to know God or our soul, either motion is good and true. God is closer to us than our own soul, for he is the foundation on which our

---

263. See p. 209.
264. So SS; P, C: 'parts'.
265. So SS, W: 'hem' (i.e., 'them'); in P, C, 'him' is defensible but less probable.

soul stands, and he is the mean which keeps the substance
and the sensuality together, so that they will never separate.
For our soul sits in God in true rest, and our soul stands in
God in sure strength, and our soul is naturally rooted in
God in endless love. And therefore if we want to have
knowledge of our soul, and communion and discourse with
it, we must seek in our Lord God in whom it is enclosed.

And of this enclosing I saw and understood more in the
sixteenth revelation, as I shall say[266], and as regards our
substance, it can rightly be called our soul, and as regards
our sensuality, it can rightly be called our soul, and that is
by the union which it has in God.

That honourable city in which our Lord Jesus sits is our
sensuality, in which he is enclosed; and our natural
substance is enclosed in Jesus, with the blessed soul of
Christ sitting in rest in the divinity. And I saw very
certainly that we must necessarily be in longing and in
penance until the time when we are led so deeply into God
that we verily and truly know our own soul; and I saw
certainly that our good Lord himself leads us into this high
depth, in the same love with which he created us and in the
same love with which he redeemed us, by mercy and grace,
through the power of his blessed Passion.

And all this notwithstanding, we can never come to the
full knowledge of God until we first clearly know our own
soul. For until the time that it is in its full powers, we
cannot be all holy; and that is when our sensuality by the
power of Christ's Passion can be brought up into the
substance, with all the profits of our tribulation which our
Lord will make us obtain through mercy and grace.

I had a partial touching[267], and it is founded in nature,

---

266. See p. 312.
267. On Julian's use of this technical term 'to convey that she is being directly affected
and moved by the Holy Spirit to experience the reality of God, in a way which is above
intellectual comprehension, but which accompanies and supports some form of inner
seeing', see *Showings*, II, 573-74 note 38.

that is to say: Our reason is founded in God, who is nature's substance. From this substantial nature spring mercy and grace, and penetrate[268] us, accomplishing everything for the fulfillment of our joy. These are our foundations, in which we have our being, our increase and our fulfillment. For in nature we have our life and our being, and in mercy and grace we have our increase and our fulfillment. This is three properties in one goodness, and where one operates all operate in the things which now pertain to us.

God wants us to understand, desiring with all our heart and all our strength to have knowledge of them, always more and more until the time that we are fulfilled; for to know them fully and to see them clearly is nothing else than endless joy and bliss, which we shall have in heaven, which God wants us to begin here in knowledge of his love. For we cannot profit by our reason alone, unless we have equally memory and love; nor can we be saved merely because we have in God our natural foundation, unless we have, coming from[269] the same foundation, mercy and grace. For from these three operating[270] all together we receive all our good, the first of which is the good of nature. For in our first making God gave us as much good and as great good as we could receive in our spirit alone; but his prescient purpose in his endless wisdom willed that we should be double.

The Fifty-Seventh Chapter

And as regards our substance, he made us so noble and so rich that always we achieve his will and his glory. When I say 'we', that means men who will be saved. For truly I saw that we are that which he loves, and that we do what is

---

268. Literally, 'spread into us'; see *Showings*, II, 574.
269. P, C, S1: 'connyng' ('knowledge') of'; but S2 has emended intelligently.
270. So SS; P, C: 'operations'.

pleasing to him, constantly, without any stinting. And from this great richness and this high nobility, commensurate powers come into our soul, whilst it is joined to our body, in which joining we are made sensual. And so in our substance we are full and in our sensuality we are lacking, and this lack God will restore and fill by the operation of mercy and grace, plentifully flowing into us from his own natural goodness. And so this natural goodness makes mercy and grace to work in us, and the natural goodness that we have from him enables us to receive the operation of mercy and grace.

I saw that our nature is wholly in God, in which he makes diversities flowing out of him to perform his will, which[271] nature preserves and mercy and grace restore and fulfil. And of these none will be destroyed, for our nature, which is the higher part, is joined to God in its creation, and God is joined to our nature, which is the lower part in taking flesh. And so in Christ our two natures are united, for the Trinity is comprehended in Christ, in whom our higher part is founded and rooted; and our lower part the second person has taken, which nature was first prepared for him.

For I saw most truly that all the works which God has done or will ever do were fully known to him and foreseen from without beginning. And for love he made mankind, and for the same love he himself wanted to become man. The next good which we receive is our faith, in which we begin to profit; and it comes from the great riches of our natural substance into our soul, which is sensual; and it is founded in us and we in it through the natural goodness of God by the operation of mercy and grace. And from that comes all our good, by which we are led and saved. For in that come the commandments of God, of which we ought to have two kinds of understanding. One is that we ought to

---

271. P, C: 'whose'; SS: 'whom'; neither is attractive.

understand and know what things he commands, to love them and to keep them. The other is that we ought to know what things he forbids, to hate them and refuse them. For in these two is all our activity comprehended. Also in our faith come the seven sacraments, one following another in the order God has ordained them in for us, and every kind of virtue. For the same virtues which we have received from our substance, given to us in nature by the goodness of God, the same virtues by the operation of mercy are given to us in grace, renewed through the Holy Spirit; and these virtues and gifts are treasured for us in Jesus Christ. For in the same time that God joined himself to our body in the maiden's womb, he took our soul, which is sensual, and in taking it, having enclosed us all in himself, he united it to our substance. In this union he was perfect man, for Christ, having joined in himself every man who will be saved, is perfect man.

So our Lady is our mother, in whom we are all enclosed and born of her in Christ, for she who is mother of our saviour is mother of all who are saved in our saviour; and our saviour is our true Mother, in whom we are endlessly born and out of whom we shall never come.

Plenteously, fully and sweetly was this shown; and it is spoken of in the first revelation[272], where it says that we are all enclosed in him, and he is enclosed in us. And it is spoken of in the sixteenth revelation[273], where he says that he sits in our soul, for it is his delight to reign blessedly in our understanding, and sit restfully in our soul, and to dwell endlessly in our soul, working us all into him. In this working he wants us to be his helpers, giving all our intention to him, learning his laws, observing his teaching, desiring everything to be done which he does, truly trusting in him, for I saw truly that our substance is in him.

---

272. See p. 186.
273. See p. 313.

The Fifty-Eighth Chapter

God the blessed Trinity, who is everlasting being, just as he is eternal from without beginning, just so was it in his eternal purpose to create human nature, which fair nature was first prepared for his own Son, the second person; and when he wished, by full agreement of the whole Trinity he created us all once. And in our creating he joined and united us to himself, and through this union we are kept as pure and as noble as we were created. By the power of that same precious union we love our Creator and delight in him, praise him and thank him and endlessly rejoice in him. And this is the work which is constantly performed in every soul which will be saved, and this is the godly will mentioned before[274].

And so in our making, God almighty is our loving Father, and God all wisdom is our loving Mother, with the love and the goodness of the Holy Spirit, which is all one God, one Lord. And in the joining and the union he is our very true spouse and we his beloved wife and his fair maiden, with which wife he was never displeased; for he says: I love you and you love me, and our love will never divide in two.

I contemplated the work of all the blessed Trinity, in which contemplation I saw and understood these three properties: the property of the fatherhood, and the property of the motherhood, and the property of the lordship in one God. In our almighty Father we have our protection and our bliss, as regards our natural substance, which is ours by our creation from without beginning; and in the second person, in knowledge and wisdom we have our perfection, as regards our sensuality, our restoration and our salvation, for he is our Mother, brother and saviour; and in our good Lord the

---

274. See p. 283.

293

Holy Spirit we have our reward and our gift for our living and our labour, endlessly surpassing all that we desire in his marvellous courtesy, out of his great plentiful grace. For all our life consists of three: In the first we have our being, and in the second we have our increasing, and in the third we have our fulfillment. The first is nature, the second is mercy, the third is grace.

As to the first, I saw and understood that the high might of the Trinity is our Father, and the deep wisdom of the Trinity is our Mother, and the great love of the Trinity is our Lord; and all these we have in nature and in our substantial creation. And furthermore I saw that the second person, who is our Mother, substantially the same beloved person, has now become our mother sensually, because we are double by God's creating, that is to say substantial and sensual. Our substance is the higher part, which we have in our Father, God almighty; and the second person of the Trinity is our Mother in nature in our substantial creation, in whom we are founded and rooted, and he is our Mother of mercy in taking our sensuality. And so our Mother is working on us in various ways, in whom our parts are kept undivided; for in our Mother Christ we profit and increase, and in mercy he reforms and restores us, and by the power of his Passion, his death and his Resurrection he unites[275] us to our substance. So our Mother works in mercy on all his beloved children who are docile and obedient to him, and grace works with mercy, and especially in two properties, as it was shown, which working belongs to the third person, the Holy Spirit. He works, rewarding and giving. Rewarding is a gift for our confidence which the Lord makes to those who have laboured; and giving is a courteous act which he does freely, by grace, fulfilling and surpassing all that creatures deserve.

Thus in our Father, God almighty, we have our being,

---

275. So SS; P, C: 'united'.

and in our Mother of mercy we have our reforming and our restoring, in whom our parts are united and all made perfect man, and through the rewards and the gifts of grace of the Holy Spirit we are fulfilled. And our substance is in our Father, God almighty, and our substance is in our Mother, God all wisdom, and our substance is in our Lord God, the Holy Spirit, all goodness, for our substance is whole in each person of the Trinity, who is one God. And our sensuality is only in the second person, Christ Jesus, in whom is the Father and the Holy Spirit; and in him and by him we are powerfully taken out of hell and out of the wretchedness on earth, and gloriously brought up into heaven, and blessedly united to our substance, increased in riches and nobility by all the power of Christ and by the grace and operation of the Holy Spirit.

The Fifty-Ninth Chapter

And we have all this bliss by mercy and grace, and this kind of bliss we never could have had and known, unless that property of goodness which is in God had been opposed, through which we have this bliss. For wickedness has been suffered to rise in opposition to that goodness; and the goodness of mercy and grace opposed that wickedness, and turned everything to goodness and honour for all who will be saved. For this is that property in God which opposes good to evil. So Jesus Christ, who opposes good to evil, is our true Mother. We have our being from him, where the foundation of motherhood begins, with all the sweet protection of love which endlessly follows.

As truly as God is our Father, so truly is God our Mother, and he revealed that in everything, and especially in these sweet words where he says[276]: I am he; that is to say: I

---

276. See p. 223.

am he, the power and goodness of fatherhood; I am he, the wisdom and the lovingness of motherhood; I am he, the light and the grace which is all blessed love; I am he, the Trinity; I am he, the unity; I am he, the great supreme goodness of every kind of thing; I am he who makes you to love; I am he who makes you to[277] long; I am he, the endless fulfilling of all true desires. For where the soul is highest, noblest, most honourable, still it is lowest, meekest and mildest.

And from this foundation in substance we have all the powers of our sensuality by the gift of nature, and by the help and the furthering of mercy and grace, without which we cannot profit. Our great Father, almighty God, who is being, knows us and loved us before time began. Out of this knowledge, in his most wonderful deep love, by the prescient eternal counsel of all the blessed Trinity, he wanted the second person to become our Mother, our brother and our saviour. From this it follows that as truly as God is our Father, so truly is God our Mother. Our Father wills, our Mother works, our good Lord the Holy Spirit confirms. And therefore it is our part to love our God in whom we have our being, reverently thanking and praising him for our creation, mightily praying to our Mother for mercy and pity, and to our Lord the Holy Spirit for help and grace. For in these three is all our life: nature, mercy and grace, of which we have mildness, patience and pity, and hatred of sin and wickedness; for the virtues must of themselves hate sin and wickedness.

And so Jesus is our true Mother in nature by our first creation, and he is our true Mother in grace by his taking our created nature. All the lovely works and all the sweet loving offices of beloved motherhood are appropriated to the second person, for in him we have this godly[278] will, whole

---

277. 'love, I am he who makes you to' from SS, W; P, C omit.
278. P: 'goodly', which is not challenged except by S2: 'kindly'; but Julian may be referring to the doctrine of the godly will which never assents to sin.

and safe forever, both in nature and in grace, from his own goodness proper to him.

I understand three ways of contemplating motherhood in God. The first is the foundation of our nature's creation; the second is his taking of our nature, where the motherhood of grace begins; the third is the motherhood at work. And in that, by the same grace, everything is penetrated, in length and in breadth, in height and in depth without end; and it is all one love.

The Sixtieth Chapter

But now I should say a little more about this penetration, as I understood our Lord to mean: How we are brought back by the motherhood of mercy and grace into our natural place, in which we were created by the motherhood of love, a mother's love which never leaves us.

Our Mother in nature, our Mother in grace, because he wanted altogether to become our Mother in all things, made the foundation of his work most humbly and most mildly in the maiden's womb. And he revealed that in the first revelation[279], when he brought that meek maiden before the eye of my understanding in the simple stature which she had when she conceived; that is to say that our great God, the supreme wisdom of all things, arrayed and prepared himself in this humble place, all ready in our poor flesh, himself to do the service and the office of motherhood in everything. The mother's service is nearest, readiest and surest: nearest because it is most natural, readiest because it is most loving, and surest because it is truest. No one ever might or could perform this office fully, except only him. We know that all our mothers bear us for pain and for death. O[280], what is

---

279. See p. 182.
280. SS: 'And'.

that? But our true Mother Jesus, he alone bears us for joy and for endless life, blessed may he be. So he carries us within him in love and travail, until the full time when he wanted to suffer the sharpest thorns and cruel pains that ever were or will be, and at the last he died. And when he had finished, and had borne us so for bliss, still all this could not satisfy his wonderful love. And he revealed this in these great surpassing words of love[281]: If I could suffer more, I would suffer more. He could not die any more, but he did not want to cease working; therefore he must needs nourish us, for the precious love of motherhood has made him our debtor.

The mother can give her child to suck of her milk, but our precious Mother Jesus can feed us with himself, and does, most courteously and most tenderly, with the blessed sacrament, which is the precious food of true life; and with all the sweet sacraments he sustains us most mercifully and graciously, and so he meant in these blessed words[282], where he said: I am he whom Holy Church preaches and teaches to you. That is to say: All the health and the life of the sacraments, all the power and the grace of my word, all the goodness which is ordained in Holy Church for you, I am he.

The mother can lay her child tenderly to her breast, but our tender Mother Jesus can lead us easily into his blessed breast through his sweet open side, and show us there a part of the godhead and of the joys of heaven, with inner certainty of endless bliss. And that he revealed in the tenth revelation[283], giving us the same understanding in these sweet words which he says: See, how I love you, looking into his blessed side, rejoicing.

This fair lovely word 'mother' is so sweet and so kind in

---

281. See p. 218.
282. See p. 223.
283. See p. 221.

itself that it cannot truly be said of anyone or to anyone
except of him and to him who is the true Mother of life and
of all things. To the property of motherhood belong nature,
love, wisdom and knowledge, and this is God. For though it
may be so that our bodily bringing to birth is only little,
humble and simple in comparison with our spiritual bringing
to birth, still it is he who does it in the creatures by whom it
is done. The kind, loving mother who knows and sees the
need of her child guards it very tenderly, as the nature and
condition of motherhood will have. And always as the child
grows in age and in stature, she acts differently, but she does
not change her love. And when it is even older, she allows it
to be chastised to destroy its faults, so as to make the child
receive virtues and grace. This work, with everything which
is lovely and good, our Lord performs in those by whom it
is done. So he is our Mother in nature by the operation of
grace in the lower part, for love of the higher part. And he
wants us to know it, for he wants to have all our love
attached to him; and in this I saw that every debt which we
owe by God's command to fatherhood and motherhood is
fulfilled in truly loving God, which blessed love Christ
works in us. And this was revealed in everything, and
especially in the great bounteous words when he says[284]: I
am he whom you love.

The Sixty-First Chapter

And in our spiritual bringing to birth he uses more
tenderness, without any comparison, in protecting us. By so
much as our soul is more precious in his sight, he kindles
our understanding, he prepares our ways, he eases our
conscience, he comforts our soul, he illumines[285] our heart

---

284. See p. 223.
285. Or, less probably in the context, 'lightens'.

and gives us partial knowledge and love of his blessed divinity, with gracious memory of his sweet humanity and his blessed Passion, with courteous wonder over his great surpassing goodness, and makes us to love everything which he loves for love of him, and to be well satisfied with him and with all his works. And when we fall, quickly he raises us up with his loving embrace and his gracious touch. And when we are strengthened by his sweet working, then we willingly choose him by his grace, that we shall be his servants and his lovers, constantly and forever.

And yet after this he allows some of us to fall more heavily and more grievously than ever we did before, as it seems to us. And then we who are not all wise think that everything which we have undertaken was all nothing. But it is not so, for we need to fall, and we need to see it; for if we did not fall, we should not know how feeble and how wretched we are in ouserlves, nor, too, should we know so completely the wonderful love of our Creator.

For we shall truly see in heaven without end that we have sinned grievously in this life; and notwithstanding this, we shall truly see that we were never hurt in his love, nor were we ever of less value in his sight. And by the experience of this falling we shall have a great and marvellous knowledge of love in God without end; for enduring and marvellous is that love which cannot and will not be broken because of offences.

And this was one profitable understanding; another is the humility and meekness which we shall obtain by the sight of our fall, for by that we shall be raised high in heaven, to which raising we might never have come without that meekness. And therefore we need to see it; and if we do not see it, though we fell, that would not profit us. And commonly we first fall and then see it; and both are from the mercy of God.

The mother may sometimes suffer the child to fall and

to be distressed in various ways, for its own[286] benefit, but she can never suffer any kind of peril to come to her child, because of her love. And though our earthly mother may suffer her child to perish, our heavenly Mother Jesus may never suffer us who are his children to perish, for he is almighty, all wisdom and all love, and so is none but he, blessed may he be.

But often when our falling and our wretchedness are shown to us, we are so much afraid and so greatly ashamed of ourselves that we scarcely know where we can put ourselves. But then our courteous Mother does not wish us to flee away, for nothing would be less pleasing to him; but he then wants us to behave like a child. For when it is distressed and frightened, it runs quickly to its mother; and if it can do no more, it calls to the mother for help with all its might. So he wants us to act as a meek child, saying: My kind Mother, my gracious Mother, my beloved Mother, have mercy on me. I have made myself filthy and unlike you, and I may not and cannot make it right except with your help and grace.

And if we do not then feel ourselves eased, let us at once be sure that he is behaving as a wise Mother. For if he sees that it is profitable to us to mourn and to weep, with compassion and pity he suffers that until the right time has come, out of his love. And then he wants us to show a child's characteristics, which always naturally trusts in its mother's love in well-being and in woe. And he wants us to commit ourselves fervently to the faith of Holy Church, and find there our beloved Mother in consolation and true understanding, with all the company of the blessed. For one single person may often be broken, as it seems to him, but the entire body of Holy Church was never broken, nor ever will be without end. And therefore it is a certain thing, and

---

286. So C, SS; P: 'the one'.

good and gracious to will, meekly and fervently, to be fastened and united to our mother Holy Church, who is Christ Jesus. For the flood of mercy which is his dear blood and precious water is plentiful to make us fair and clean. The blessed wounds of our saviour are open and rejoice to heal us. The sweet gracious hands of our Mother are ready and diligent about us; for he in all this work exercises the true office of a kind nurse, who has nothing else to do but attend to the safety of her child.

It is his office to save us, it is his glory to do it, and it is his will that we know it; for he wants us to love him sweetly and trust in him meekly and greatly. And he revealed this in these gracious words[287]: I protect you very safely.

The Sixty-Second Chapter

For at that time he revealed our frailty and our falling, our trespasses and our humiliations, our chagrins and our burdens and all our woe, as much as it seemed to me could happen in this life. And with that he revealed his blessed power, his blessed wisdom, his blessed love, and that he protects us at such times, as tenderly and as sweetly, to his glory, and as surely to our salvation as he does when we are in the greatest consolation and comfort, and raises us to this in spirit, on high in heaven, and turns everything to his glory and to our joy without end. For his precious love, he never allows us to lose time; and all this is of the natural goodness of God by the operation of grace.

God is essence in his very nature; that is to say, that goodness which is natural is God. He is the ground, his is the substance, he is very essence or nature, and he is the true Father and the true Mother of natures. And all natures which he has made to flow out of him to work his will, they

287. See p. 241.

will be restored and brought back into him by the salvation of man through the operation of grace. For all natures which he has put separately in different creatures are all in man, wholly, in fulness and power, in beauty and in goodness, in kingliness and in nobility, in every manner of stateliness, preciousness and honour.

Here we can see that we are all bound to God by nature, and we are bound to God by grace. Here we can see that we do not need to seek far afield so as to know various natures, but to go to Holy Church, into our Mother's breast, that is to say into our own soul, where our Lord dwells. And there we should find everything, now in faith and understanding, and afterwards truly, in himself, clearly, in bliss.

But let no man or woman apply this particularly to himself, because it is not so. It is general, because it is our precious Mother Christ, and for him was this fair nature prepared for the honour and the nobility of man's creation, and for the joy and the bliss of man's salvation, just as he saw, knew and recognized from without beginning.

The Sixty-Third Chapter

Here we may see that truly it belongs to our nature to hate sin, and truly it belongs to us by grace to hate sin, for nature is all good and fair in itself, and grace was sent out to save nature and destroy sin, and bring fair nature back again to the blessed place from which it came, which is God, with more nobility and honour by the powerful operation of grace. For it will be seen before God by all his saints in joy without end that nature has been tried in the fire of tribulation, and that no lack or defect is found in it.

So are nature and grace of one accord; for grace is God, as uncreated nature is God. He is two in his manner of operation, and one in love, and neither of these works

303

without the other, and they are not separated. And when we by the mercy of God and with his help reconcile ourselves to nature and to grace, we shall see truly that sin is incomparably worse, more vile and painful than hell. For it is in opposition to our fair nature; for as truly as sin is unclean, so truly is sin unnatural. All this is a horrible thing to see for the loving soul which would wish to be all fair and shining in the sight of God, as nature and grace teach. But do not let us be afraid of this, except insofar as fear may be profitable; but let us meekly lament to our beloved Mother, and he will sprinkle us all with his precious blood, and make our soul most pliable and most mild, and heal us most gently in the course of time, just as it is most glory to him and joy to us without end. And from this sweet and gentle operation he will never cease or desist, until all his beloved children are born and brought to birth; and he revealed that when he gave understanding of the spiritual thirst which is the longing in love which will last till the day of judgment[288].

So in our true Mother Jesus our life is founded in his own prescient wisdom from without beginning, with the great power of the Father and the supreme goodness of the Holy Spirit. And in accepting our nature he gave us life, and in his blessed dying on the Cross he bore us to endless life. And since that time, now and ever until the day of judgment, he feeds us and fosters us, just as the great supreme lovingness of motherhood wishes, and as the natural need of childhood asks. Fair and sweet is our heavenly Mother in the sight of our soul, precious and lovely are the children of grace in the sight of our heavenly Mother, with gentleness and meekness and all the lovely virtues which belong to children by nature. For the child does not naturally despair of the mother's love, the child does not naturally rely upon itself, naturally the child loves the mother and either of them the other.

---

288. See p. 230.

These, and all others that resemble them, are such fair virtues, with which our heavenly Mother is served and pleased. And I understood no greater stature in this life than childhood, with its feebleness and lack of power and intelligence, until the time that our gracious Mother has brought us up into our Father's bliss. And there it will truly be made known to us what he means in the sweet words when he says[289]: All will be well, and you will see it yourself, that every kind of thing will be well. And then will the bliss of our motherhood in Christ be to begin anew in the joys of our Father, God, which new beginning will last, newly beginning without end.

The Fifteenth Revelation[290]
The Sixty-Fourth Chapter

So I understood that all his blessed children who have come out of him by nature ought to be brought back into him by grace.

Before this time[291], I had great longing and desire of God's gift to be delivered from this world and from this life. For often I beheld the woe that there is here and the good and the blessed being that is there; and if there had been no pain in this life except the absence of our Lord, it seemed to me sometimes that that was more than I could bear, and this made me to mourn and diligently long[292], and also over my

---

289. See p. 229.
290. For the editors' reasons for following SS in beginning Revelation XV here, and not P, C, which begin it with 'And then will the bliss of our motherhood. . .' (chapter 63, p. 305), see *Showings*, II, 619.
291. Correspondence with the short text, chapter xx, resumes. See p. 160.
292. The rest of this sentence is not in the short text.

own wretchedness, sloth and weariness, so that I had no pleasure in living and labouring as was my duty.

And to all this our courteous Lord answered, to give me comfort and patience, and said these words: Suddenly you will be taken out of all your pain, all your sickness, all your unrest and all your woe. And you will come up above, and you will have me for your reward, and you will be filled full of joy and bliss, and you will never again have any kind of pain, any kind of sickness, any kind of displeasure, no lack of will, but always joy and bliss without end. Why then should it afflict you to endure awhile, since it is my will and to my glory?

And in these words: Suddenly you will be taken, I saw that God rewarded man for the patience which he has in awaiting God's will and his time, and that man has patience to endure throughout the span of his life, because he does not know when the time for him to die will come. This is very profitable, because if he knew when that would be, he would set a limit to his patience. Then, too, it is God's will that so long as the soul is in the body it should seem to a man that he is always on the point of being taken. For all this life and this longing we have here is only an instant of time, and when we are suddenly taken into bliss out of pain, then pain will be nothing.

And in this time[293] I saw a body lying on the earth, which appeared oppressive and fearsome and without shape and form, as it were a devouring pit of stinking mud[294]; and suddenly out of this body there sprang a most beautiful creature, a little child, fully shaped and formed, swift and lively and whiter than the lily, which quickly glided up to heaven.

The pit which was the body signifies the great wretchedness of our mortal flesh; and the smallness of the

---

293. The next four paragraphs are not in the short text.
294. For the editors' justification of this translation, see *Showings*, II, 622-23 notes 32-33.

child signifies the cleanness and the purity of our soul. And I thought: In this body there remains none of this child's beauty, and in this child there remains none of the body's foulness. It is most blessed for man to be taken from pain, more than for pain to be taken from man; for if pain be taken from us, it may return. Therefore this is a supreme comfort and a blessed contemplation for a longing soul, that we shall be taken from pain. For in this promise[295] I saw a merciful compassion which our Lord has for us because of our woe, and a courteous promise of a clean[296] deliverance, for he wants us to be comforted in surpassing joy. And that he revealed in these words: And you will come up above, and you will have me for your reward, and you will be filled full of joy and bliss.

It is God's will that we focus our thought on this blissful contemplation, as often as we can and for as long as we can continue in it with his grace, for to the soul who is led by God, this contemplation is blissful and greatly to God's glory whilst it lasts.

And when we fall back into ourselves, through depression and spiritual blindness and our experience of spiritual and bodily pains, because of our frailty, it is God's will that we know that he has not forgotten us. And this is what he means and says for comfort in these words: And you will never again have pain of any kind, any kind of sickness, any kind of displeasure, any lack of your will, but always joy and bliss without end. Why then should it have afflicted you to endure for awhile, since it is my will and to my glory?

It is God's will[297] that we accept his commands and his consolations as generously and as fully as we are able; and he also wants us to accept our tarrying and our sufferings as

---

295. That is, 'Suddenly you will be taken out of all your pain. . .'
296. C: 'clear'.
297. Correspondence with the short text resumes; see p. 161.

lightly as we are able, and to count them as nothing. For the more lightly that we accept them, the less importance we ascribe to them because of our love, the less pain shall we experience from them and the more thanks and reward shall we have for them.

The Sixty-Fifth Chapter

And so I understood that any man or woman who voluntarily chooses God in his lifetime for love[298], he may be sure that he is endlessly loved with an endless love which makes that grace in him[299]. For he wants us to pay true heed to this[300], that we are as certain in our hope[301] to have the bliss of heaven whilst we are here as we shall be certain of it when we are there.

And always, the more delight and joy that we accept from this certainty, with reverence and humility, the more pleasing it is to God. For as it was revealed[302], this reverence which I mean is a holy courteous fear of our Lord to which humility is joined; and that is that a creature should see the Lord marvellously great, and herself marvellously little. For these virtues are endless brought[303] to God's beloved, and when this happens, it can now to some extent be seen and felt through our Lord's gracious presence. In every circumstance this presence is most desired, for it creates that wonderful security in true faith and certain hope, by a greatness of love in fear which is sweet and delectable.

It is God's will that I see myself as much bound to him

---

298. 'For love' is not in the short text; see p. 161.
299. The short text has: 'may be sure that he too is chosen'.
300. The short text has: 'Pay true heed to this'.
301. The short text has: 'in our trust'.
302. What follows departs from the short text.
303. Literally, 'had'.

in love as if everything which he has done he had done for me; and so[304] should every soul think with regard to his lover. That is to say, the love of God creates in us such a unity that when it is truly seen, no man can separate himself from another. And so each soul ought to think that God has done for him all that he has done. And he reveals this to make us love him, and delight in him, and fear nothing but him.

For it is his will that we know that all the[305] power of our enemy is shut in the hand of our friend, and therefore a soul which knows this to be certain will fear nothing but him whom she[306] loves. All other fears she counts among the sufferings and bodily sicknesses and fantasies which she must endure; and therefore, though we be in so much pain, woe and unrest that it seems to us that we can think of nothing at all but the state we are in or what we are feeling, let us, as soon as we may, pass it over lightly and count it as nothing. Why? Because God wants to be known, and because if we know him and love him and reverently fear him[307], we shall have patience and be in great rest. And all that he does would be a great delight to us; and our Lord revealed this in these words: Why then should it grieve you to endure for awhile, seeing[308] that it is my will and to my glory?

Now I have told you[309] of fifteen revelations, as God vouchsafed to administer them to my mind, which have been renewed by illuminations and inspirations, from the same spirit, I believe, which revealed them all; of these fifteen revelations, the first began early in the morning, about the hour of four, and it lasted, revealing them in a determined

---

304. Correspondence with the short text resumes; see p. 161.
305. So C, SS; P: 'our'.
306. C, S2: 'he'; S1: 'she', altered to 'he'.
307. 'And reverently fear him' is an addition to the short text.
308. SS: 'since', which agrees with the short text.
309. This last paragraph is not in the short text.

order[310], most lovely and calm, each following the other, until it was three o'clock in the afternoon[311] or later.

The Sixteenth Revelation
The Sixty-Sixth Chapter

And after this the good Lord showed the sixteenth revelation on the following night, as I shall afterwards tell; and this sixteenth revelation was a conclusion and confirmation to all the fifteen. But first I must tell you about my weakness, wretchedness and blindness. I have told of this at the beginning, where it says[312]: Suddenly all my pain was taken from me, and I had no sorrow or distress from this pain so long as the fifteen revelations were being shown. And at the end all was hidden, and I saw no more[313]; and soon I felt that I should live[314] longer. And presently my sickness returned, first in my head, with a sound and a din; and suddenly all my body was filled with sickness as it was before[315], and I was as barren and dry as if the consolation which I had received before were trifling, and, as the wretched creature that I am, I mourned grievously for the bodily pains which I felt, and for lack of spiritual and bodily consolation.

Then a man of religion came to me and asked me how I did, and I said that during that day I had been raving. And he laughed aloud and heartily[316]. And I said that it seemed

---

310. Literally, 'by process'; see *Showings*, II, 631 note 39.
311. Literally, 'noon of the day'; see Matthew 27.45, and *Showings*, II, 631, notes 39-40.
312. See p. 180.
313. Compare the short text, p. 162.
314. Compare the short text, p. 162.
315. 'And presently. . .before' is not in the short text.
316. For the editors' reasons for preferring this to P's 'inwardly', see *Showings*, II, 633, note 17.

to me[317] that the cross which stood in front of my face bled profusely; and when I said this the cleric I was speaking to became very serious, and was surprised. And at once I was very ashamed of my imprudence, and I thought: This man takes seriously every word I could say, who saw no more of this than I had told him[318]. And when I saw that he treated it so seriously and so respectfully, I was greatly ashamed, and wanted to make my confession. But I could not tell it to any priest, for I thought: How could a priest believe me, when I, by saying that I had been raving[319], showed that I did not believe our Lord God? Notwithstanding, I did believe him truly at the time when I saw him, and it was then my will and my intention to do so forever. But like a fool, I let it pass from my mind.

See how wretched I was! This was a great sin and a great ingratitude, that I was so foolish, because of a little bodily pain that I felt, as to abandon so imprudently the strength of all this blessed revelation from our Lord God. Here you can see what I am in myself; but our courteous Lord would not leave me so. And I lay still until night, trusting in his mercy, and then I began to sleep.

The Sixty-Seventh Chapter

And as soon as I fell asleep, it seemed to me that the devil set himself at my throat, thrusting his face[320], like that of a young man, long and strangely lean, close to mine. I never saw anything like him; his colour was red, like a newly baked tile, with black spots like freckles, uglier than a tile. His hair was red as rust, not cut short in front[321], with

---

317. See the short text, p. 162, which makes Julian say that the cross did bleed.

318. This is what the long text seems to mean, but it is probably a corruption of what in the short text is given as 'and he says nothing in reply'.

319. This makes clear, as the short text does not, the precise fault which Julian imputes to herself.

320. The following details of the apparition are not in the short text.

321. SS: 'clipped in front'.

side-locks hanging at his temples. He grinned at me with a vicious look, showing me white teeth so big that it all seemed the uglier to me. His body and his hands were misshapen, but he held me by the throat with his paws, and wanted to stop my breath and kill me, but he could not.

This ugly apparition[322] came when I was sleeping, as none of the others did; and in all this time I trusted to be saved and protected by the mercy of God. And our courteous Lord gave me grace to wake[323], more dead than alive. The people who were with me watched me, and wet my temples, and my heart began to gain strength. And then a little smoke came in at the door, with great heat and a foul stench. And then I said: Blessed be the Lord! Is everything on fire here? And I thought that it must be actual fire, which would have burned us all to death. I asked those who were with me if they were conscious of any stench. They said no, they were not. I said: Blessed be God! for then I knew well that it was the devil who had come to tempt[324] me. And at once I had recourse to what our Lord had revealed to me on that same day, and to all the faith of Holy Church, for I regarded them both as one, and I fled to them as to my source of strength. And immediately everything vanished, and I was brought to great rest and peace, without sickness of body or fear of conscience.

The Sixty-Eighth Chapter

And then our good Lord opened my spiritual eye, and showed me my soul in the midst of my heart. I saw the soul as wide as if it were an endless citadel, and also as if it were

---

322. Literally, 'showing', the term Julian frequently uses for the revelations; but she is careful to distinguish this event from them.
323. Correspondence with the short text resumes; see p. 163.
324. SS: 'tempest' ('assail'), which agrees with the short text.

a blessed kingdom, and from the state which I saw in it, I understood that it is a fine city. In the midst of that city sits our Lord Jesus, true God and true man, a handsome person and tall, highest bishop, most awesome king, most honourable lord. And I saw him splendidly clad in honours. He sits erect there in the soul, in peace and rest, and he rules and guards[325] heaven and earth and everything that is. The humanity and the divinity sit at rest, the divinity rules and guards[326], without instrument or effort. And the[327] soul is wholly occupied by the blessed divinity, sovereign power, sovereign wisdom and sovereign goodness.

The place which Jesus takes in our soul he will nevermore vacate, for in us is his home of homes and his everlasting dwelling[328]. And in this[329] he revealed the delight that he has in the creation of man's soul; for as well as the Father could create a creature and as well as the Son could create a creature, so well did the Holy Spirit want man's spirit to be created, and so it was done. And therefore the blessed Trinity rejoices without end in the creation of man's soul, for it saw without beginning what would delight it without end.

Everything which God has made shows his dominion, as understanding was given at the same time by the example of a creature who is led to see the great nobility and the rulership which is fitting to a lord, and when it had seen all the nobility beneath, then in wonder it was moved to seek up above for that high place where the lord dwells, knowing by reason that his dwelling is in the most honourable place. And thus I understood truly that our soul may never have rest in anything which is beneath itself. And when it comes

---

325. P. C: 'giveth', which is a mistake for 'gemeth' ('guards'), as SS and the short text, p. 164, show.
326. *Ibid*.
327. The short text has 'my'.
328. The short text has 'and it is the greatest delight to him to dwell there'.
329. The rest of this paragraph and the next two are not in the short text.

above all creatures into itself, still it cannot remain contemplating itself; but all its contemplation is blessedly set in God, who is the Creator, dwelling there, for in man's soul is his true dwelling.

And the greatest light and the brightest shining in the city is the glorious love of our Lord God, as I see it. And what can make us to rejoice more in God than to see in him that in us, of all his greatest works, he has joy? For I saw in the same revelation that if the blessed Trinity could have created man's soul any better, any fairer, any nobler than it was created, the Trinity would not have been fully pleased with the creation of man's soul. But because it made man's soul as beautiful, as good, as precious a creature as it could make, therefore the blessed Trinity is fully pleased without end in the creation of man's soul. And it wants our hearts to be powerfully lifted above the depths of the earth and all empty sorrows, and to rejoice in it.

This was a delectable sight and a restful showing, which is without end, and to contemplate it while we are here is most pleasing to God and very great profit to us. And this makes the soul which so contemplates like to him who is contemplated, and unites it in rest and peace. And it was a singular joy and bliss to me that I saw him sitting, for the truth[330] of sitting revealed to me endless dwelling; and he gave me true knowledge that it was he who had revealed everything to me before. And when I had contemplated this with attention, our Lord very humbly revealed words to me, without voice and without opening of lips, just as he had done before, and said very sweetly[331]: Know it well, it was no hallucination which you saw today, but accept and believe it and hold firmly to it, and comfort yourself with it and trust in it[332], and you will not be overcome.

---

330. SS: 'certainty'.
331. The short text has 'seriously'.
332. 'And comfort. . .trust in it' not in the short text.

These last words were said to me to teach me perfect
certainty that it is our Lord Jesus who revealed everything to
me; and just as in the first words which our good Lord
revealed, alluding to his blessed Passion: With this the fiend
is overcome, just so he said in the last words, with perfect
fidelity[333], alluding to us all: You will not be overcome. And
all this teaching and this true strengthening apply generally
to all my fellow Christians, as is said before, and so is the
will of God.

And these words: You will not be overcome, were said
very insistently and strongly, for certainty and strength
against every tribulation which may come. He did not say:
You will not be troubled[334], you will not be belaboured, you
will not be disquieted; but he said: You will not be
overcome. God wants us to pay attention to these words,
and always to be strong in faithful trust[335], in well-being and
in woe, for he loves us and delights in us, and so he wishes
us to love him and delight in him and trust greatly in him,
and all will be well.

And soon all was hidden, and I saw no more after this.

The Sixty-Ninth Chapter

The devil returned with his heat and his stench, and
kept me very busy. The stench was vile and painful, and the
physical heat was fearful and oppressive; and I could also
hear in my ears a conversation, as if between two speakers,
and they seemed to be both talking at once, as if they were
conducting a confused debate, and it was all low muttering.
And I did not understand what they said, but all this, it
seemed, was to move me to despair[336], and they seemed to

---

333. The short text has 'certainty'.
334. The short text has 'assailed'.
335. The short text has 'in our certainty'.
336. The rest of this paragraph is not in the short text.

be mocking us when we say our prayers lamely, lacking all the devout attention and wise care which we owe to God in our prayer.

And our good Lord God gave me grace to trust greatly in him, and to comfort my soul by speaking words aloud, as I should have done to another person who was so belaboured. It seemed to me that this commotion could not be compared with any natural event.

The Seventieth Chapter

I set my eyes on the same cross in which I had seen comfort before, my tongue to speaking of Christ's Passion and repeating the faith of Holy Church, and my heart to clinging to God with all my trust and strength, so that I thought privately to myself: Now you have plenty to do to keep yourself in the faith, so that you may not be caught by your enemies[337]. If from now on you would be so busy in keeping yourself free of sin, that would be a most excellent occupation. For I truly thought that if I were safe from sin, I should be very safe from all the devils of hell and the enemies of my soul.

And so he occupied me all that night and into the morning, until it was a little after sunrise, and then all at once had gone and disappeared, leaving nothing but their stench, and that persisted for a little while. And I despised him, and so I was delivered from him by the strength of Christ's Passion. For it is so that the fiend is overcome, as our Lord Jesus Christ said before.

In all this blessed revelation[338], our good Lord gave me to understand that the vision would pass, and it is faith

---

337. 'So that. . .enemies' is not in the short text.
338. The rest of this chapter is original to the long text, and replaces the apostrophe, 'O, wretched sin, what are you?. . .' in the short text.

which preserves the blessed revelation through God's own good will and his grace; for he left with me neither sign nor token whereby I could know it. But he left with me his own blessed word truly understood, commanding me most forcefully to believe them, and so I do, blessed may he be.

I believe that he is our saviour who revealed it, and that what he revealed is of the faith, and therefore I love it, and I am bound to this, always rejoicing, by everything which he intended, and by the words which follow next[339]: Hold firmly to it and comfort yourself with it and trust in it.

So I am obliged to keep it in my faith; for on the same day that it was revealed, when the vision had passed, like a wretch I denied it, and openly said that I had been raving. Then our Lord Jesus in his mercy would not allow it to perish, but he revealed it all again in my soul, more completely in the blessed light of his precious love, saying these words[340] most powerfully and most meekly: Know it well now, it was no hallucination which you saw today, as if he had said: Because the vision had passed away from you, you lost it, and you did not know how or you were not able to keep it. But know it now, that is, now that you see it.

This was said not only for that one occasion, but so as to found on this my faith, where he goes on to say: But accept it and believe[341] it and hold firmly to it, and comfort yourself with it and trust in it, and you will not be overcome.

---

339. See p. 164.
340. See p. 164.
341. So SS ('leve'), which is superior to P, C: 'learn'. See p. 164.

The Seventy-First Chapter[342]

In the six words[343] which follow, when he says: Accept
it, he means us to fix it faithfully in our hearts; for he wants
it to abide with us in faith to the end of our lives and
afterwards, in fulness of joy, wishing us always to have
faithful trust in his blessed promises, knowing his goodness,
for our faith is opposed in various ways by our own
blindness and our spiritual enemies, internal and external.
And therefore our precious lover helps us with spiritual
light[344] and true teaching, in various ways, from within and
from without, by which we may know him. And therefore,
however he teaches us, he wants us to perceive him wisely,
and sweetly receive him, and to keep ourselves faithfully in
him. For above the faith no goodness is kept in this life, as I
see it; and beneath the faith there is no health[345] of soul. But
in the faith is where our Lord wants us to keep ourselves,
for we are obliged by his goodness and his own action to
keep ourselves in the faith, and he suffers us to have our
faith tried by our spiritual enemies and to be made strong.
For if there were no enmity to our faith, it would deserve no
reward, as I understand our Lord to mean.

Glad and merry and sweet is the blessed and lovely
demeanour of our Lord towards our souls, for he saw[346] us
always living in love-longing, and he wants our souls to be
gladly disposed towards him, to repay him his reward. And
so I hope that by his grace he lifts up[347] and will draw our
outer disposition to the inward, and will make us all at unity

---

342. The next two chapters are not in the short text.
343. That is, 'accept', 'believe', 'hold', 'comfort', 'trust', 'overcome'.
344. SS: 'sight'. Either reading makes excellent sense.
345. SS: 'help', again also giving equally good sense.
346. Perhaps a mistake for 'sees'.
347. For the editors' conjecture that this is what P's 'hayth' means, see *Showings*, II,
656, note 22.

with him, and each of us with others in the true, lasting joy
which is Jesus.

I recollect three kinds of demeanour in our Lord. The
first is that of his Passion, as he revealed when he was with
us in this life, dying; and although to contemplate this be
sorrowful and grievous, still it is glad and joyful, because he
is God. The second is pity and ruth and compassion, and
this he reveals to all his lovers, with the certainty of
protection which necessarily belongs to his mercy. The third
is that blessed demeanour as it will be without end, and this
was most often revealed, and continued the longest time.
And so in the time of our pain and our woe he reveals to us
the aspect of his Passion and his Cross, helping us to bear it
by his own blessed power. And in the time of our sinning he
shows to us the demeanour of ruth and pity, mightily
protecting us and defending us against all our enemies. And
these are the two usual aspects which he reveals to us in this
life, mingling with them the third, and that is his blessed
demeanour, partly like what it will be in heaven; and that is
when through grace we are touched by sweet illuminations
of the life of the Spirit, through which we are kept in true
faith, hope and love, with contrition and devotion and also
with contemplation and every kind of true joys and sweet
consolations. The blessed demeanour of our Lord God works
this in us through grace.

The Seventy-Second Chapter[348]

But now I must tell how I saw that sin is deadly in
creatures who will not die for sin but live in the joy of God
without end. I saw that two opposites ought not to be

---

348. So SS, but P, C omit the chapter number.

together in one place. The two greatest oppositions which exist are the highest bliss and the deepest pain. The highest bliss there is, is to possess God in the clarity of endless light, truly seeing him, sweetly feeling him, peacefully possessing him in the fulness of joy; and a part of this blessed aspect of our Lord God was revealed. In this revelation I saw that sin was the greatest opposition to this, so much so that as long as we have anything to do with any kind of sin, we shall never clearly see the blessed face of God. And the more horrible and grievous our sins may be, the deeper are we for that time fallen from this blessed sight.

And therefore it often seems to us as if we were in danger of death and in some part of hell, because of the sorrow and the pain which sin is to us, and so for that time we are dead to the true sight of our blessed life. But in all this I saw truly that we are not dead in the sight of God, nor does he ever depart from us; but he will never have his full joy in us until we have our full joy in him, truly seeing his fair, blessed face. For we are ordained to this by nature, and brought to it by grace.

So I saw how sin is for a short time deadly to the blessed creatures of endless life, and always, the more clearly that the soul sees the blessed face by the grace of loving, the more it longs to see it in fulness, that is to say in God's own likeness. For even though our Lord God dwells now in us, and is here with us, and embraces us and encloses us for his tender love, so that he can never leave us, and is nearer to us than tongue can tell or heart can think, still we can never cease from mourning and weeping, seeking and longing, until we see him clearly, face to his blessed face, for in that precious sight no woe can remain, no well-being can be lacking.

And in this I saw matter for mirth and matter for mourning[349]—matter for mirth, that our Lord, our maker is

---

349. SS: 'moaning', equally defensible.

so near to us and in us, and we in him, because of his great goodness he keeps us faithfully; matter for mourning[350], because our spiritual eye is so blind, and we are so burdened with the weight of our mortal flesh and the darkness of sin that we cannot see clearly the blessed face of our Lord God. No, and because of this darkness, we can scarcely believe or have faith in his great love and his faithfulness, with which he protects us. And so it is that I say that we can never cease mourning[351] and weeping.

This weeping does not only mean the outpouring of tears from our mortal eyes, but it has a more spiritual understanding; for the natural desire of our soul is so great and so immeasurable that if all the nobility which God ever created in heaven and on earth were given to us for our joy and our comfort, if we did not see his own fair blessed face, still we should never cease to mourn and to weep in the spirit, because, that is, of our painful longing, until we might see our Creator's fair blessed face. And if we were in all the pain that heart can think or tongue can tell, if we could at that time see his blessed face, all this pain would not grieve us.

So is that blessed vision the end of every kind of pain to loving souls, and the fulfillment of every kind of joy and bliss; and that he revealed in the great, marvellous words when he says[352]: I am he who is highest, I am he whom you love, I am he who is all.

We ought to have three kinds of knowledge. The first is that we know our Lord God. The second is that we know ourselves, what we are through him in nature and in grace. The third is that we know humbly that our self is opposed[353] to our sin and to our weakness. And all this revelation was made, as I understand it, for these three.

---

350. *Ibid*.
351. *Ibid*.
352. See p. 223.
353. SS: 'with regard', which is erroneous.

The Seventy-Third Chapter

All this blessed teaching[354] of our Lord God was shown in three parts, that is to say by bodily vision, and by words formed in my understanding and by spiritual vision. About the bodily vision I have said as I saw, as truly as I am able. And about the words, I have repeated them just as our Lord revealed them to me. And about the spiritual vision, I have told a part, but I can never tell it in full; and therefore I am moved to say more about this spiritual vision, as God will give me grace.

God showed two kinds of sickness that we have[355]. One is impatience or sloth[356], because we bear our labour and our pain heavily. The other is despair or doubtful fear[357], as I shall say afterwards. He showed sin generally, in which all sin is comprehended; but he showed no sins in particular but these two[358], and it is these two which most belabour and assail us, by what our Lord showed me, of which he wants us to be amended. I am speaking of such men and women as for the love of God hate sin and dispose themselves to do God's will. Then by our spiritual blindness and bodily sluggishness we are most inclined to these[359]; and therefore it is God's will that they should be known, and then we should reject them as we do other sins.

And for help against this[360], very meekly our Lord showed what patience he had in his cruel Passion, and also the joy and delight that he has in that Passion, because of love. And he showed me this as an example of how we

---

354. Correspondence with the short text resumes; see p. 167.
355. The short text's 'of which he wants us to be cured' is omitted.
356. 'Or sloth' is not in the short text.
357. The short text reads 'coming from doubtful fear'.
358. 'He showed. . .these two' not in the short text.
359. This replaces the short text's 'So these are two secret sins, extremely busy in tempting us'.
360. The short text has 'And so'.

ought gladly and easily to bear our pains, for that is very pleasing to him and an endless profit to us. And the reason why we are oppressed by them is because of our ignorance of love. Though the three persons of the blessed Trinity be all alike in the self[361], the soul received most understanding of love. Yes, and he wants us in all things to have our contemplation and our delight in love. And it is about this knowledge that we are most blind, for some of us believe that God is almighty and may do everything, and that he is all wisdom and can do everything, but that he is all love and wishes to do everything, there we fail. And it is this ignorance which most hinders God's lovers, as I see it; for when we begin to hate sin and to amend ourselves according to the laws of Holy Church, there still persists a fear which hinders us, by looking at ourselves and at our sins committed in the past, and some of us because of our everyday sins, because we do not keep our promise or keep the purity which God has established us in, but often fall into so much wretchedness that it is shameful to say it. And the perception of this makes us so woebegone and so depressed that we can scarcely see any consolation. And sometimes we take this fear for humility, but it is a reprehensible blindness and weakness; and we do not know how to despise it like any other sin which we recognize, and this comes through lack of true judgment, and it is contrary to truth. For of all the attributes of the blessed Trinity, it is God's will that we have most faithfulness and delight in love.

For love makes power and wisdom very humble to us; for just as by God's courtesy he forgets our sin from the time that we repent, just so does he wish us to forget our sin with regard to our unreasonable depression and our doubtful fears.

---

361. Some of what follows in this paragraph is not in the short text; see p. 168.

323

The Seventy-Fourth Chapter

For I understand[362] four kinds of fear. One is fear of assault, which comes to a man suddenly through timidity. This fear does good, for it helps to purge a man, as does bodily sickness or such other pains which are not sinful; for all such pains help one if they are patiently accepted. The second is fear of pain, through which a man is stirred and wakened from the sleep of sin; for anyone fast asleep in sin is not for that time able to receive the gentle strength of the Holy Spirit, until he has accepted[363] this fear of pain from bodily death and from spiritual enemies[364]. And this fear moves us to seek comfort and mercy of God; and so this fear helps us as an approach[365], and enables us to have contrition by the blessed touching[366] of the Holy Spirit. The third is doubtful fear[367]. God wants to have doubtful fear, inasmuch as it induces to despair, turned in us into love by true knowledge of love, that is to say that the bitterness of doubt be turned into the sweetness of gentle love by grace, for it can never please our Lord that his servants doubt in his goodness. The fourth is reverent fear, for there is no fear in us which fully pleases God but reverent fear, and that is gentle. For[368] the more it is obtained, the less is it felt, because of the sweetness of love.

Love and fear are brothers, and they are rooted in us by the goodness of our Creator, and they will never be taken from us without end. It is our nature to love, and we are given grace to love; and it is our nature to fear, and we are

---

362. The short text has 'I saw'; see p. 169.
363. The short text has 'obtained'; SS: 'has understanding of'.
364. 'From bodily. . .enemies': the short text has 'and of the fire of purgatory'.
365. Literally, 'an entry'; see the short text, 'as though by chance' ('an anntre'); but there may well be corruption in one text or both.
366. The short text has 'teaching'.
367. The short text's treatment of 'doubtful fear' differs considerably.
368. 'For the more. . .to love him for his goodness' is not in the short text.

given grace to fear. It is proper to God's lordship and his
fatherhood to be feared, as it is proper to his goodness to be
loved; and it is proper to us who are his servants and his
children to fear him, for his lordship and fatherhood, as it is
proper to us to love him for his goodness. And yet this
reverent fear and love are not the same, but they are
different in kind and in effect, and neither of them may be
obtained without the other.

And therefore I am sure that he who loves, he fears,
though he may feel little of this. Whatever kinds of fear be
suggested to us other than reverent fear, though they appear
disguised as holiness, they are not so true; and this is how
they can be recognized apart. The fear[369] that makes us
hastily to flee from everything that is not good, and to fall
into our Lord's breast, as the child into the mother's arms[370],
with all our intention and with all our mind, knowing our
feebleness and our great need, knowing his everlasting
goodness and his blessed love, seeking only in him for
salvation, cleaving to him with faithful trust, that fear which
leads us in this direction is gentle and gracious and good and
true; and all that is opposed to this is either wrong or mixed
with wrong.

So this is the remedy, to recognize them both and to
refuse the wrong; for the natural attribute of fear which we
have in this life by the grace-giving operation of the Holy
Spirit will be the same in heaven before God, gentle,
courteous, most sweet; and thus in love we shall be familiar
and close to God, and in fear we shall be gentle and
courteous to God, and both the same, in the same way.

So let us desire of our Lord God to fear him reverently
and love him meekly and trust him strongly; for when we
fear him reverently and love him meekly, our trust is never

---

369. At this point correspondence with the short text ceases; the rest of the long text
is original.
370. SS: 'barme' ('bosom'), which may be superior.

in vain. For the more that we trust and the more strongly that we trust, the more we please and honour our Lord in whom we trust; and if this reverent fear and meek love is lacking in us, as God forbid it should be, our trust will soon in that time be misdirected. And therefore we have much need to pray to our Lord for grace, that we may have this reverent fear and meek love as his gift, in our hearts and in our deeds, for without this no man can please God.

The Seventy-Fifth Chapter[371]

I saw that God can do everything which is necessary for us; and these three necessities which I shall describe compel us to long in love. Pity and love protect us in the time of our need; and the longing in the same love draws us into heaven, for God's thirst is to have man, generally, drawn into him, and in that thirst he has drawn his holy souls who are now in bliss. And so, getting[372] his living members, always he draws and drinks, and still he thirsts and he longs.

I saw three kinds of longing in God, and all to the same end, and we have the same in us, and from the same power, and for the same end[373]. The first is because he longs to teach us to know him and to love him always more and more, as is suitable and profitable to us. The second is that he longs to bring us up into bliss, as souls are when they are taken out of pain into heaven. The third is to fill us with bliss, and that will be fulfilled on the last day, to last forever. For I saw what is known in our faith, that pain and sorrow will be ended then for those who will be saved. And

---

371. The opening sentences of this chapter have been much corrupted, and they are translated here as they have been edited in *Showings*, with the least emendation possible. Consultation of other translations, and especially of Walsh, *Revelations*, will show how variously they can be interpreted.

372. See *Showings*, II, 679 note, for the editors' suggestion that this may be a corruption of 'gathering', a favourite term of Julian's.

373. 'And we have. . .the same end' from SS; P, C omit.

not only shall we receive the same bliss which souls have had already in heaven, but also we shall receive a new bliss, which will be plenteously flowing out of God into us, and will fill us full.

And those are the good things which he has ordained from without beginning to give us. These good things are treasured and hidden in himself, for until that time, the creature has not the power or merit to receive them. In this we should truly see the cause of all the deeds which God has done; and furthermore, we should see the cause of all the things which he has permitted; and the bliss and the fulfillment will be so deep and so high that, out of wonder and marvelling, all creatures ought to have for God so much reverent fear, surpassing what has been seen and felt before, that the pillars of heaven will tremble and quake.

But this kind of trembling and fear will have no kind of pain, but it is proper to God's honourable majesty so to be contemplated by his creatures, trembling and quaking in fear, because of their much greater joy[374] endlessly marvelling at the greatness of God, the Creator, and at the smallest part of all that is created.

For the contemplation of this makes the creature marvellously meek and mild; and therefore God wants us, and it is also proper to us, both by nature and by grace, to want to have knowledge of this, desiring the vision and the action. For it leads us in the right way, and keeps us in true life, and unites us to God.

And as good as God is, so great is he; and as much as it is proper to his divinity to be loved, so much is it proper to his great exaltedness to be feared. For this reverent fear is the fairer courtesy which is in heaven before God's face; and by as much as he will be known and loved, surpassing how he now is, by so much will he be feared, surpassing how he

---

374. SS: 'their meekness'.

now is. Therefore it must necessarily be that all heaven, all earth will tremble and quake when the pillars will tremble and quake.

The Seventy-Sixth Chapter

I say very little about this reverent fear, for I hope that it may be seen in what has been said before. But I know well that our Lord revealed to me no souls but those who fear him, for I know well that the soul which truly accepts the teaching of the Holy Spirit hates sin more, for its vileness and horribleness, than it does all the pain which is in hell. For the soul which contemplates the gentleness of Jesus does not hate any hell, but the sin of hell[375], as I see it. And therefore it is God's will that we recognize sin, and pray busily and labour willingly and seek meekly for teaching, so that we do not fall blindly into it, and if we fall, so that we quickly rise. For the greatest pain that the soul can have is at any time to turn from God through sin.

The soul which wants to be in rest should, when other men's sins come to mind, flee that as the pain of hell, seeking from God help against it. For the contemplation of other men's sins makes as it were a thick mist before the soul's eye, and during that time we cannot see the beauty of God, unless we can contemplate them[376] with contrition with him[377], with compassion on him, and with holy desires to God for him. For without this it harasses and troubles and hinders the soul which contemplates them[378]; for I understand this in the revelation of God's compassion[379].

---

375. This is the editors' emendation; see *Showings*, II, 684-85. P, C: 'but hell is sin' (which is nonsensical in this context); SS omit (probably for this reason).
376. That is, a man's sins.
377. That is, the sinner.
378. A man's sins.
379. See p. 231.

In this blessed revelation of our Lord I have understanding of two contraries. One is the wisest act which any creature can perform in this life, the other is the most foolish. The wisest act is for a creature to do according to the will and the counsels of his greatest and supreme friend. This blessed friend is Jesus, and it is his will and counsel that we keep with him and fasten ourselves closely to him, in whatever state we may be. For whether we be foul or clean, we are always the same in his love; for well or for woe, he wants us never to flee from him. But because of our own inconstancy, we often fall into sin. Then by the prompting of our enemy and by our own folly and blindness we come to this. For they say: You know well that you are a wretch, a sinner and also unfaithful, because you do not keep your covenant. Often you promise our Lord that you will do better, and then you fall again into the same state, especially into sloth and wasting of time, for that, as I see it, is the beginning of sin, and especially to creatures who have given themselves to serve our Lord by the inward contemplation of his blessed goodness. And this makes us afraid to appear before our courteous Lord.

Thus it is our enemy who wants to retard us with his false suggestions of fear about our wretchedness because of the pain which he threatens us with. For it is his purpose to make us so depressed and so sad in this matter that we should forget the blessed contemplation of our everlasting friend.

The Seventy-Seventh Chapter

Our good Lord showed the fiend's enmity, by which I understood that everything which is opposed to love and to peace is from the fiend and from his side. We are liable through our feebleness and our folly to fall, and we are able through the mercy and the grace of the Holy Spirit to rise to greater joy. And if our enemy gains anything from us by our falling, which is his delight[380], he loses many times more in our rising by our charity and our meekness; and this glorious rising is to him such great sorrow and pain, because of the hatred which he has for our souls, that he burns constantly in envy. And all this sorrow which he would make us have will come back to him, and this was why our Lord scorned him, and revealed that he will be scorned; and this made me to laugh greatly[381].

So this is the remedy, that we acknowledge our wretchedness and flee to our Lord; for always, the more abased we are, the more profitable it is for us to touch him. And let us then in intention say this: I know well that I have deserved pain; but our Lord is almighty, and may punish me greatly, and he is all wisdom, and can punish me wisely, and he is all goodness, and loves me tenderly. And it is profitable for us to remain in this contemplation; for it is a most lovely humility in a sinful soul, made by the mercy and grace of the Holy Spirit, when we are willing and glad to accept the scourging and the chastising which our Lord himself wishes to give us. And it will be very tender and very easy, if we will only keep ourselves content with him and with all his works.

As to the penance which one takes upon oneself, that was not revealed to me; that is to say, it was not revealed to me specifically. But what was revealed, specially and greatly and in a most loving manner, is that we ought meekly and patiently to bear and suffer the penance which God himself gives us, with recollection of his blessed Passion. For when we recall his blessed Passion, with pity and love, then we suffer with him as his friends did who saw it. And this was

---

380. All the witnesses have 'likeness', but this is plainly a corruption of 'liking'. See *Showings*, II, 689 note.
380. See p. 201.

revealed in the thirteenth revelation, near the beginning, where it speaks of pity[382].

For he says: Do not accuse yourself that your tribulation and your woe is all your fault; for I do not want you to be immoderately depressed or sorrowful. For I tell you that whatever you do, you will have woe. And therefore I want you wisely to understand the penance which you are continually in, and to accept that meekly for your penance. And then you will truly see that all your life is profitable penance.

This place is prison, this life is penance, and he wants us to rejoice in the remedy.

The remedy is that our Lord is with us, protecting us and leading us into the fulness of joy; for our Lord intends this to be an endless joy, that he who will be our bliss when we are there is our protector whilst we are here, our way and our heaven in true love and faithful trust. And he gave understanding of this in everything, and especially in the revelation of his Passion, where he made me to choose him with all my strength for my heaven[383].

Let us flee to our Lord, and we shall be comforted. Let us touch him, and we shall be made clean. Let us cleave to him, and we shall be sure and safe from every kind of peril. For our courteous Lord wants us to be as familiar with him as heart may think or soul may desire; but let us beware that we do not accept this familiarity so carelessly as to forsake courtesy. For our Lord himself is supreme familiarity, and he is as courteous as he is familiar, for he is true courtesy. And he wants to have the blessed creatures who will be in heaven with him without end like himself in all things, and to be perfectly like our Lord is our true salvation and our greatest bliss. And if we do not know how we shall do all

---

382. See p. 226.
383. See p. 211.

this, let us desire it from our Lord, and he will teach us, for that is his own delight and his glory, blessed may he be.

The Seventy-Eighth Chapter

Our Lord in his mercy reveals our sin and our feebleness to us by the sweet gracious light of his own self, for our sin is so foul and so horrible that he in his courtesy will not reveal it to us except by the light of his mercy.

It is his will that we have knowledge of four things. The first is that he is the foundation from whom we have our life and our being. The second is that he protects us mightily and mercifully, during the time that we are in our sin, among all our enemies who are so fierce against us; and we are in so much more peril because we give them occasion for this, and we do not know our own need. The third is how courteously he protects us and makes us know that we are going astray. The fourth is how steadfastly he waits for us, and does not change his demeanour[384], for he wants us to be converted and united to him in love, as he is to us.

And so by knowledge and grace we may see our sin, profitably, without despair. For truly we need to see it, and by the sight we should be made ashamed of ourselves, and broken[385] down from our pride and our presumption. For truly it behoves us to see that in ourselves we are nothing at all but sin and wretchedness. And so by the sight of the less which our Lord reveals to us, the more which we do not see is dispelled. For he in his courtesy measures the sight for us; for it is so foul and so horrible that we should not endure to see it as it is.

And so by this meek knowledge, through contrition and grace we shall be broken down from everything which is not

---

384. This could perhaps mean 'does not go away'; see *Showings*, II, 697 note.
385. So SS; P, C: 'breaking'.

our Lord. And then will our blessed saviour cure us perfectly and unite us to him. This breaking and this curing our Lord intends for men in general, for he who is highest and closest to God may see himself sinful and needy along with me. And I who am the least and the lowest of those who will be saved may be comforted along with him who is highest. So has our Lord united us in charity.

When he revealed to me that I should sin, what for the joy that I had in contemplating him, I did not attend promptly to that revelation, and so our courteous Lord paused there, and did not wish to teach me any more until he had given me the grace and will to attend. And by this I was taught that though we may be lifted up high into contemplation by the special gift of our Lord, still, together with this, we must necessarily have knowledge and sight of our sin and of our feebleness; for without this knowledge we may not have true meekness, and without this we cannot be safe. And I also saw that we cannot have this knowledge through ourselves or through any of our spiritual enemies, for they do not wish so much good to us. For if it were according to their will, we should never see it until our last day. Then are we much indebted to God, who is willing himself for love to show it to us, in the time of mercy and of grace.

The Seventy-Ninth Chapter

I also had more understanding of his revealing to me that I should sin. I applied it merely to my own single self, because at that time I was not otherwise moved, but by the great and gracious comfort of our Lord which followed afterwards, I saw that he intended it for general man, that is to say every man, who is sinful and will be until the last day. Of which man I am a member, as I believe, by the mercy of God, for the blessed comfort which I saw is generous enough for us all. And there I was taught that I ought to see my own sin and not other men's, unless it may be for the comfort and help of my fellow Christians.

And also in the same revelation, where I saw that I should sin, I was taught to be fearful because of my own uncertainty, because I do not know how I may fall, nor do I know the measure or the greatness of my sin. For in my fearfulness I wanted to know that, and I had no answer to it.

Also at that same time our courteous Lord revealed, most sweetly and most powerfully, the endlessness and the unchangeability of his love, and also his great goodness and his gracious protection of our spirit, so that the love between him and our souls will never be parted into eternity. And so in the fear I have matter for meekness, which saves me from presumption, and in the blessed revelation of love I have matter for true comfort and for joy, which saves me from despair.

All this familiar revelation of our courteous Lord is a lesson of love and a sweet, gracious teaching from himself, in comforting of our soul. For he wants us to know by the sweetness of his familiar love that all which we see or feel, within or without, which is in opposition to this is from the enemy and not from God, and in this way. If we are moved to be more careless about our way of life or about the custody of our heart, because we have knowledge of this plentiful love, then we have great need to beware of this impulse, should it come. It is false, and we ought to hate it greatly, for it has no resemblance to God's will. And when we have fallen through weakness or blindness, then our courteous Lord, touching us, moves us and protects us. And then he wants us to see our wretchedness and meekly to acknowledge it; but he does not want us to remain there, or to be much occupied in self-accusation, nor does he want us to be too full of our own misery. But he wants us quickly to attend to him, for he stands all alone, and he waits for us continually, moaning and mourning until we come. And he hastens to bring us to him, for we are his joy and his delight, and he is the remedy of our life[386].

Where I say that he stands all alone, I neglect to speak of the blessed company in heaven, and speak of his office and his work here on earth, according to the circumstances of the revelation.

The Eightieth Chapter

Man endures in this life by three things, by which three God is honoured and we are furthered, protected and saved. The first is the use of man's natural reason. The second is the common teaching of Holy Church. The third is the inward grace-giving operation of the Holy Spirit; and these three are all from one God. God is the foundation of our natural reason; and God is the teaching of Holy Church, and God is the Holy Spirit, and they are all different gifts, and he wants us to have great regard for them, and to accord ourselves to them. For they work continually in us, all together, and those are great things; and of this greatness he wants us to have knowledge here, as it were in an ABC. That is to say that we can have a little knowledge of that of which we shall have the fulness in heaven, and that is to further us.

We know in our faith that God alone took our nature, and no one but he, and, furthermore, that Christ alone performed all the great works which belong to our salvation, and no one but he; and just so, he alone acts now in the last end, that is to say he dwells here in us, and rules us, and cares for us[387] in this life, and brings us to his bliss. And so he will do as long as any soul is on earth who will come to

---

386. SS: 'our remedy and our life'; see *Showings*, II, 706 note.
387. See p. 313, note 325.

heaven; and so much so that if there were no such soul on earth except one, he would be with it, all alone, until he had brought it up into his bliss.

I believe and understand the ministration of holy angels, as scholars tell, but it was not revealed to me; for God himself is nearest and meekest, highest and lowest, and he does everything, and not only all that we need, but also he does everything which is honourable for our joy in heaven; and when I say that he waits for us, moaning and mourning, that means all the true feelings which we have in ourselves, in contrition and in compassion, and all the moaning and mourning because we are not united with our Lord. And as such is profitable, it is Christ in us; and though some of us feel it seldom, it never leaves Christ until the time when he has brought us out of all our woe.

For love never allows him to be without pity; and when we fall into sin, and neglect recollection of him and the protection of our own soul, then Christ bears all alone the burden of us. And so he remains, moaning and mourning. Then it is for us in reverence and kindness to turn quickly to our Lord, and not to leave him alone. He is here alone with us all; that is to say, he is here only for us. And when I am distant towards him through sin, despair or sloth, then I leave my Lord to remain alone, inasmuch as he is in me. And this is the case with us all who are sinners; but though it may be that we act like this often, his goodness never allows us to be alone, but constantly he is with us, and tenderly he excuses us, and always protects us from blame in his sight.

The Eighty-First Chapter

Our good Lord revealed himself to his creature in various ways, both in heaven and on earth; but I saw him take no place except in man's soul. He revealed himself on earth in the sweet Incarnation and his blessed Passion, and he showed himself in other ways on earth, where I said[388] that I saw God in an instant of time; and he showed himself in another way on earth, as if it were on[389] pilgrimage, that is to say that he is here with us, leading us, and will be until he has brought us all to his bliss in heaven.

He revealed himself several times reigning, as is said before[390], but principally in man's soul; he has taken there his resting place and his honourable city. Out of this honourable throne he will never rise or depart without end. Marvellous and splendid is the place where the Lord dwells; and therefore he wants us promptly to attend to the touching of his grace, rejoicing more in his unbroken love than sorrowing over our frequent fallings.

For it is the greatest glory to him of anything which we can do that we live gladly and happily for love of him in our penance. For he regards us so tenderly that he sees all our life here to be penance; for the substantial and natural longing in us for him is a lasting penance in us, and he makes this penance in us, and mercifully he helps us to bear it. For his love makes him long, his wisdom and his truth with his justice make him to suffer us here, and he wants to see this in us in this way. For this is our loving penance, and the greatest, as I see it, for this penance never leaves us until the time when we are fulfilled, when we shall[391] have him for our reward.

And therefore he wants us to set our hearts on our passing over, that is to say from the pain which we feel to the bliss which we trust.

---

388. See p. 197.
389. So SS; P, C: 'a'.
390. See pp. 203, 278.
391. So SS; P, C: 'should'.

The Eighty-Second Chapter

But here our courteous Lord revealed the moaning and the mourning of our soul, with this meaning: I know well that you wish to live for my love, joyfully and gladly suffering all the penance which may come to you; but since you do not live without sin, you are depressed and sorrowful, and if you could live without sin, you would suffer for my love all the woe which might come to you, and it is true. But do not be too much aggrieved by the sin which comes to you against your will.

And here I understood that the lord looked on the servant with pity and not with blame; for this passing life does not require us to live wholly without sin. He loves us endlessly, and we sin customarily, and he reveals it to us most gently. And then we sorrow and moan discreetly, turning to contemplate his mercy, cleaving to his love and to his goodness, seeing that his is our medicine, knowing that we only sin.

And so by the meekness which we obtain in seeing our sin, faithfully recognizing his everlasting love, thanking him and praising him, we please him. I love you and you love me, and our love will never be divided in two; and it is for your profit that I suffer. And all this was revealed in spiritual understanding, he saying these blessed words: I protect you very safely[392].

And by the great desire which I saw in our blessed Lord that we shall live in this way, that is to say in longing and rejoicing, as all this lesson of love shows, I understood that all which is opposed to this is not from him, but it is from enmity. And he wants us to know it by the sweet light of grace of his substantial and natural love.

---

392. See p. 154.

If there be any such liver[393] on earth, who is
continually protected from falling, I do not know, for it was
not revealed to me. But this was revealed, that in falling and
in rising we are always preciously protected in one[394] love.
For we do not fall in the sight of God, and we do not stand
in our own sight; and both these are true, as I see it, but the
contemplating of our Lord God is the higher truth. So we
are much indebted to him, that he will in this way of life
reveal to us this high truth, and I understood that while we
are in this way, it is most profitable to us that we see these
both together. For the higher contemplation keeps us in
spiritual joy and true delight in God; the other, which is the
lower contemplation, keeps us in fear, and makes us
ashamed of ourselves.

But our good Lord always wants us to remain much
more in the contemplation of the higher, and not to forsake
the knowledge of the lower, until the time that we are
brought up above, where we shall have our Lord Jesus for
our reward, and be filled full of joy and bliss without end.

The Eighty-Third Chapter

In this matter I had touching, sight and feeling of three
properties of God, in which consist the strength and the
effect of all the revelation. And it was seen in every
revelation, and most exactly in the twelfth, where it says
repeatedly: I am he[395]. The properties are these: life, love
and light. In life is wonderful familiarity, in love is gentle
courtesy, and in light is endless nature.

These three properties were seen in one goodness, to
which goodness my reason wanted to be united and to cleave

---

393. SS: 'lover'.
394. So SS; P, C: 'our'.
395. See p. 223.

with all my powers. I contemplated with reverent fear, greatly marvelling at the sight and the feeling of the sweet harmony, that our reason is in God, understanding that this is the highest gift that we have received, and its foundation is in nature.

Our faith is a light, coming in nature from our endless day, which is our Father, God; in which light our Mother, Christ, and our good Lord the Holy Spirit lead us in this passing life. This light is measured with discretion, and it is present to us in our need in the night. The light is the cause of our life, the night is the cause of our pain and all our woe, in which woe we deserve endless reward and thanks from God; for we by his mercy and grace willingly know and believe our light, walking therein wisely and mightily. And at the end of woe, suddenly our eyes will be opened, and in the clearness of our sight our light will be full, which light is God, our Creator, Father, and the Holy Spirit, in Christ Jesus our saviour.

So I saw and understood that our faith is our light in our night, which light is God, our endless day.

The Eighty-Fourth Chapter

This light is charity, and the measuring of this light is performed for us to our profit by the wisdom of God; for the light is not so generous that we can see clearly our blessed day, nor is it all shut off from us, but it is such a light as we can live in meritoriously, with labour deserving the honourable thanks of God. And this was seen in the sixth revelation, where he says[396]: I thank you for your service and your labour. So charity keeps us in faith and in hope. And faith and hope lead us in charity, and in the end everything will be charity.

---

396. See p. 203.

I had three kinds of understanding in this light of charity. The first is uncreated charity, the second is created charity, the third is given charity. Uncreated charity is God, created charity is our soul in God, given charity is virtue, and that is a gift of grace in deeds, in which we love God for himself, and ourselves in God, and all that God loves for God.

The Eighty-Fifth Chapter

And I marvelled greatly at this vision, for despite our foolish living and our blindness here, still endlessly our courteous Lord regards us, rejoicing in this work. And we can please him best of all by wisely and truly believing it, and rejoicing with him and in him. For as truly as we shall be in the bliss of God without end, praising and thanking him, so truly have we been in God's prevision loved and known in his endless purpose from without beginning. In this love without beginning he created us; and in the same love he protects us, and never allows us to be hurt, by which our bliss might be decreased. And therefore when the judgment is given, and we are all brought up above, we shall then clearly see in God the mysteries which are now hidden from us. And then shall none of us be moved to say in any matter: Lord, if it had been so, it would have been well. But we shall all say with one voice: Lord, blessed may you be, because it is so, it is well; and now we see truly that everything is done as it was ordained by you before anything was made.

The Eighty-Sixth Chapter

This book is begun by God's gift and his grace, but it is not yet performed, as I see it. For charity, let us all join with God's working in prayer, thanking, trusting, rejoicing, for so will our good Lord be entreated, by the understanding which I took in all his own intention, and in the sweet words where he says most happily[397]: I am the foundation of your beseeching. For truly I saw and understood in our Lord's meaning that he revealed it because he wants to have it better known than it is. In which knowledge he wants to give us grace to love him and to cleave to him, for he beholds his heavenly treasure with so great love on earth that he will give us more light[398] and solace in heavenly joy, by drawing our hearts from the sorrow and the darkness which we are in.

And from the time that it was revealed, I desired many times to know in what was our Lord's meaning. And fifteen years after and more, I was answered in spiritual understanding, and it was said: What, do you wish to know your Lord's meaning in this thing? Know it well, love was his meaning. Who reveals it to you? Love. What did he reveal to you? Love[399]. Why does he reveal it to you? For love. Remain in this, and you will know more of the same. But you will never know different, without end.

So I was taught that love is our Lord's meaning. And I saw very certainly in this and in everything that before God made us he loved us, which love was never abated and never will be. And in this love he has done all his works, and in this love he has made all things profitable to us, and in this love our life is everlasting. In our creation we had beginning, but the love in which he created us was in him from without

---

397. See p. 157.
398. 'With so great. . .more light' from SS; P, C omit.
399. 'What did. . .Love' from SS; P, C omit.

beginning. In this love we have our beginning, and all this shall we see in God without end.

Thanks be to God. Here ends the book of revelations of Julian the anchorite of Norwich, on whose soul may God have mercy.[400]

May Jesus grant us this. Amen. So ends the revelation of love of the blessed Trinity, shown by our saviour Jesus Christ for our endless comfort and solace, and also that we may rejoice in him in the passing journey of this life. Amen. Jesus. Amen. I pray almighty God that this book may not come except into the hands of those who wish to be his faithful lovers, and those who will submit themselves to the faith of Holy Church and obey the wholesome understanding and teaching of men who are of virtuous life, settled age and profound learning; for this revelation is exalted divinity and wisdom, and therefore it cannot remain with him who is a slave to sin and to the devil. And beware that you do not accept one thing which is according to your pleasure and liking, and reject another, for that is the disposition of heretics. But accept it all together, and understand it truly; it all agrees with Holy Scripture, and is founded upon it, and Jesus, our true love and light and truth, will show this to all pure souls who meekly and perseveringly ask this wisdom from him. And you to whom this book will come, give our saviour Christ Jesus great and hearty thanks that he made these showings and revelations for you and to you out of his endless love, mercy and goodness, for a safe guide and conduct for you and us to everlasting bliss, which may Jesus grant us. Amen. Here end the sublime and wonderful revelations of the unutterable love of God, in Jesus Christ vouchsafed to a dear lover of his, and in her to all his dear friends and lovers whose hearts like hers do flame in the love of our dearest Jesus.

---

400. What follows is the colophon found only in S1 and S2, plainly the work of some devout seventeenth-century scribe-editor.

Bibliography

(of works cited in Introduction)

Augustine: *Sancti Aurelii Augustini enarrationes in Psalmos* (ed. Dekkers, Eligius, and Fraipont, Jean, Corpus Christianorum Series Latina 38-40, 1956).

Augustine: *S. Aurelii Augustini. . .epistulae* (Corpus Scriptorum Ecclesiasticorum Latinorum 34, 44, 57, 58, 1895-   ).

Bazire, Joyce, and Colledge, Eric, ed.: *The Chastising of God's Children and The Treatise of Perfection of the Sons of God* (Oxford, 1957).

Bede: *Bedae Venerabilis opera II: opera exegetica* (ed. Hurst, David, CCSL 120, 1960).

Bernard: *S. Bernardi opera* (ed. Leclercq, Jean, Talbot, Charles H. and Rochais, Henri-M., Rome, 1957-   ).

Blomefield, Francis, continued by Parkin, Charles: *An Essay towards a Topographical History of the County of Norfolk* (5 vols., Fersfield and Lynn, 1739-1775).

Cabassut, André: 'Une dévotion médiévale peu connue: la dévotion à "Jésus nôtre mère" ' (*Revue d'Ascétique et de Mystique* 25, 1949, 234-245).

Chatillon, François: 'Hic, ibi, interim' (*RAM* 25, 1949, 194-199).

Colledge, Edmund, and Walsh, James: 'Editing Julian of Norwich's *Revelations*: a Progress Report' (*Mediaeval Studies* 38, 1976, 404-427).

Cressy, Serenus, ed.: *Revelations of divine Love shewed to a devout Servant of God called Mother Juliana* (no place of publication, 1670).

De Lubac, Henri: *Exégèse médiévale: les quatre sens de l'Ecriture* (4 vols. in 3, Paris, 1959-1964).

Dumontier, Pierre: *S. Bernard et la Bible* (Paris, 1953).

Foucard, Betty: 'A Cathedral Manuscript' (*Westminster Cathedral Chronicle* 50, 1956, 41-43, 59-60, 74-75, 89-90, 108-110).

Gregory: *Sancti Gregorii Magni homiliae in Hiezechihelem Prophetam* (ed. Adriaen, Marcus, CCSL 142, 1971).

Harford, Dundas: *Comfortable Words to Christ's Lovers* (London, 1911).

Hodgson, Phyllis, ed.: *The Cloud of Unknowing and The Book of Privy Counselling* (Early English Text Society, Original Series 218, 1944, 1958).

Hudleston, Roger: *Revelations of Divine Love* (London, 1927).

Irenaeus: *Sancti Irenaei. . .libri quinque adversus haereses* (Cambridge, England, 1858; Ridgewood, New Jersey, 1965).

Leclercq, Jean, trans. Misrahi, Catherine: *The Love of Learning and the Desire for God* (New York, 1961).

Meech, Sanford B., and Allen, Hope E., ed.: *The Book of Margery Kempe* (EETS OS 212, 1940).

Meunier, Gabriel ('un bénédictin de Farnborough'): *Julienne de Norwich. . .Révélations de l'amour de dieu* (Paris, 1910).

Owen, Hywel W.: 'Another Augustine Baker Manuscript' (Ampe, Albin, ed.: *Dr. L. Reypens-Album*, Antwerp, 1964, 269-280).

Poiret, Pierre: *Bibliotheca mysticorum selecta* (Amsterdam, 1708).

Rahner, Karl, trans. Donceel, Joseph: *The Trinity* (New York, 1970).

Rupert of Deutz: *Ruperti Tuitiensis de Sancto Trinitate et operibus eius* (ed. Haacke, Hraban (Corpus Christianorum Continuatio Medievalis 21-24, 1971-   ).

Stanley, David: 'Contemplation of the Gospels. Ignatius Loyola and the Contemporary Christian' (*Theological Studies* 29, 1968, 417-443).

Tanner, Norman P.: *Popular Religion in Norwich* (Oxford D.Phil. dissertation, 1973).

Thomas Aquinas: *Doctoris angelici Divi Thomae Aquinatis. . .opera omnia* (34 vols., Paris, 1871-1880).

Walsh, James: *The Revelations of Divine Love of Julian of Norwich* (London, 1961).

William of St. Thierry: *Un traité de la vie solitaire: Epistola ad Fratres de Monte Dei* (Paris, 1940).

Wolters, Clifford: *Julian of Norwich: Revelations of Divine Love* (Harmondsworth, 1966).

Index to Preface and Introduction

Index to Texts

Adam, blissfully restored, 282; brought out of hell, 275; compassion for, 271; fall of, 274, 280, 282; like all men, 274; as servant, 269, 274; his sin, 149, 194, 228, 261, 266; and Son are one, 275.

Atonement, 176, 184, 213; as glorious, 282; as pleasing to God, 150, 228.

Beseeching, cf. Prayer and Trust.

Blame, not imputed, 149, 154, 226, 245, 257, 266, 271, 281, 282, 336, 338; in parable, 268; from Christ's pain, 271; sin deserving of, 257, 259, 266; taken by Jesus, 275; turned to honour, 282.

Bliss, cf. also Joy, Heaven, Christ, Delight; Christ as ours, 209, 318, 333; Christ's bearing us, as, 298; Christ's in heaven, 127, 145, 146, 218; in contemplation, 164, 218, 314; correspondence with sin, 154, 242; degrees of, 139, 160; desire for, 160; enclosed in God, 272; as endless, 127, 179, 194, 269, 278, 298, 306, 307, 341; fullness of, 271, 321, 326, 327; as heavenly, 271; Jesus as, 143, 175, 303; man made for, 258; from mercy and grace, 295; of mother Jesus, 305; in opposition to pain, 320; of Our Lady, 222; in our salvation, 219, 221; ours, in heaven, 179, 181, 211, 227, 238, 242, 252, 283, 306, 326, 327, 341; in possessing God, 320; of

Son, 286; trust in, 337; we are Christ's bliss, 145, 151, 216, 219, 220, 230, 335.

Blood of Christ, cf. also Christ's Passion; to cleanse us, 137, 200; as delight to him, 146; as healing, 304; and prayer, 185; as precious, 200, 220, 302, 304; vision of, 129, 132, 137, 181, 183, 187, 188, 190, 193, 199, 207, 208, 218; vision of as lovely, 188; vision of as fearful, 188.

Certainty, cf. Trust.

Charity, cf. Love, Christ's Love, God's Love; created, 341; and faith and hope, 340; given, 341; and God's working, 342; uncreated, 341.

Christ, cf. Son, Lord; as brother, 279, 293, 296; as church, 302; desires to become man, 195, 291; draws us, 280, 299, 330; Father in, 295; as friend, 329; gentleness of, 328; as heaven, 143, 211, 212, 216; his body, 230, 276; his divinity, 274, 275, 276, 288, 291, 300, 313; his humanity, 230, 274, 275, 276, 280, 288, 291, 292, 297, 300, 304, 313; is life, 176, 209, 223, 339; is love, 301, 339; and man in heaven, 216; as mediator, 283; as Mother, 292, 293, 294, 295, 296, 298, 299, 301, 302, 303, 304, 319, 340; opposes good to evil, 295; our being from, 295, 332; our fulfillment, 147, 236, 299; our head, 230, 276; our portion, 228;

our sensuality in, 295; our way, 286; protector, 331; saviour, 240, 279, 292, 293, 296, 302, 317, 340, 343; as Son, 274; as teacher, 236; in us, 292, 313, 335, 336; wants our love, 299, 302; we are in, 286, 292; willing to die again, 217; is with us, 280, 331.

Christ's blessed Passion, cf. also Pain, Suffering; Christ's joy and delight in, 168, 216, 218, 219, 280, 322; as comfort to us, 149, 180, 225, 316, 319; as greatest pain, 148, 214, 225; humiliation of, 227; as labour, 202, 218, 219; memory of, 300; and mercy, 302; as overcoming devil, 164, 165, 201, 202, 316; patience in, 168, 322; power of, 256, 280, 289, 294, 316; and prayer, 185; recollection of (vision), 125, 126, 129, 136, 137, 141, 175, 176, 177, 189, 190, 193, 206, 213, 214, 234, 288, 315, 318, 330, 331, 337; as restoring us, 184, 246; sharing in, 129, 141-2; and sin, 225, 322; and Trinity, 219; turned to consolation, 148, 227; as way to heaven, 143, 276.

Christ's joy, in his labour for us. 146, 218, 219, 298; in his Passion, 216; we are, 151, 216.

Christ's love, as all-encompassing, 130; as choosing Passion, 214, 230, 280, 298; as everlasting, 144, 184, 334, 338, 343; giving grace, 251; as joy in Passion, 146, 214, 217, 298, 322; not withheld by sin, 156, 245; operation of, in man, 299-300; as redeeming us, 289; revelation of, 302; as strength, 247; as surpassing pain, 144, 217; unchanging, 334; willing to become man because of, 181.

Christ's lovers, 125, 177, 234, 249, 343; Christ's compassion for, 319; compassion of, 126, 178; ignorance of, 323; profit to, 238, 343; suffering of, 142, 178, 330; we are, 300.

Christ's pain, cf. Pain.

Clothing, significance of, in parable, 272, 275, 276, 278.

Color, significance of, in parable, 272.

Comfort, alternating with failure, 205, 302; cross as, 316; end of pain, 307; lacking, 204, 279; Lord as, 151, 154, 157, 183, 212, 229, 271, 280, 307, 331, 333; in salvation, 218, 232, 333; seeking, in God, 169, 324; and soul, 316; revelation as, 182, 190, 191, 192, 221, 229, 307, 314, 317, 333, 334, 343.

Commandments, acceptance of, 307; what God commands, 292, 317; what he forbids, 292.

Compassion, cf. Christ's Lovers, Our Lady St. Mary; for Adam, 280; for Christ, 181, 226, 330, 331; Christ's, for us, 149, 152, 213, 226, 231, 235, 262, 271, 301, 307, 319, 326, 336, 338; Christ's unending, 262; in contemplation, 214; as earthly, 271; of Father, 271; for fellow Christians, 149, 226, 328; God's, for us, 262, 281, 328; as goodness, 231; as grace, 244, 296; leading to longing, 129, 180, 231, 245, 336; in parable, 268, 271; as wound, 127, 129, 180.

Consolation, acceptance of, 307; and grace, 241, 319; lack of, 267, 310; in pain, 227; revelation as, 162, 269; in seeing God with man, 193; and sin, 247.

Contemplation, of Christ, 195; of
Christ in soul, 164, 314; of God,
187, 191, 198, 255, 314, 327,
339; through grace, 214, 319;
higher and lower, 339; as honour
to soul, 196; as joy, 238, 241,
307; of Lord's works, 198; as
love, 258, 323; by Mary, 131,
182, 187; of Passion, 214, 217,
218, 319; and prayer, 159, 254,
255; of revelation, 190, 192, 201,
287, 288; of sin, 328.

Contrition, as cleansing, 245, 331;
and contemplation, 214, 328; as
grace, 244, 281, 336; and Holy
Spirit, 155, 169, 244, 246, 319,
324.

Courtesy, contemplation of God's,
236, 327; of Father, 189, 216,
286; of God, 168, 204, 263, 281,
282, 323; of Holy Spirit, 294; of
Lord, 153, 218, 227, 331, 332; of
man to God, 325; of Mother,
301.

Creatures, cf. Man, Soul; all
creatures are in man, 303; as
cared for, 231; and endless life,
320; from God, 198; as good,
132-3, 190; as little, 133, 256,
308, 327; made for love, 133,
190, 256, 342; as nothing, 131-2;
preserved by love, 130, 133, 190,
252, 256; as rightful, 198; sharing
in Passion, 210; wise act of, 328.

Creation, honour of, 303; man's
first, 286, 290, 293, 296; Trinity
rejoices in, 313.

Crown, we are Christ's, 145, 278.

Crown of thorns, 129, 298;
revelation of, 175, 181, 187, 207,
208.

Cross, Christ dying on, 304; Christ
on, in joy, 144, 215; as image of
Christ, 128, 180, 215; as soul's
safety, 143, 165, 211, 316, 319;

vision of Passion through, 162,
193, 311.

Damnation, danger of, 320; of
devils, 233, 234; of men, 233,
234, 240.

David, 242.

Death, of Christ, 141, 176, 194,
202, 206, 207, 277, 280; Christ
accounts his as nothing, 145, 217;
of Christ in his humanity, 219;
Christ's love for us in, 145, 217,
230; Christ's, and prayer, 185;
Christ's, as shameful, 144, 213,
298, 304, 318; desire to avoid,
178, 179; longing for, 127, 129,
160, 190; at point of, 126, 127,
128, 136, 142, 178, 179, 180,
190, 306; power of Christ's, 294.

Delight, cf. Joy, Bliss, Heaven; in
Christ's familiarity, 188, 189;
Christ's, in his suffering, 146,
168, 219; Christ's, in our
salvation, 221; Christ as ours,
147, 162, 176, 188, 223; Christ's,
in us, 219, 221, 235, 292, 313,
331, 335; in contemplating God,
153, 161, 255; of God, 152, 158,
185, 205, 315; of Holy Spirit,
146, 218, 278, 286; and love,
323; and Our Lady, 222, 223;
ours, in God, 239, 293, 309, 315,
339; ours, in our salvation, 218;
in revelation, 191; and trust, 204,
308.

Desire, Christ's, for us, 231, 338;
for death, 178, 305; for faith,
234; as gift, 253, 254; and God,
255, 261, 296, 308, 325; ours, for
Christ, 147, 151, 193, 223, 254,
321; for salvation, 264; of soul,
184; to understand, 257, 261;
way to heaven, 276.

Despair, alternating with
recklessness, 281; and love, 324,

334, 336; as sickness, 167, 322; and sin, 245, 332; as spiritual pain, 142, 178; temptation to, 165, 315, 323, 324, 329.

Devil, assault of, 126, 163, 165; damned, 202, 233, 234; fear of, 211, 324; God's scorn for, 138, 201, 202, 330; malice of, 138, 201, 202, 329, 330; as nothing, 201; opposed to faith, 318; opposed to love, 329; overcoming of, 138, 164, 175, 201, 315, 316, 332; power of, 309, 343; presence of, 128, 143, 180, 311, 315; protection from, 130, 245, 312, 316; as stench, 163, 165, 312, 315, 316; temptations of, 130, 170, 178, 182, 247, 250, 312, 315, 329, 334.

Disciples, 210; cf. Christ's lovers.

Divinity, 288; attributes of, 270; Christ's, 230, 274, 275, 276, 277; of Father, 276; giving strength to Christ's suffering, 213; no labour in, 276; love for, 300, 327; as noble, 213; please by atonement, 228; power of, 200, 230; and revelation, 343; soul of Christ, 285, 289; as sovereign power, wisdom and goodness, 164, 190; and understanding, 182, 220.

Easter, 277.

Essence, God is, 302.

Faith, and Christ's humanity, 230, 335; as comfort, 205, 232, 280, 316; as gift, 157, 189, 285, 291, 303, 319, 340; and God's word, 233; and grace, 233, 286; of Holy Church, 192, 316, 343; and joy, 318; keep in, 316, 318; love for, 317; from love, 286, 340; and miracles, 241; opposed to blindness, 318; as power, 285; as

preserver of revelation, 189, 317, 318; and revelation, 317, 318, 326; in seeking God, 195, 312; tried, 318, 321; as trust, 211, 232, 286, 308, 317, 323.

Father, attributes of, 145, 151, 216, 229, 283, 294, 295, 296, 304; bliss of, 145, 216, 218, 271, 275; compassion of, 271; courtesy of, 189, 216, 286; as Creator, 189, 293, 313; enclosed in us, 289; as familiar, 272; gives us to Son, 286; joy of, 145, 146, 218, 271, 276, 286, 305; and nature, 294, 302, 340; is not man, 272; our being from, 294; our protection and bliss, 293; permitting Son's suffering, 277; receives us from Christ, 286; as rewarding Jesus, 145, 216; we enclosed in him, 285; wills, 296.

Fatherhood, our debt to, 299; property of, in God, 293, 296, 325.

Fear, in allegory, 267, 268; alternating with consolation, 241; of assault, 169, 324; as blindness, 168; of Christ's pain, 208; of conscience, 312; of devils, 211, 324; as doubt, 169, 253, 261, 323, 324; as false, 325, 329; four kinds of, 169, 324; of God, 325; and grace, 325, 326; of ignorance, 266; leading to despair, 167, 168; of Lord, 181, 308, 329; and love, 324, 325; and nature, 324; of pain, 169, 324; as profitable, 304, 324; as reverent, 169, 187, 190, 238, 250, 308, 309, 324, 325, 326, 327, 328, 340; of sin, 149, 154, 334, 339; as suffering, 161, 309; as true, 264, 325.

Feeling, afflicted by Adam, 279; of Christ, 336; and comfort, 261,

286, 301; common experience, 260; as experience of God, 255, 279, 288, 308, 320, 327; of grace, 280, 336; lack of, 261; in parable, 267; of sin, 261, 334; as vision (spiritual sight), 260, 261, 288, 339, 340.

Gabriel, 131, 182.

Glory, Christ's desire for God's, 276; of God and prayer, 157, 307; of God in his wisdom, 197, 239; to live for God's, 178, 179, 234, 290, 306, 307, 309, 337; of our Lord, 147, 223, 230, 302, 304, 331, 337; of our Lord's work, 252, 255; ours, in heaven, 176, 215.

God, cf. Goodness, Joy; and anger, 159, 201, 246, 264; closeness of, 288, 320, 321, 325; as creator, 134, 166, 175, 183, 190, 192, 198, 237, 252, 255, 285, 288, 291, 293, 297, 314, 320, 321, 327, 340; desire of, to be known, 132, 134, 161, 184, 235, 238, 251, 260, 307, 309, 318, 326, 342; desire of, for our love, 167, 170, 186, 235, 238, 239, 254, 308, 326; as doer of everything, 166, 175, 197, 199, 236, 237, 253, 323, 326, 336; dwells in us, 285, 286, 320, 321; encloses us, 320; as everlasting, 184, 293; as everything, 166, 184, 192, 321; in everything, 166, 197, 199; face of, 327; is Father, 272, 279, 293, 295, 296, 340; is grace, 303; his friendship, 244, 264; as Holy Church, 152, 236, 259, 335; is Holy Spirit, 335; knowledge of, 288, 289, 321, 327; is love, 256, 259, 323; majesty of, 327; is Mother, 279, 293, 295, 297; has not forgotten us, 307; is One,

285, 293, 296, 303; our being is, 296, 297; is peace, 259, 265; presence of, 308; as protector, 265; as righteous, 234; substantial nature of, 284, 303; is Trinity, 181, 293, 296; is truth, 256, 259; is unchanging, 198; union of, with us, 183, 291, 292; is wisdom, 256, 259, 323.

God's love, 232; as abundant, 263; creates unity, 309; as creator, 183, 194, 289, 291, 300; as endless, 281, 284, 285, 289, 308; for everything, 192; our ignorance of, 168, 186, 321; not affected by our offenses, 300; as perfect, 159; as protecting us, 262, 284, 340; as unchanging, 159, 167, 254; for us, 192, 194, 247, 290, 293, 296, 309, 315, 333; as without beginning, 283, 284, 341, 342, 343.

God's mercy, and blood of Christ, 302; as gift, 258, 295; and goodness, 237, 291, 295; hope of, 155, 244; as leading us, 262, 265, 286, 287, 304, 333, 340; as property of love, 262, 286; as purging, 178, 246, 256, 265, 302; recognizes our sin, 300; seeking of, 169, 225, 296, 324; and sins, 246, 260, 263, 329, 330; and Son, 294; trust in, 163, 179, 180, 234, 251, 279, 311, 312, 338; understanding of, 260; in works of Lord, 198; and wrath, 260, 263.

God's power, 201, 237, 247, 259, 264, 313, 323.

God's will, 126; acceptance of, 160, 161, 179, 238; bound to us, 308; to have us, 186; permitting temptation, 130, 182, 201, 238, 300; and prayer, 157, 158, 178, 250; as providence, 137, 197,

199, 224, 232, 233, 237, 262, 283, 293, 341; to save man, 156, 247; and suffering, 161, 307, 309; that we believe, 194, 235, 323; that we be comforted, 152, 307; that we know and love, 186, 194, 241; that we preserve delight, 140; that we recognize his deeds, 152, 235; that we recognize sin, 168, 170.

Goodness, of Christ, 298, 329, 330, 334, 336, 338, 343; as compassion, 231; as divinity, 164, 313; fullness of, 185, 236; is God, 259, 296; of God, 133, 134, 153, 176, 184, 190, 192, 193, 231, 232, 236, 237, 246, 249, 259, 262, 264, 269, 281, 282, 291, 302, 318, 321, 324, 325, 327; God's, and sin, 238; as longing, 231; love for, 266; and mystery, 239; opposed to evil, 295; pray for God's, 185.

Grace, as bond, 303; causes bliss, 295; Christ as our mother in, 296, 297; Christ's word as, 298; as consolation, 241; as destroyer of sin, 303; developing natural, 210, 318; and forgiveness, 246, 265; as generosity, 263; as gift, 125, 177, 185, 186, 212, 219, 234, 237, 238, 249, 250, 251, 256, 264, 290, 295, 316, 324, 340, 342; from God's goodness, 291, 295, 302; from Holy Spirit, 189, 246, 255, 256, 287, 288, 294, 296, 325, 329, 330; as illuminating, 147, 176, 186, 192, 193, 194, 214, 233, 240, 252, 254, 258, 263, 265, 266, 281, 282, 304, 305, 319, 322, 332, 333, 340; in Lord's work, 198; and mercy, 265, 294, 296; and nature, 303, 304, 320, 321, 327; in parable, 268; as protector, 281,

286; as transformer, 263, 332; trust in, 279; to wish for, 157.

Heaven, cf. Bliss, Joy; begins here, 290, 308, 335; as bliss, 271, 276, 290, 298, 306, 308, 327, 331, 337, 339; with Christ in, 215, 220; Christ's ascension to, 200; and earth, 286; enclosed in God, 272; and fear, 325, 327; Christ's humanity as, 145; Jesus as, 143, 211, 212, 331, 339; as joy, 238, 276, 290, 298, 306, 331, 336, 339; enables us to know clearly, 300; possessing God in, 255; and purity, 281; three heavens, 145-6, 216, 218, 275; vision of, 154; way to, 245, 276, 286, 295, 304, 326, 331, 343.

Hell, cf. also Adam, Man, Sin; bonds broken, 200; Christ in, 277; creatures condemned to, 233; pain of, 247, 328; sight of, 234; and sin, 244, 247, 304, 328; we as taken from 295.

Holy Church, 148, 149; assent to, 163, 234, 257, 301; body of, 301; is Christ, 302; faith in, 165, 176, 192, 257, 258, 301, 312, 316, 343; God as, 152, 236; laws of, 323; life of, 155, 244; as Mother, 259, 301, 302, 303; and penance, 155; rites of, 126, 127, 155, 178, 179, 244; as teacher, 135, 147, 228; teachings of, 125, 134, 148, 152, 157, 178, 191, 192, 194, 196, 223, 233, 235, 236, 257, 258, 266, 281, 298, 335; in tribulation, 226; union with, 302.

Holy Scripture, 343.

Holy Spirit, confirms, 296; delight of, 146, 218, 286; desiring creation, 313; as drawing us, 150, 151, 184, 195, 228, 229, 262, 286, 287, 288; as giver of grace,

189, 255, 256, 286, 292, 294, 295, 296, 319, 325, 329, 335; as goodness, 283, 293, 295, 304; as grace, 294; enclosed in us, 285; as illuminator, 195, 257, 285, 319, 340; leads us to contrition, 155, 169, 244, 246, 260, 319; as love in Father and Son, 274; as our fulfillment, 294, 295; as our reward, 294; in our soul, 261; as protector, 261; strength of, 324; as teacher, 153, 155, 169, 196, 244, 328.

Honour, of Christ, 146, 164, 176, 195, 213, 218, 278, 326; to God, 153, 185, 196, 236, 238, 335; of God and prayer, 185; God's, 269; and grace, 303; in heaven, 238, 242, 265; of man, 195, 239, 242, 280, 295, 302, 303; of Our Lady, 147, 223; in parable, 269, 273, 274; regard for Christ's, 144, 176; as reward for pain, 203, 226, 227, 265; as reward for shame, 245, 263; of the soul for service to God, 139, 203, 204; and trust, 251, 326; we are Christ's, 216, 230.

Hope, in Christ's love, 261; as comfort, 205; and faith, 286, 308, 340; as gift, 157, 189, 244, 318, 319; and heaven, 308; in search for God, 195.

Humility, of Christ, 297; false, 168, 323; and fear, 308, 334; of Mary, 187; and nature, 296; and penance, 330, 331; and sin, 300, 321, 338; of soul, 196, 244, 296, 308, 327, 330, 333, 343.

Image, of bottom of sea, 193; of cheerful giver, 219; of hazelnut, 183; of mud, 306; of purse, 186.
Incarnation, 201, 219, 275, 276, 277, 292, 297, 336.

Intermediaries, 288; and prayer, 185.

Jews, and Christ's death, 234.
Joy, cf. Bliss, Heaven, Delight; alternating with pain, 140, 176, 205, 279; in Christ, 193, 223, 255; of contemplation, 164, 190, 237, 238, 255, 314, 333, 339; and cross, 144, 215; destroys pain, 282; enclosed in God, 272; as endless, 265, 302, 304, 306, 307, 331; in familiarity of Christ, 188, 189; of Father, 145, 146, 218, 271, 276, 286, 305; fullness of, 232, 237, 320, 321, 331; in God, 256, 265, 320; God's, in us, 314, 320; in God's works, 239, 283, 314; heavenly, increased by woe, 202, 226; incomplete, 321; and love, 205, 334; man made for, 258; and mother Jesus, 298; of Our Lady, 147, 223; in our salvation, 240, 303; ours, in Church, 258; ours, in heaven, 155, 160, 186, 215, 226, 238, 249, 298, 302, 304, 307, 327, 336, 342; in Passion, 168, 176, 188, 218, 220, 322; in revelation, 191, 218, 224; soul's, in finding God, 195; Trinity's, in man's salvation, 286; and trust, 308.
Judgement, of God, 257, 263, 341; of Holy Church, 257; true, 323.
Judgement Day, 212, 230, 231, 232, 233, 304, 326.
Justice, Christ's, 337; God's, 201, 256, 281; God's, from love, 257.

Knowledge, of God, 127.

Light, and Christ, 332, 339, 343; clarity of, 320; as faith, 340; is God, 340; and grace, 338, 342; is love, 296, 314, 317; and mother

Christ, 340; spiritual, 318.

Longing, for bliss, 252, 258; for
Christ, 147, 223, 224, 246, 255,
337, 338; Christ's, in love, 151,
230, 231, 246, 271, 276, 280,
304, 334, 336; comes from
knowledge, 258; as compassion,
231; for death, 160, 305; for
God, 129, 320, 321; God makes
us to long, 296; God's, for man,
326; as grace, 244, 258, 320;
made worthy by, 245; man's, for
love, 318, 326; as natural, 258; as
seeking, 195, 320; soul as, 307,
318; as way to heaven, 276.

Lord, cf. Christ; as alone, 336;
brings us to himself, 335, 337; as
comfort, 183; as courteous, 136,
163, 188, 196, 218, 223, 235,
246, 254, 267, 271, 300, 306,
307, 311, 312, 329, 331, 332,
333, 334, 338, 339, 341; as
everything good, 183; as
everything to us, 223, 236; as
familiar, 136, 183, 188, 196, 223,
331, 339; as God and man, 164,
181, 230, 275, 278, 313; his
mercy, 281, 317, 329, 330, 331;
his work, 299, 300, 302, 330,
335; as king of bliss, 267; as
maker, 320; moves us, 334, 337,
339; permits us to fall, 300; as
protector, 154, 245, 246, 279,
331, 332, 334, 336, 338; punishes
us, 330; is One, 285, 293; as our
brother, 221, 329; as our creator,
221; as our reward, 177, 236,
250, 306, 307; as our saviour,
221, 229, 240, 319, 333; as
receiver of prayer, 249; as
strength, 157, 300, 319; teaching
of, 135, 223, 318, 332, 333, 334;
is true God, 313.

Lord and Servant, Lord is God,
270, 274; parable of, 267-269,

272-274; servant is Adam, 269,
270, 274; servant is Son, 274.

Lordship, property of, in God,
293, 325.

Love, cf. Christ, God; Christ is,
130, 156, 247, 331; Christ's, as
courteous, 130, 155, 182, 191,
245; Christ's, as everlasting, 221,
245, 338; Christ's, for Our Lady,
222; Christ's, in our salvation,
220, 225, 238, 298; Christ's, for
us, 130, 155, 168, 176, 217, 220,
221, 226, 230, 231, 241, 242,
245, 281, 298, 318, 330, 334,
338, 343; as comfort, 205; for
creation, 192; is delight in God,
256; and fear, 169, 187, 308, 325,
326; for fellow Christians, 134,
136, 154, 156, 187, 190, 191,
241; as gift, 157, 189, 324, 342;
for God, 127, 134, 161, 179, 186,
187, 191, 279, 293, 296, 299,
308, 309, 315, 319, 321, 325,
327, 338, 340, 343; God for God,
340; God makes us to, 296, 300,
309, 326; God's, 186, 300; God's,
as giving being, 130; as grace,
342; and hate as contraries, 281;
ignorance of, 323; is life-giving,
263; and Mother, 299; as natural,
210; ours, for Christ, 223, 299,
300, 343; ours, for Church, 258;
ourselves in God, 340; in
parable, 267, 268, 273; protecting
us, 286, 326, 339; revelation of,
186, 197; as unity, 191.

Man, cf. Soul; accuses himself,
281, 282, 329, 330, 334; being in
God, 264; as blinded, 270, 271,
272, 279, 281, 307, 318, 321,
322, 323, 329, 334, 341; body
made from earth, 284; as child of
God, 286, 294, 301, 304, 305,

mother of Christ, 275, 292; our delight in, 222; as our Mother, 292; position of, 131, 147, 182, 187, 222; qualities of, 131, 182, 222; sorrow of, 213, 234; soul of, 256; vision of, 131, 147, 176, 182, 187, 190, 222, 223, 256, 297.

Pain, cf. also Suffering, Oppression, Christ's pain; of absence of God, 160, 305; as alternating with joy, 140, 176, 205, 242, 279, 305, 306, 320, 337; bodily, 126, 129, 141, 160, 162, 178, 180, 207, 267, 307; Christ's, 126, 129, 136, 141, 144, 178, 193, 206, 207, 208, 209, 213, 214, 227, 230, 275, 298; consolation of, 227; deliverance from, 139, 160, 177, 180, 244, 306, 307, 321, 326, 337; as exceeding mortal death, 142; fear of, 169, 324; not to be pursued, 140, 205; patience in, 168, 169, 307, 319, 322, 323; rewarded by joy, 215, 221, 265, 340; sharing in Christ's, 129, 142-3, 209, 210, 226; and sin, 156, 159, 163, 227, 242, 247, 320, 328; spiritual, 126, 141, 142, 160, 178, 207, 267, 279, 307, 310.

Patience, awaiting death, 160; Christ's, in his Passion, 168, 322; lacking in, 204, 266; and love, 162, 168; and mercy, 296; in our pains, 168, 169, 309, 324; and penance, 330; rewarded, 306; revelation concerning, 162; in seeking God, 196.

Paul, 140, 142, 154, 205, 243.

Penance, life is, 331, 337; patience in, 330, 338; for sin, 155, 244.

Peter, 140, 154, 205, 243.

Pilate, 211.

Pity, cf. Compassion.

Power, of Christ, 277, 280, 295, 302, 319, 330; as divinity, 166, 313; of God, 176, 323, 326, 343; of man, 270, 302, 327, 340; of Trinity, 294.

Prayer, and devil, 316; in dryness, 249, 280; and faith, 234; for fellow Christians, 157; fittingness of, 246; for forgiveness, 264; giving joy to Lord, 249; and God's will, 157, 178, 252, 253, 254, 328; for help, 266; and intermediaries, 185; led to, by Holy Spirit, 246, 249; as life-giving, 185; for mercy, 296; need for, 254, 326; not cause of grace, 249, 251; origins of, 251, 253; our duty in regard to, 252, 253, 316; and our joy in heaven, 249; to our Mother, 296; as pleasing to God, 158, 177, 249; revelation concerning, 157, 177, 248, 250; as trust, 248; as uniting man and God, 158, 159, 249, 254, 255, 342; what we pray for, 185, 251, 252, 253.

Pride, the breaking of, 332; of devils, 233; prevention of, 226.

Purgatory, pain of, 247; sight of, 234.

Recollection, cf. Vision, Revelation, Sight; as bodily sight, 129, 130; from Christ, 129; as comfort, 130; of Passion, 129, 130, 142, 177, 178, 180; as revelations, 125, 126, 129.

Redemption, 219, 252, 283, 289.

Rejoicing, of Christ, 279, 302; of Christ in compassion, 226; of dwelling of God in us, 285; of God, 279; in heaven, 263; in Holy Church, 258; of the Lord in man, 228, 256, 314, 340; of man in God, 225, 260, 279, 293, 314, 342; of man in the Lord, 221, 228, 229, 232, 239, 240, 256, 279, 337, 338, 340, 343; our dwelling in the Lord as, 285; in parable, 268; in penance, 331; of Trinity in creation, 313, 314; in trust, 261, 317.

Rest, cf. Comfort; on earth, 271; in heaven, 271, 278.

Resurrection, 219, 294.

Revelation, cf. also Vision, Recollection; assent to, 163; from Christ, 129, 175, 181, 184, 299, 309, 311, 312, 314, 317, 319; 321, 328, 342; of Christ, 336, 337; as comfort, 138, 182, 292, 312; of consolation, 154; as delight, 139; as gift/grace, 129, 189, 255, 259, 309; of God as King, 203; as joy, 181, 224; Julian's, as applying to all Christians, 133, 191, 315; lack of belief in, 162, 163, 194, 310, 311, 317; list of sixteen in long text, 175; of love, 334, 342; meaning of, 342; not desiring any, 181; of prayer, 157; as recollection, 125, 126, 129, 177; renewed by illuminations, 309; of sin, 153, 154, 302, 320, 321, 332, 333; sixteenth, a conclusion, 310; as spiritual, 191, 269; as strength, 311; she trusts in her own, 164, 189, 234, 258, 300, 312, 314; as understanding, 131, 132, 282, 297, 308, 329, 330, 340, 342.

Reverence, 308; cf. Fear.

Reward, Christ as ours, 337, 339; of Father to Jesus, 145; for faith, 318; God as ours, 153; from grace, 263; from Holy Spirit, 294; ours, in heaven, 155, 158, 160, 176, 177, 178, 204, 242, 245, 263, 265, 306, 308, 337, 339; in parable, 268; for prayer, 248, 249, 252, 253; repaying Christ with his, 318; to servant, 269; for service, 203, 204, 294, 340; for suffering, 308, 340; we are Christ's, 145, 216, 230.

Sacraments, Eucharist, as food, 298; rites of dying, 126, 127; seven, 292, 298.

Salvation, Christ's delight in, 221; Christ's labour in ours, 145, 216, 218, 219, 221, 245, 277, 298, 335; our delight in, 218, 219, 240, 303; as glorious deed, 275; and love of Christ, 220, 230, 301, 304; of man, 200, 220, 228, 239, 247, 265, 275, 276, 283, 284, 303, 304, 314, 315, 325, 326, 331, 333, 335, 337, 340; through mercy and grace, 290, 302; of only one man, 161; and pain, 209; and Trinity, 219.

St. Cecilia, 27.

St. Denis of France, 211.

St. John of Beverly, revelation of, 243.

Seeking, through grace, 193, and Holy Spirit, 195, 236; as honour to soul, 196; and knowledge of soul, 289; man's, of God, 236, 303, 320, 324; as pleasing to God, 195; through prayer, 250.

Self, of Christ, 331 and God, 258; knowledge of, 288, 289, 321; known in faith, 258; love for, 282; opposed to sin, 321; in Trinity, 323.

Sensuality, Christ in, 289, 294; God in, 287; of man, 286, 287, 289, 291, 293, 294, 295; and nature, 287, 296.

Servant, as Adam, 269, 274, 275, 280; as Christ's humanity, 274; compassion for, 338; fall of, 281;

God dwells in, 285, 289; God's love for, 159, 247, 287, 288, 299; and holiness, 284, 289, 307, 314; and Holy Spirit, 261, 328; importance of each, 161, 231, 242, 285, 309, 335, 336; knowledge of, 288, 289; led by God, 307; like God, 158, 251, 253, 284, 287, 314; love for God, 256; as loving, 304; made by God, 256, 283, 284, 287, 289; made righteous, 237; man's love for, 247; a place of Jesus, 164, 166, 287, 289, 292, 303, 313, 314, 336, 337; and power, 211, 291; received in joy, 246, 256; rest of the soul, 223, 246, 261, 289, 309, 312, 313, 314, 328; salvation of, 265; seeking God, 195, 307; as sensual, 285, 287, 289; and sin, 244, 328; spouse of God, 279, 293; union with God, 159, 166, 186, 246, 259, 262, 279, 283, 284, 285, 287, 289, 292; united to body, 287, 289, 291; vision of, as city, 163, 272, 289, 312, 313, 337.

Spouse, God is, 279, 293; Son is, 278.

Substance, of God, 284, 285, 302, 338; of man, 285, 287, 289, 290, 291, 292, 293, 294, 295, 296, 337; nature's, 290.

Suffering, cf. also Pain, Oppression, Despair; acceptance of, 161, 268, 307; barrenness, 310; Christ's, 125, 129, 176, 177, 181, 206, 207, 209, 213, 218, 277; Christ's accounting his, as nothing, 217, 219; of Christ's lovers, 125, 126, 178, 210; Christ's satisfaction of his own, 144, 216, 219, 221; Christ's willingness for greater, 144, 145, 216, 217, 218, 298; Christ's, for

us, 213, 214; end of Christ's, 220; fear as, 309; Jesus as comfort in, 143; Julian's, 127, 212, 310; man's, 270, 302; man's count as nothing, 308, 309; for pain of the Passion, 142; in parable, 268; as passing, 215; in seeking God, 195; seen as not good, 148; sharing in Christ's, 129, 180, 210.

Thanksgiving, from God, 340; to God, 293, 296, 338, 341, 342; in heaven, 284; as prayer, 250, 252; as rejoicing, 279; for revelations, 343; and reward, 263, 308.

Thomas of India, 243.

Touchings, as experience of God, 331; of grace, 279, 281, 300, 324, 330, 334, 337; memory as, 300; as spiritual sights, 255, 289, 339.

Trinity, attributes of, 168, 181, 323; in Christ, 181, 291; as creator, 152, 181, 194, 233, 283, 293, 313, 314; delight in Christ's Passion, 176, 219; dwells in us, 177; as good, 154, 232; goodness of the Trinity is Lord, 285; is God, 181, 295, 296; knowledge of, 296; and love, 168, 343; love of the Trinity is Lord, 294; is Mother, 285, 294; and mysterious deeds of, 232, 239; our substance in, 295; pleased with its works, 199; and power, 232, 294; revelation of, 175, 177, 181; our salvation in, 146, 151, 219, 229, 233, 283; second Person of, 287; unity of, 151, 229, 278, 323; at work in Passion, 219; work of, 293.

Truth, and God, 256.

Treasure, in parable, 273, 274.

Trust, in Christ, 229, 280, 301, 318, 331; in Christ's familiarity,